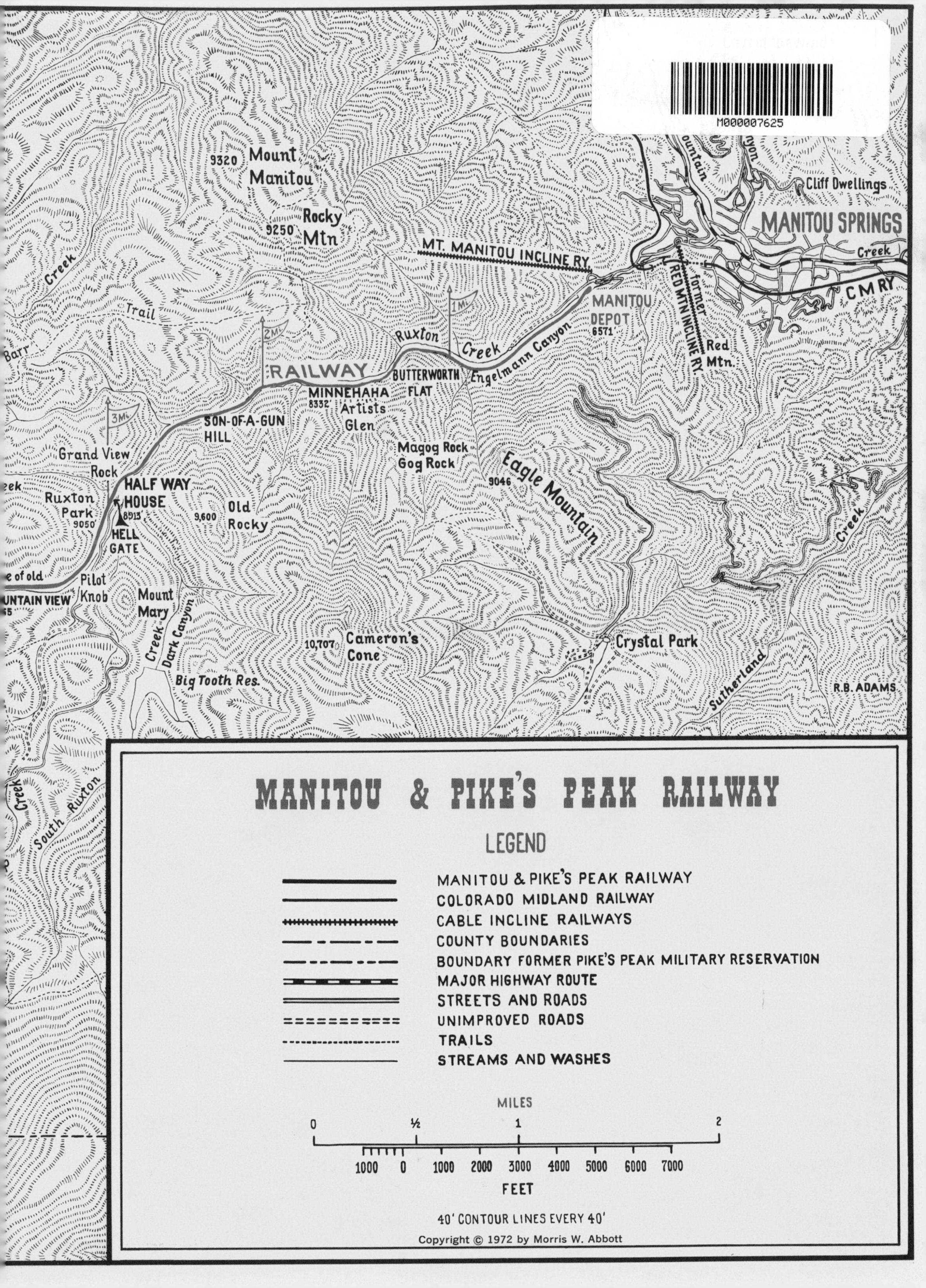

M000007625
Mount Manitou
9320
Rocky Mtn
9250
MT. MANITOU INCLINE RY
Cliff Dwellings
MANITOU SPRINGS
Creek
CM RY
former
RED MTN INCLINE RY
Red Mtn.
MANITOU DEPOT
6571
Creek
Trail
Barr
2 Mi
1 Mi
Ruxton
Creek
Engelmann Canyon
RAILWAY
BUTTERWORTH FLAT
MINNEHAHA
8332
Artists Glen
3 Mi
SON-OF-A-GUN HILL
Magog Rock
Gog Rock
Eagle Mountain
9046
Grand View Rock
HALF WAY HOUSE
8913
Ruxton Park
9050
HELL GATE
Old Rocky
9,600
Creek
Pilot Knob
Mount Mary
Creek
Dark Canyon
Big Tooth Res.
10,707
Cameron's Cone
Crystal Park
Sutherland
R.B. ADAMS
Creek
South Ruxton
MANITOU & PIKE'S PEAK RAILWAY
LEGEND
MANITOU & PIKE'S PEAK RAILWAY
COLORADO MIDLAND RAILWAY
CABLE INCLINE RAILWAYS
COUNTY BOUNDARIES
BOUNDARY FORMER PIKE'S PEAK MILITARY RESERVATION
MAJOR HIGHWAY ROUTE
STREETS AND ROADS
UNIMPROVED ROADS
TRAILS
STREAMS AND WASHES
MILES
0
½
1
2
1000
0
1000
2000
3000
4000
5000
6000
7000
FEET
40' CONTOUR LINES EVERY 40'

CENTENNIAL EDITION

THE PIKE'S PEAK COG ROAD

MORRIS W. ABBOTT

PULPIT ROCK PRESS
855 Pulpit Rock Circle South
Colorado Springs, CO 80918
U.S.A.

Reprinted - 1990 in the U.S.A.
Library of Congress Catalog Card Number
89-92264
ISBN 0-9624008-2-3
First published in 1972 by Golden West Books, San Marino, CA
(ISBN 87095-039-8, LC Catalog Card Number 77-190175)

ACKNOWLEDGMENTS

No one writes a book like *The Pike's Peak Cog Road* without the unselfish assistance of countless friends. There are writers who have recorded their research in published books; there are libraries and museums where original material, long out of print documents and pictures are available. A complete acknowledgment is impossible.

I wish to particularly express appreciation to William W. Abbott, Robert W. Barrell, Gerald M. Best, the late William S. and Mrs. Crosby, Clarence Coil, Thomas E. Daniels, Donald Duke, Mrs. Kenneth Englert, Mallory Hope Ferrell, the late Jack Haley, the late G. H. Hibbard, F. H. Hollenback, Mrs. Mary P. Hoe, the late Harry J. Holt, Richard B. Jackson, Lee D. Jamison, Richard H. Kindig, Michael Koch, Robert A. LaMassena, Mrs. Frank C. Martin, the late Carl F. Mathews, the late William H. McKay, Mrs. Clyde C. McReynolds, Steve Maguire, William C. Mason, Robert L. Morrison, Proctor W. Nichols, Charles B. O'Brien, Herbert O'Hanlan, Robert W. Richardson, Harold T. Seely, Grant G. Simmons, Grant G. Simmons, Jr., Miss Dorothy E. Smith, Frank J. and Mrs. Smith, Mrs. Helen Wilson Stewart, the late Brough J. Taggart, Jackson C. Thode, H. L. Voss and Lester L. Williams M.D.

Also to the Baldwin Locomotive Works and present day Baldwin-Lima-Hamilton Corporation, the City of Colorado Springs (Department of Public Utilities), Colorado Springs Chamber of Commerce, DeGolyer Foundation Library, Denver Public Library, General Electric Company (Railroad and Car Department), Library of Golden West Books, Manitou Springs Chamber of Commerce, Martin R. Frick (General Manager) and the employees of the Manitou & Pike's Peak Railway Co., Pioneers Museum of Colorado Springs, State Historical Society of Colorado, Swiss National Tourist Office, Tutt Library of Colorado College, Verkehrshaus der Schweiz, Luzern, Switzerland, and the Swiss Locomotive & Machine Works.

Special thanks to Robert B. Adams for his map of the railway and to railroad artist Howard Fogg for his realistic scene of the Cog Road appearing on the dust jacket.

The need for a definitive history of the unique Pike's Peak Cog Railway was filled by the publication of this classic book by Morris W. Abbott. However, it has been out of print for a number of years, and Abbott died in May, 1978. It is a pleasure to make this CENTENNIAL EDITION available through the cooperation of the estate of the late Morris W. Abbott, and Golden West Books. A CENTENNIAL EDITION is appropriate. Construction of the Cog Road began in 1889: the last spike was driven and there were scheduled trains as far as the Halfway House in 1890; and regular service to the summit of Pikes Peak began in 1891.

Pulpit Rock Press
855 Pulpit Rock Circle South
Colorado Springs, CO 80918

To
Martin R. Frick
General Manager — Manitou & Pike's Peak Railway
and to the men whose
great service to the Cog Road
should be recognized
and appreciated.

Back in 1930 when steam was still king of the rails on the Manitou & Pike's Peak Railway, a cog train moves toward timber line as it tackles the Big Hill at Grecian Bend. — BERT WARD COLLECTION

PREFACE

ONE WOULD be challenged to find a more interesting railroad in North America than the Manitou & Pike's Peak Railway. The Cog Road, whose history has been synonymous with that of the Rocky Mountain region of Colorado since 1888, has carried well over a million passengers to the summit of Pike's Peak and holds the distinction of being the highest railroad in the United States.

The story of the Manitou & Pike's Peak Railway differs in many respects from the average railroad. During their early years, most railroads were so involved in corporate shenanigans and financial pinwheeling that one reading their history is overwhelmed by the mass of uninteresting corporate detail.

The Cog Road had no struggles for control, no proxy fights, no bankruptcy. Ownership changed only once, and then it was a clear-cut sale. Neither Daniel Drew, Jim Fisk nor Jay Gould had a hand in its construction or operation — just the Simmons family of mattress fame, and Spencer Penrose, a distinguished local citizen, and his associates. The road was not even a pioneer in rack railroading, though a lot had to be learned by trial and error in its construction and early operation.

In a way the Manitou & Pike's Peak Railway runs from nowhere to nowhere. It didn't open up any virgin territory of the American West nor serve any industries, and has never been anything but a tourist attraction. It has had no rail competition, and the automobile road to the top of the peak hasn't mattered that much.

The almost complete lack of company records has hampered and prolonged research. The Simmons family confesses to not having been preservers of records or memorabilia. The present operators view the railroad with more interest in its current operations than its earlier history, which is understandable and by no means a reprehensible trait.

Way back in the 1940's, I was fortunate in being able to examine two scrapbooks containing considerable information about the road's early days. These books were lent to me by the then president of the road, the late H. J. Holt, and were later returned to him. In recent years I have made several attempts to locate the scrapbooks or learn who owned them, but without success.

Equally unfortunately, I have been unable to locate any photographs or illustrations made during the construction of the road, though I know photographs were taken. It should be obvious some local photographer made a photograph of the driving of the last spike.

My personal acquaintance with the Cog Road dates back to when I was a boy and the railroad was still a teenager. On August 1, 1907, with my parents I rode up from Manitou to the Half Way House, where we spent the rest of the summer. I remember clearly the thrill of the slow, jerky start up Engelmann Canyon, of watching the steam spurt from first one and then another of the engine's cylinder cocks. I would experience the same thrill today if it were possible to repeat the ride in front of a steam locomotive.

There is no small amount of personal nostalgia in this account of *The Pike's Peak Cog Road.*

MORRIS W. ABBOTT

Milford, Connecticut
June 1971

Pike's Peak, 14,110 feet above sea level, is shown in a famous view through the gateway rocks of the Garden of the Gods, adjacent to Colorado Springs. In this unusual setting Red Morrison sandstone juts out of the ground as much as 300 feet to form the Garden. The Cog Road, not visible in this scene, climbs up and around the shoulder of the Peak at the left in its ascent to the top. — STEWARTS COMMERCIAL PHOTOGRAPHERS

TABLE OF CONTENTS

One of the most important events in American history was the purchase of Louisiana Territory in 1803. With one stroke the United States doubled her territory and acquired a vast and fertile region of expansion. In July 1806, Lieutenant Pike and 26 men left St. Louis on an official journey of discovery. By mid-November the troop first noticed the peak and later made an attempt to reach the top. Though Pike never did reach the summit of the high peak which later carried his name, he was the first American to describe it. He did not name it for himself, but modestly called it "The Great Peak" on his maps, believing it to be at least 18,000 feet in height. It was called James' Peak by Major Long after James climbed it in 1820. Then trappers came later insisting on calling it *Pike's Peak* and it has become Colorado's most famous mountain.

1

PIKE'S PEAK

LIEUTENANT Zebulon Montgomery Pike was a comparative newcomer as far as concerns the mountain that bears his name. The Spanish had been the first white men to see it, perhaps a century earlier, and James Purcell, a Kentucky trader, found gold in South Park, just west of Pike's Peak, in 1803, or at least that is what he told Lieutenant Pike.

Pike's Peak is undoubtedly the best known mountain in North America, in spite of the fact that there are many others that surpass it in elevation. Actually, it ranks only 32nd even in its own State of Colorado, which counts more than 50 peaks that exceed 14,000 feet of elevation above sea level, yet it enjoys an international reputation.

It became so well known because of its location. While most of the high Rockies are well back amongst their fellow mountains, Pike's Peak stands at the edge of the plains, in the Front Range. Thus it was visible for many miles to the east and became a landmark for the gold seekers, a sort of lighthouse of the plains. In fact, "Pike's Peak" was applied to the whole Colorado mountain region, where, it was said, gold could be scooped up by the shovelful.

Pike was in command of an official U. S. Army party of exploration of 26 men, looking for the source of the Arkansas River, which was the boundary between the newly acquired Louisiana and Spanish territory, and the powers in Washington did not know just where that river ran. At two o'clock in the afternoon of November 15, 1806, he first saw the big mountain. With a few soldiers and in spite of the lateness of the season, he set out to climb it. They approached from the south, and after a long, wearying struggle through snow, they reached the top of one of the foothills (possibly Cheyenne Mountain), where they gave it up.

With what instruments he had at hand he arrived at the figure of 18,581 feet as its elevation above sea level, an error of about 4,500 feet, basing his estimate on the assumption that the plains were 8,000 feet above the sea, and the mountain 10,581 feet above the plains. That was one of his errors. Another was of wandering into Spanish territory, where he and his men were arrested and packed off to Santa Fé. However, he did take advantage of this opportunity to learn something about the country and its people, and it may be that he knew very well where he was going and what he was doing.

Pike was commissioned major in 1808, colonel in 1812, and brigadier general in 1813. He personally led his troops in a successful attack on the British at York (Toronto) in the War of 1812, but died April 27, 1813, a few hours after their powder

The second U.S. Army Signal Station (i.e., weather observatory) on Pike's Peak was built in 1882 and discontinued in 1889. This structure shown above was later incorporated into the Summit House. Note the huge wood storage pile at the right. —MIKE KOCH COLLECTION (BELOW) C. F. Schneider and — Sherwood, presumably of the Signal Service, at the weather station on Pike's Peak. The lattice covered affair housed instruments and protected them from direct sunlight, rain, hail and snow. —NATIONAL ARCHIVES

magazine exploded. He was taken aboard a U. S. ship and died there, with his head pillowed on a captured British flag, which later hung in the U. S. Naval Academy at Annapolis.

The next official party to visit the region was that of Major Stephen H. Long, at which time the mountain was climbed by Dr. Edwin James, the expedition's botanist-physician, and two companions who reached the summit on July 14, 1820. For some time it was known as James' Peak, but the name was later given to an even higher mountain nearer Denver. So, in spite of Pike's doubts that the foot of man would ever tread its summit, the peak was scaled within a few years, and in August 1858 the first ascent by a woman was made by Julia Anna Holmes of Lawrence, Kansas. A rude trail is said to have existed as early as 1852.

For some years and until they decided that the weather on Pike's Peak had little relation to that down on earth, the U. S. Signal Service (forerunner of the Weather Bureau) maintained a weather station on the summit. A 17-mile trail had been built, a stone house was constructed at the top of the peak, and a single telegraph wire strung along the trail. This trail, which was built in 1871 under the supervision of engineer E. S. Nettleton and improved in 1873, followed up Bear Creek through Jones' Park to Lake Moraine and Seven Lakes. About 1874 it was widened into a wagon road as far as Seven Lakes, and rest houses or small hotels were built at Lake Moraine and Seven Lakes. One four-room house was called the Half Way House, a not uncommon name. A new trail was built about 1882 by the Signal Service, running up the narrow and steep canyon of Ruxton Creek from Manitou, to join ultimately the old trail. The government maintained a guarded and padlocked gate near Manitou, where toll was collected by the guard, a practice that ceased before 1889.

Both trails attracted a certain number of tourist mountaineers, later known as hikers, and the Ruxton trail proved popular, being considerably shorter, though steeper. There was also a so-called Fremont trail, which Fremont had had nothing to do with, via a shoulder of Mt. Manitou, where the Mt. Manitou Incline Railway now runs. In 1882 there was a telegraph instrument and relay at Booth's (later the Half Way House) for the benefit of those who used the Ruxton trail.

Between the years 1914 and 1918 a new trail was laid out and built by Fred Barr, who had the burro concession at the upper station of the Mt. Manitou Incline Railway. This trail led across Cabin Creek into the Sheep Creek drainage and then struck out up the east face of Pike's Peak, zigzagging back and forth to gain altitude. Barr was also a charter member of the Ad-Am-An Club of Colorado Springs, formed in 1923 to climb to the top of the Peak each New Year's Eve to set off fireworks, an organization that is still going strong.

In December 1883 articles of incorporation were filed for a $30,000.00 company to be known as the Ute Pass & Pike's Peak Signal Station Toll Road Company. This may or may not have been the one that completed and opened a carriage road in 1887 from Cascade, a few miles above Manitou in Ute Pass. For a few years a more or less thriving business was done hauling tourists to the summit and back by carriage, which was easier on the human frame than riding a burro or mule. The firm of Hundley & Carlile operated such a carriage line from the Colorado Midland Railway depot in Cascade. With the opening of the cog road, the carriage road trade fell off and eventually ceased, but the road itself was, after many improvements, reopened in October 1915 as the Pike's Peak Auto Highway, a toll road that still carries many automobiles during the summer season. An annual event is the Pike's Peak Hill Climb, first run in 1916, when the great Barney Oldfield managed to place twelfth.

The office of the Signal Station at the summit looks very comfortable for the time, but the snowshoes on the wall were not just for decoration. When the ink froze in the inkwell, it was too cold to enjoy the guitar. —PIONEERS MUSEUM, COLORADO SPRINGS

The living room of the Signal Station was made liveable by a woodburning stove, which saw daily duty. The barrel-like affair was called a "drum," and contained baffles which slowed down the passage of smoke in order to extract the last bit of heat before it went up the chimney. — PIONEERS MUSEUM, COLORADO SPRINGS

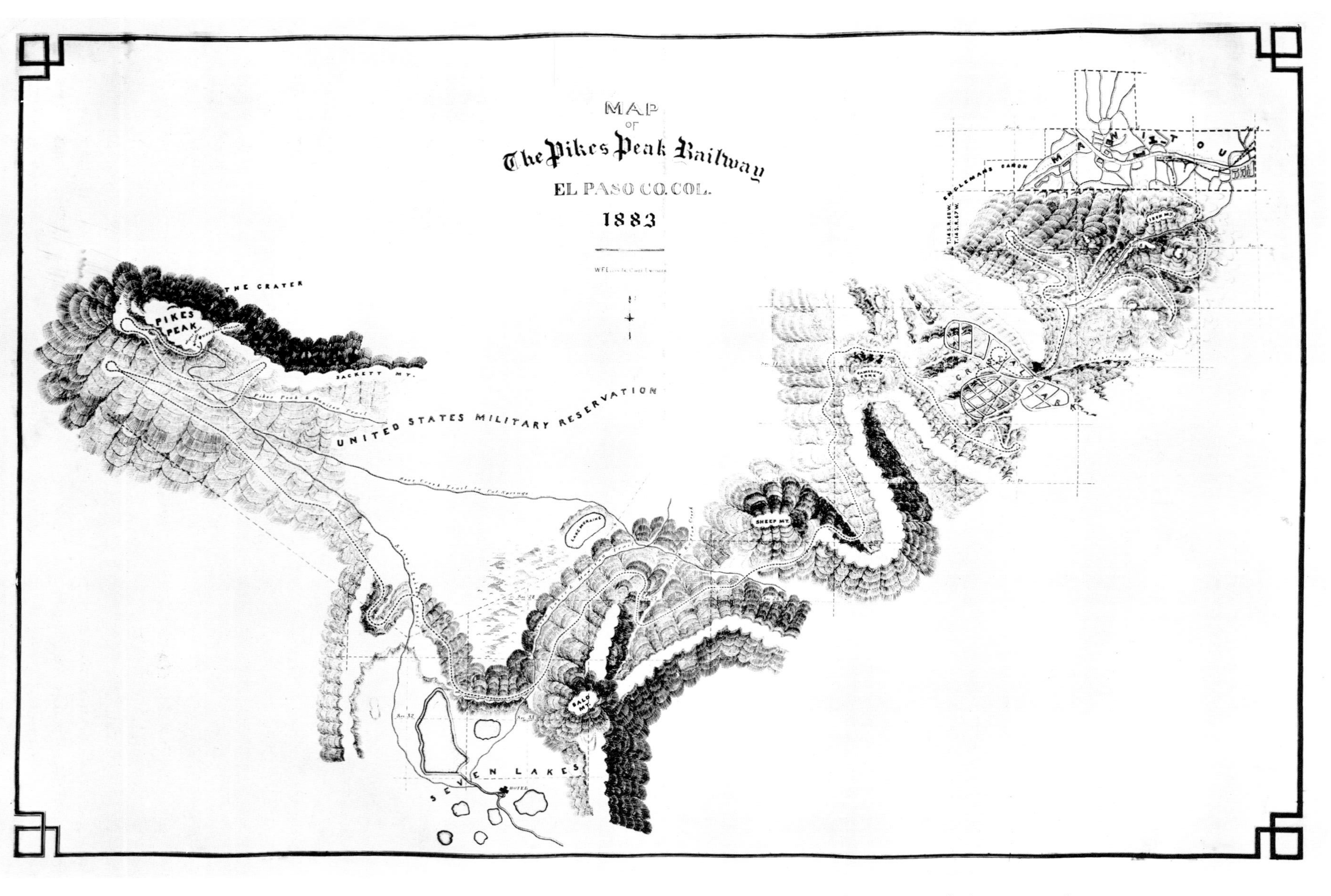

This is a reduction of a large map drawn in 1883 by W. F. Evans, chief engineer of the proposed narrow gauge railway to the summit of Pike's Peak. Starting from Manitou in the upper right hand corner, the road zig-zagged up to Crystal Park by means of two switchbacks. It then looped over itself, passed north of Cameron's Cone, then south of Sheep Mountain, and thence curled its way to the top. Note that the region was still considered a portion of the U.S. Military Reservation on account of the weather station in 1882. — WILLIAM C. MASON COLLECTION

2

FIRST PROJECTED RAILROAD

JAMES Hutchinson Kerr, M.A. (Yale) may not have been the first to dream of rails to the top of Pike's Peak, but he was the first to do anything about it. Born in Chambersburg, Pennsylvania in 1837, he was professor of chemistry and geology, a mining and metallurgical engineer, and president the first 15 years of Colorado College in Colorado Springs. Before that he had been a civil engineer for the Pennsylvania Railroad.

Kerr had friends and influence, and some of these friends had money or had other friends who had it or knew where to get it. The first proposal was for an aerial tramway for freight and passengers from Manitou to the summit of Pike's Peak, an idea that was revived as late as 1911. In April 1883 the firm of Martin, Kerr & Co. displayed a model of the tramway, and a meeting was held to discuss the matter. Professor Kerr presided, and Charles M. Huson, inventor of the type of tramway to be used, "gave full information," while E. S. McKinlay of the South Pueblo Machinery Co. presented an estimate of about $100,000.00 for an eight-mile line, which was to go via Lake Moraine.

Later in April the articles of incorporation were filed with the Secretary of State in Denver for the Pike's Peak Railway & Improvement Company, which was to have broad powers, including the building of a railroad or tramway, telegraph and telephone lines, laying out and sale of townsites, etc. The officers were Kerr, president; Irving Howbert, vice-president; T. J. Fisher, secretary; Orlando Metcalf (Pittsburgh steel magnate), treasurer. Hanson Riply, General Palmer's attorney, was also interested in the venture.

With considerable optimism, inventor Huson said he would contract "to complete the line by July 15, 1883, and positively by August 1, 1883," and resorts would be built along the line. By July, however, it was found that the Huson system could not be used, since it appeared to conflict with patents held by a California firm.

Undismayed, the company hired as engineer W. F. Ellis, city engineer for Colorado Springs, who proceeded at once to make preliminary surveys for a narrow gauge adhesion railroad, which "from Manitou passes eastward, curves around Iron Mountain, takes a westerly course to a projection on the side of the high mountains to the south of Engelmann Canyon, 1,000 feet above the Iron Spring. Here a semi-circle is described, and the road runs again east and south and pursues a tortuous way onward and upward to Crystal Park." The survey then proposed to take the road to Bear Creek, Lake Moraine, Seven Lakes and Sachett

Mountain, where timberline was to be reached.

This road was to be about 27 miles long and have a maximum gradient of 300 feet in a mile, was expected to cost $300,000.00, and Kerr reported that the Pullman Company told him that three cars could be made, each weighing three tons, with a capacity of about 120 persons each, and that a 16.5 ton locomotive could handle them. Later figures (the following April) estimated 30 miles, 316 feet rise per mile with an average of 200, numerous 40 degree curves and one of 42 degrees to describe a three-quarter circle, longest tangent 300 feet, and a cost of $12,000-$15,000 per mile. It was proposed also to use H. K. Porter & Co. locomotives "like those on the Lima & Oroya Ry., where grades are 448 feet per mile, and they operate at 18 m.p.h." Switchbacks were included in the plans.

A brief notice in the April 24, 1884 issue of the *Cadillac* (Michigan) *Weekly News* read: "E. Shay has made a bid for furnishing an engine on the famous Pike's Peak road. The grade averages 242 feet to the mile for 33 miles, and it will require a good machine to do the business. Mr. Shay says his engine can make it go."

Considerable work was actually done, and by mid-December 1883 three miles had been graded

This Packard sight-seeing bus, better known as a "rubberneck wagon," is on the turntable at Inspiration Point on the road to Crystal Park. The Crystal Park Road followed more or less the route of the proposed narrow gauge Pike's Peak Railway. Pike's Peak is faintly visible in the distance, and a short stretch of the Cog Road may be seen at the extreme right. Vehicles of this type were built on truck chassis made by Packard, White, Pierce-Arrow and others. — STEWARTS COMMERCIAL PHOTOGRAPHERS

and about 50 men were at work, which by April 1884 had risen to 80 men on the payroll, two-thirds of the grading to Crystal Park was completed, and the company cheerfully expected to operate trains that far by July, and another 18 miles (to timberline) by the end of the year.

Professor Kerr issued in 1884 a *Brief Statement Relating to The Pike's Peak Railway*. In it he mentioned that no rival road to the summit could be built for less than $50,000 per mile, painted a glowing picture of the expected increase in the tourist business, the natural resources to be made available (timber, building stone, grazing lands, mineral properties), resort locations, and the enthusiasm with which the road would be greeted by other railroads. "The Pike's Peak Railway & Improvement Company was organized . . . to build and operate a railway from Manitou to the summit of Pike's Peak. Capital stock $1,500,000. The present franchises of the Company are valued at $500,000." He went on to say that the net profit the first year could not possibly be "less than 10 percent of the capital stock, and each succeeding year must greatly increase the profits to the stockholder."

It appears that Professor Kerr did not trust the local banks, and he therefore caused the money received from the sale of stock to be deposited in the Marine National Bank of New York City, which closed its doors that very afternoon, never to reopen, due at least in part to the failure at that precise moment of the firm of Grant & Ward. That was early in May 1884, and it was the end of the line for the Pike's Peak Railway & Improvement Company.

The copy of the *Brief Statement* or prospectus, which is now in the Tutt Library of Colorado College, bears a rather pathetic notation written and signed by Kerr, which reads: "These surveys were all made at my expense. The surveys, promotion expenses &c cost me thirty thousand dollars every cent of which was lost through the failure of Grant and Ward and President Tenney's Colorado College Land Scheme. The latter being unable to return borrowed money."

The estimated cost of this narrow gauge road to the summit, as stated in 1891 when Colonel Ervay proposed a standard gauge line over about the same route, was as follows:

First division, Manitou to Crystal Park, 7.75 miles	$ 80,073	
Second division, to Bear Creek divide via Rosemont Park, 8 miles	97,670	
Third division, to timberline, 8.5 miles	108,905	
Fourth division, to summit, 5.75 miles	110,420	$397,068
Thirty miles telegraph line	7,500	
Buildings, etc.	10,000	
Real estate for right-of-way, depots, townsites, engineering offices, salaries, etc.	40,000	57,500
Four engines at $8000	32,000	
Six coaches at $3000	18,000	
Three 2nd class coaches at $2000	6,000	
Forty freight cars at $400	16,000	72,000
	Total	$526,568

Much of the old grade of the Pike's Peak Railway & Improvement Company's line was utilized in the construction in 1910 of a road to Crystal Park by the Crystal Park Auto Highway Company, under the supervision of William H. Bartlett (later El Paso County road commissioner), financed by William C. Dotterer (traffic manager of the M. & P.P.) and J. H. Van Nostrum, who was then president of the Bon Ton Bank of New York City.

At one point a turntable was installed so that the big tourist coaches could negotiate the switchback, failing which they would have dropped into Manitou. It was said that there was a mile of roadway in a 20-acre area, though another account said it was 30 acres. Either way it was and is impressive, but the company never made money, went into bankruptcy and was taken over in 1919 by the Cog Road.

Before the completion of the Manitou & Pike's Peak Railway, the only way to reach the summit was by burro, shank's mare or the carriage road. This burro party headed for Pike's Peak posed for the camera at the toll gate just above the present Cog Road depot in Manitou. —DENVER PUBLIC LIBRARY, WESTERN COLLECTION

3

THE MANITOU & PIKE'S PEAK RAILWAY

ALL ACCOUNTS seem to agree that the instigator of the movement to build a cog railway up Pike's Peak was Major John Hulbert of Manitou, Civil War veteran originally from Michigan. He apparently had the courage of his convictions, for although he had been an investor in the ill-fated Pike's Peak Railway & Improvement Company of 1883-4, he was the capable and successful promoter of the Cog Road.

Like Professor Kerr, he had friends or found the right kind of supporters, and on September 29, 1888, he and a few well-chosen gentlemen organized the Manitou & Pike's Peak Railway Company (some accounts reverse the names), with a capitalization of $500,000. The cast of characters is rather impressive, for amongst the incorporators we find Major Hulbert, Dr. William A. Bell (English backer of General Palmer's Denver & Rio Grande Railway), Louis Ehrich (wealthy New Yorker), Albert E. Pattison of Colorado Springs, and B. F. Crowell (ex-Leadville silver magnate).

The board of directors consisted of these: Major Hulbert, Ransom R. Cable (president of the Rock Island), Major Jerome Byron Wheeler (silver millionaire from Aspen and Leadville, banker, first vice-president of the Colorado Midland), David H. Moffat (banker, mine owner and president of the Denver & Rio Grande), J. B. Glasser (cashier of Wheeler's bank in Manitou), and possibly also Henry Watson. The officers were: Hulbert as president, Cable as vice-president, Wheeler secretary and treasurer. Zalmon G. Simmons was the majority stockholder, and others included Governor Roswell Pettibone Flower of New York, H. H. Porter (president of the Chicago & Eastern Illinois Railroad), Edward E. Nichols (owner of the Cliff House, Manitou's famous hostelry), and the Estate of David Dow, deceased. Without mentioning any names, Hulbert said in 1890 that a large amount of stock had been subscribed by local capitalists.

Simmons was the power behind the throne, guiding genius and supplier of cash. When the Civil War broke out, he had to choose between going to war or finishing what he was doing — extending the telegraph lines in the country north and west of Chicago. He chose the latter, did such a good job that the G.A.R. made him an honorary member, the only man save presidents to receive this honor. In the process, he made himself a fortune, acquired another from Wisconsin cheese, and finally heaped up additional monies as head of the famous Simmons mattress business in Kenosha, Wisconsin, which his descendants now operate.

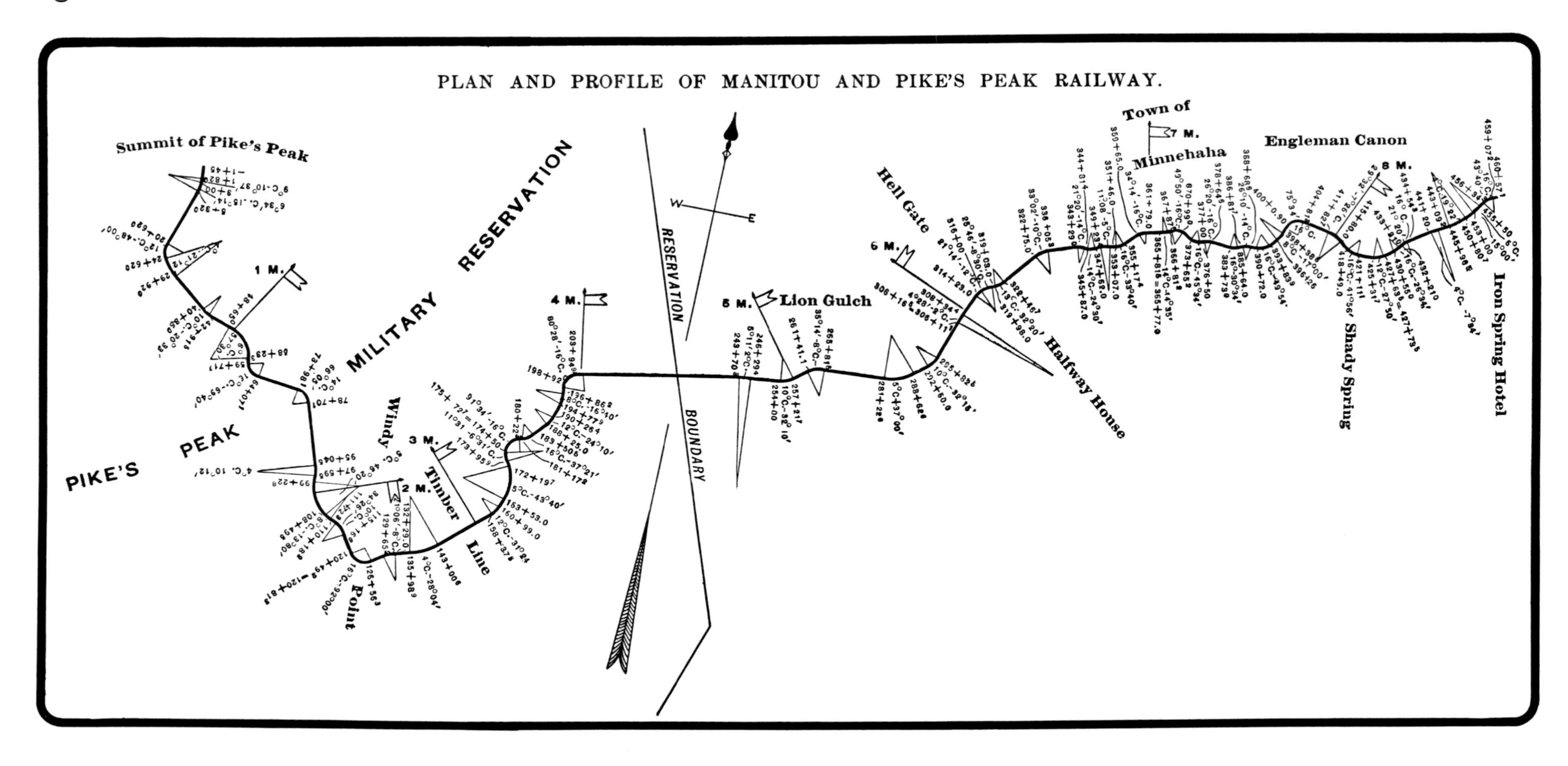

In 1894 Thomas F. Richardson, C.E., the engineer of the Manitou & Pike's Peak Railway, prepared a paper on the construction, design, equipment and early operation of the Cog Road, and presented it before the Boston Society of Civil Engineers. This plan of the line is reproduced from his paper later reprinted in the *Journal of The Association of Engineering Societies.* The plan shows the present day route, with Manitou at the right, Grecian Bend the first curve below milepost 3, and Ruxton Park just below the 6-mile marker.

Simmons had been a guest at Ed Nichols' Cliff House and was probably exposed there to Hulbert's persuasive discourse on the prospects of a railroad to the top of the world, with the desired results. Family tradition persists that he was persuaded to make the trip on board a mule yclept Balaam, doing so clad in his customary high silk hat and frock coat. Anybody who has ever ridden a burro or mule down hill knows what happened, since the animal of necessity descends stiff-legged, which does certain things to the rider's sitting and walking muscles. Anyway, that experience is said to have played an important part in his decision to become a benefactor of mankind by building a railway to the top of Pike's Peak, which he proceeded to do forthwith.

Marshall Sprague, in his *Newport in the Rockies,* tells of Simmons' opposition to the use of profanity, and how, on one occasion, he used the word "damn" on the telephone, but hastily apologized and excused his lapse by explaining that there was a burglar in the room.

After Hulbert and Simmons got their heads together, the Cog Road resulted. The other big names were additional frosting on the cake, as Simmons really put up the money, but a master stroke was their choice of Hiram S. Cable as superintendent of the Cog Road. He was the 23 year old son of the president of the Chicago, Rock Island & Pacific Railroad, and soon became general manager. The Rock Island had not long before been extended into Colorado Springs and could easily feed passenger traffic to the Cog Road, as could the Denver & Rio Grande Railway and the Colorado Midland Railway, represented respectively by David Moffat and Jerome Wheeler.

The chief engineer during the construction of the Manitou & Pike's Peak Railway was Roswell E. Briggs, who had recently resigned as chief engineer of the Denver & Rio Grande. However, the engineer actually on the job was Thomas F. Richardson, C. E. He was a member of the American Society of Civil Engineers, the Boston Society of Civil Engineers, and the Engineers Club of New York, and died in Rutherford, New Jersey in January 1916. He was credited with having built the Canyon Diablo bridge for the Santa Fe Railway in Arizona, and also "the largest bridge in New Mexico," and played an important role in the construction of the Wasachusetts dam and aqueduct in Massachusetts.

Zalmon G. Simmons, builder and first owner of the Manitou & Pike's Peak Railway, whose ascent of the mountain on a mule is said to have led him to build the railway. — DENVER PUBLIC LIBRARY, WESTERN COLLECTION

Major John Hulbert, promoter of the Cog Road and its first president. The first locomotive was named for him, later becoming No. 1. — DENVER PUBLIC LIBRARY, WESTERN COLLECTION

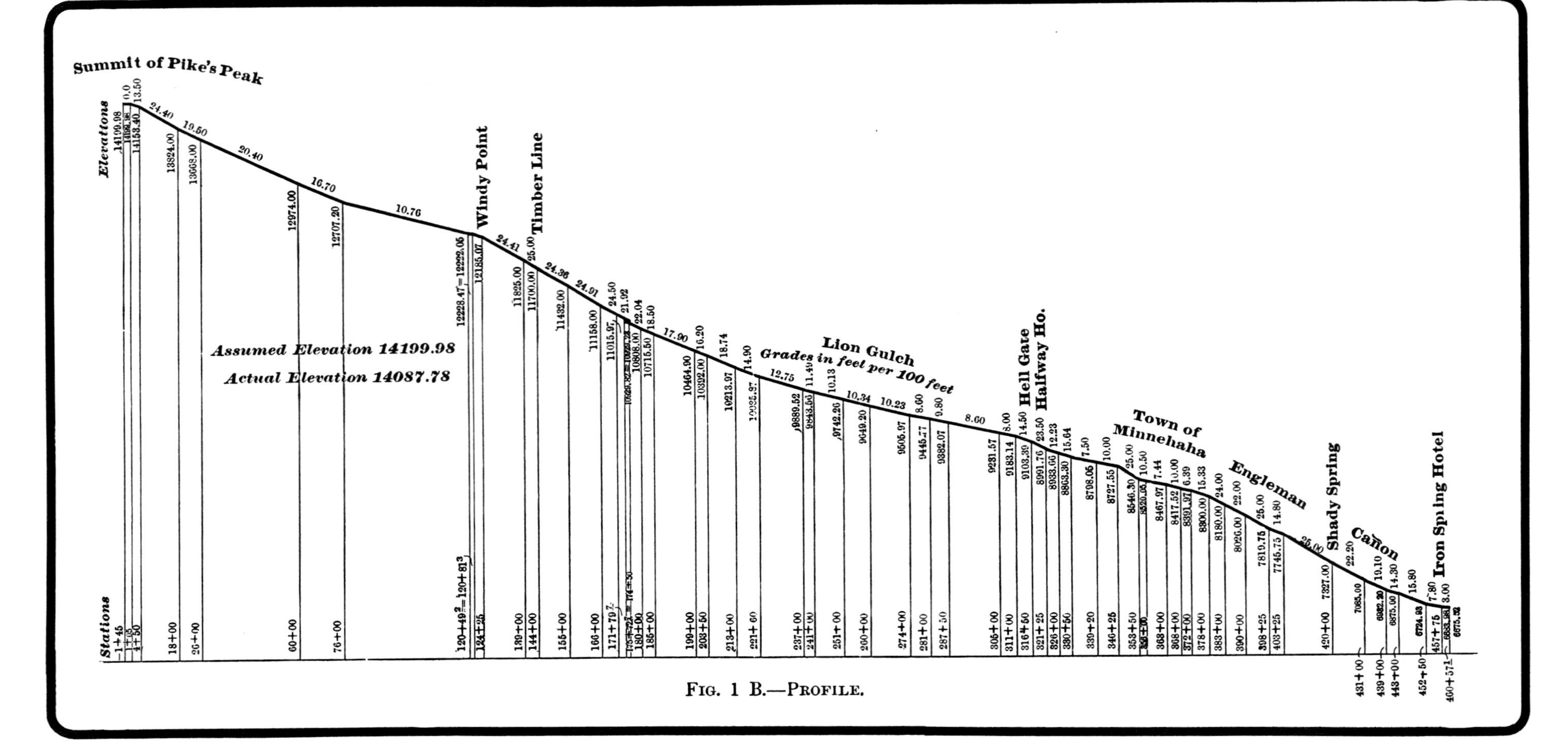

Fig. 1 B.—Profile.

This profile of the Manitou & Pike's Peak Railway, like the plan on page 20, was prepared by Thomas F. Richardson and appeared in the *Journal of The Association of Engineering Societies.* The elevations shown in his profile do not agree with those of more recent surveys. The first 25 percent grade is below Minnehaha, the next is Son-of-a-Gun Hill. The Big Hill ranges from 22.04 to 25 percent for a brief stretch, and in addition there is a short stretch of 24.4 percent grade near the summit.

Richardson read a paper before a meeting of the Boston Society of Civil Engineers on February 21, 1894, and this was printed in the August issue of the *Journal of The Association of Engineering Societies.* This paper covered so thoroughly the construction, design, equipment and early operations that the present writer has had no choice but to draw on Richardson's account at great length.

Young men are always advised that they must begin at the bottom and work up, but the survey was started at the top on April 3, 1889. Loaded with supplies and camp equipment for six weeks, a train of 30 burros went up the carriage road from Cascade on that day. Camp was pitched that night three and one-half miles from the summit.

Twelve of the strongest burros were chosen to carry the men's blankets and four days' supplies, and they reached the then abandoned signal station at the summit in the middle of the next afternoon. As April is apt to be a bad snow month on the peak, they were afraid they might be caught in a storm, and they were. In the night it began to snow, and this continued without letup for four days. On the fifth morning they fashioned makeshift sleds from an old ladder and a packing case, loaded their gear and started for their camp, three and one-half miles below, in a blinding snowstorm. There was no danger of getting lost, however, as they could and did follow the line of telegraph poles. That night they made camp at timberline, a mile from the main camp, and while they slept they were covered with another foot of snow, but got to their destination at noon.

Because of the steep grades and rough mountain slopes, their work progress was slow. Although preliminary lines and estimates were made in late June, deep snow delayed the location of the uppermost two miles until August.

When completed, the line was 46,292 feet in length, four and one-half feet shorter than the estimated 46,296.6 feet. It was found that timberline was at 11,630 feet, and that the highest spring or source of water was at an elevation of 10,110 feet, 22,000 feet distant from the summit. Some others of Richardson's statistics are of interest. The average grade is 16.23 percent, meaning a vertical rise of 16.23 feet in a horizontal distance of 100 feet. Of the total length of the road, 40 percent is on curves, and the longest tangent (straight track) is 3,975.4 feet. Curvature totals 1,844 degrees, 48 minutes (870 degrees 20 minutes right and 972 degrees 28 minutes left).

Following the submission to the owners of cost estimates, Wilhelm Hildebrand was engaged to represent Roman Abt (whose system was being used) for the rack rails and fastenings, as well as to be consulting engineer, and contracts were let to the Baldwin Locomotive Works for three engines, to the Wason Manufacturing Company for six coaches, and to B. Lantry & Sons for grading and ties.

The survey is said actually to have envisioned a lower terminus in Manitou near Red Rocks, not far above Colorado City, the surveying party having its abode in a Denver & Rio Grande maintenance-of-way car at the Manitou depot of that road, and at one time the company gave some thought to extending the line down Ruxton Creek, to have its lower terminus "where Gillis Bros. lumber yard now stands, which would be an admirable place for a depot."

As late as 1939 the management again pondered the feasibility of running the line down into town, this time to the disused Denver & Rio Grande Western depot in Manitou, beautiful in its Victorian way and now demolished. They thought of utilizing the rails and right-of-way of their Manitou Electric Railway & Casino Company part of the way, and went so far as to have the General Electric Company plan on designing their projected diesel-electric locomotive as a combination rack and adhesion type. This was in fact done, but proved mechanically disappointing, which, as it turned out, did not matter, as the extension never materialized, possibly because Spencer Penrose became seriously ill and died before any decision was made. The extension would have been about 1.5 miles in length, and it is at least interesting that America almost had its second combination rack-adhesion railway. The grading contract called for completion by May 1, 1890, so work was begun at the top on September 25, 1889, since it was desirable to get the upper end finished before winter set in, if possible. However, the contractor had to leave much of the grading above timberline unfinished in November, when there was a four foot snowfall, and it was early June before operations could be resumed there.

Most of the heavy work was near the lower end, which may seem odd, and all grading below timberline was finished on time. Nevertheless, the difficulties and problems of work and supply were many and troublesome. All supplies and equipment had to be brought up by pack train, as there were no roads, other than the carriage road near the top. There were two steam drills in Manitou waiting for somebody to figure out how to get them up to the job, but they never made it. The lower three miles cost more to grade than the top six miles. The labor turnover was high, as the lack of oxygen at the higher elevations made work difficult and unattractive, though men who stayed on the job two or three weeks were thereafter able to do a good day's work without much discomfort. It seemed that there were always three gangs — one leaving, one working and one coming.

Because of the grade and rough terrain, it was impracticable to use horses, so the work was nearly all done with pick, shovel and wheelbarrow. While there were frequent snow storms, Pike's Peak is generally free of snow most of the year, but, as we shall mention later, they found permanent ice two feet below the surface.

A time book of construction days found years later showed that top wages were 25 cents and common labor 18 cents per hour. Richardson mentioned two dollars per day as the going rate for labor, and said that, under the contract, grading was to be paid for at the rate of 15 cents per cubic yard for earth, 32 cents for loose rock and 90 cents for solid rock. He went on to say that this rate was far too low in view of the difficulities, and should have been 25 to 30 percent higher to give the contractor a fair deal. One practice, however, did favor the contractor. If he used excavation for fill, he was paid 32 cents per yard when he excavated and another 32 cents when he used the same material for an embankment. All ballast is coarse gravel (disintegrated granite) from gravel slides along the right of way.

There were at least five labor camps along the route, and the number of men employed was said to be as high as 1,000, which was probably an overstatement for publicity purposes. One camp was above timberline, probably at or near the Saddle and not far above Windy Point. Within the writer's memory there stood there, on the left of the track, the remains of the "cement house," and hardened blocks of what had been cloth bags of cement were scattered about. Two other camps were above the Half Way House, and if you know where to look you can identify one of the sites today.

Camp No. 5 was one and one-quarter miles above the old toll gate, which should place it about at Butterworth Flat, though there is not much room anywhere in Engelmann Canyon for the buildings described. In December 1889 two newspapermen, one from Colorado Springs and the other from Denver, went to within a mile of the summit, and described Camp 5 as having accommodations for 200 men: viz., three bunk houses each 50x16 feet, a cook house 90x30 feet, all built of logs up four feet from the ground and canvas above that. Ordinary tents had proven too flimsy and cold.

Up to that time six men had lost their lives on the job, two from heart failure, three from blasts, and one, an engineer by the name of G. C. Huntington, was crushed by a falling boulder. One of the deaths occurred on Sunday, December 7, 1889, when the men were at dinner. The dynamite blasts were customarily set off at that time, and on this day the fuses were lighted for a blast 900 feet away. A 60-pound piece of granite fell into the tent and shattered, one piece injuring a man's foot, another striking one Antonio Jose Farrilla in the left shoulder, severing the jugular vein. He died in a few minutes, and was buried at company expense in Evergreen Cemetery.

Most of the laborers were foreigners, and the Italians usually dug themselves caves to sleep in. Breakfast was at 5 a.m., supper at 6 p.m. The pay was, according to these reporters, $2 per day for week days, $2.50 for Sundays, board and lodging $4.50 per week. Because of the elevation, few men could work every day, and the contractor stated in print that, because of the altitude, effective labor cost one dollar per hour, an unheard of wage in 1889-90.

The presence of so many men in Engelmann Canyon during construction and the frequent use of dynamite caused such a muddying of the waters of Ruxton Creek that water-drinking folks in Colorado Springs had much fault to find. When the mayor and an alderman went to Manitou to protest, the contractor assured them that "the camps are removed from the creek, use only spring water, not creek water, garbage is buried," etc. Those who have journeyed up the Ruxton will wonder where, below the Half Way House, a camp could be set up and not be close to the creek.

The contract for grading also included the "second-class" masonry for the four iron bridges, and this work was at $11 per cubic yard. The total cost of grading, log culverts of red spruce and masonry

A popular post card subject in the 1890's, this burro carried a conglomeration of tools and supplies, with a sign reading, "I HELPED TO BUILD THE PIKE'S PEAK RAILROAD." It never is a problem to get a burro to stand still! — MORRIS W. ABBOTT COLLECTION

came to $150,000, but this included considerable cost that Richardson felt should have been charged to buildings.

The four iron bridges were supplied by the Edgemoor Bridge Works of Wilmington, Delaware, and one wonders why it was necessary to go so far afield for such small and simple iron girders. These bridges were located as follows: one beside the shops in Manitou, one just below Minnehaha, and two above Son-of-a-Gun Hill a few hundred yards below the Half Way House.

There was a bit of a controversy between the grading contractor (referred to variously as Lantry Brothers, Langton & Sons, and B. Lantry & Sons, of Joliet, Illinois, Topeka or Strong City, Kansas) and the company. In September 1890 Lantry put a lien of $61,000 on the Cog Road because of a dispute over the meaning of the contract terms. Lantry claimed 90 cents a cubic yard for rock cut plus another 90 cents when the same was used as fill, while Simmons agreed to the 90 cents for the cut, but only 32 cents more when it was used as fill. At this time, all but two miles had been graded, and the telephone line completed to "Timber Line Camp." In November 1891 (the courts were slow then, too), when the amount had grown to $65,000 (one account says $76,000), President Hulbert went to Chicago to meet with Simmons, and attended the hearing of the suit. The company had chosen as arbitrator H. A. Parker, general manager of the Rock Island, while Lantry had picked A. A. Robinson, general manager and vice-president of the Santa Fe. Together they agreed upon a third, O. Chanute. The Colorado Springs papers did not report, as far as the writer can learn, as to the outcome, which could very well have been a compromise.

In November 1890 the *Colorado Springs Gazette* reported the completion, at a cost of $2,000, of the cog road's new repair shop. It was "like the railroad, diminutive, but good," and included the usual blacksmith and pattern shops, machine shop with lathe, planer and drill press. The machinists were then engaged in putting the machinery in good repair for the next season.

Richardson's paper gives great detail and descriptions of the bearing and rack rail. The rails are ordinary 40-lb. T-rails laid on standard gauge wooden ties with the rail spacing to the standard gauge measure of four feet eight and one-half inches. The Abt rack rail is laid in the center between them, and consists of two toothed steel bars, fastened side by side in specially designed chairs. These bars are 80 inches long, four and five-eighths inches deep, and vary in thickness depending upon the grade. On all grades under 12.5 percent the

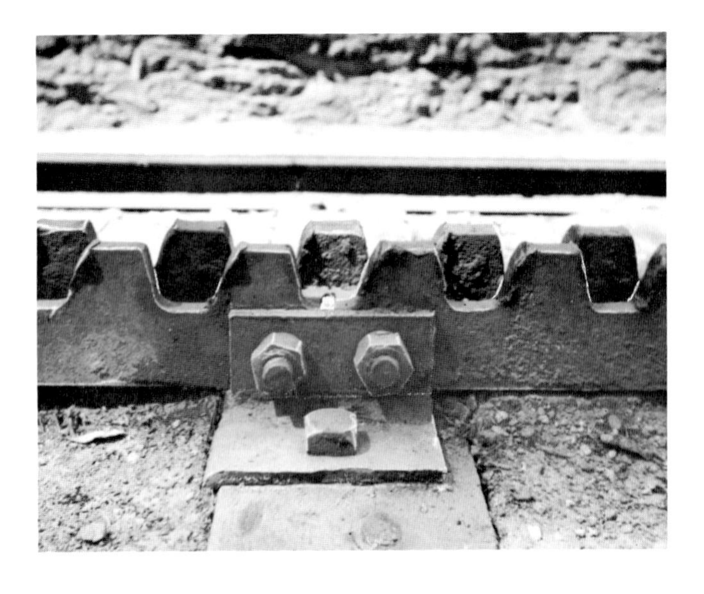

The basic design of the cog track is one of the interesting features of the Manitou & Pike's Peak Railway. This illustration shows how the rack rails are fastened together and to the supporting tie. The ends of the two nearer rack bars, and the center portion of the farther rack bar meet here, and all are held firmly in the chair. Note how the plate is bent downward and around the uphill edge of the tie, and that the upper faces of the rack teeth are battered by wear. — MORRIS W. ABBOTT

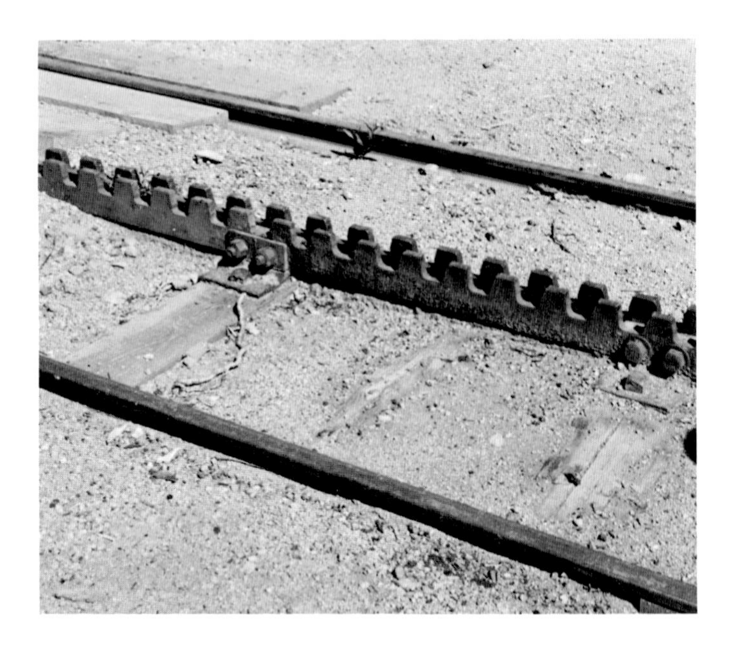

This illustration shows the rack in relation to the running rails. The rack rail (actually two rack rails each offset) is located midway between the two standard running rails which do little more than carry the weight of the train and guide it. — MORRIS W. ABBOTT

bars have a thickness of seven-eighths inch, on grades 12.5 to 15.5 percent they are one inch thick, one and one-eighth inch on 15.5 to 19.5 percent one and three-sixteenths inch on grades 19.5 to 22.5 percent, and one and one-quarter inches on steeper grades. The teeth of the bars are 2 inches deep, with a pitch distance of 2.35295 inches. They are of steel to stand a tensile strain of 70,000 lbs. per square inch. They cost, in 1890, 4.5 cents per pound, f.o.b. the factory.

In later years it was found that the rack bars, after becoming battered on the upper side of the teeth, could be turned end for end and thus their useful life could be doubled. When unfit for main line service, they could be and were used on sidings and in the sheds.

Abroad most Abt systems used steel ties, but, as we have noted, the Pike's Peak road followed standard American practise and used hewn red spruce ties nine feet long by seven by eight inches. To maintain the correct relative height of the T-rails and rack rails, an ordinary jointer-planer was used to plane each tie where the chairs were to be located, at a cost of nine cents per tie.

The engines as first built were powerful enough to allow track material for 210 feet to be run up to the farthest point where the rack rail had been secured. Each load included the correct number and sizes of rack bars, chairs, bolts, washers, nuts, cover plates, ties and anchorage material for the grade on which the track was laid. The material was then loaded on light cars drawn by two mules, a load consisting of nine ties and two 30-foot rails on heavy grades. To prevent these light cars from rolling backwards downhill in case of breakage of traces, etc., two stout pieces of oak were hinged on behind and dragged over the ties. This arrangement also allowed the mules to rest, permitting the load to roll back upon the oak blocks. It was found best to keep the T-rails somewhat ahead of the rack rail.

Tracklaying began on June 11, and was completed on October 20, 1890, lacking five days of being 13 months from the time the grading had been started. The cost of tracklaying was about $4,275 per mile, totalling $38,100 and this included engine service, the cost of installing switches, and everything except engineering. Richardson was convinced that the cost would have been less if the material had been more simply designed, by which it can be assumed that he felt there were too many

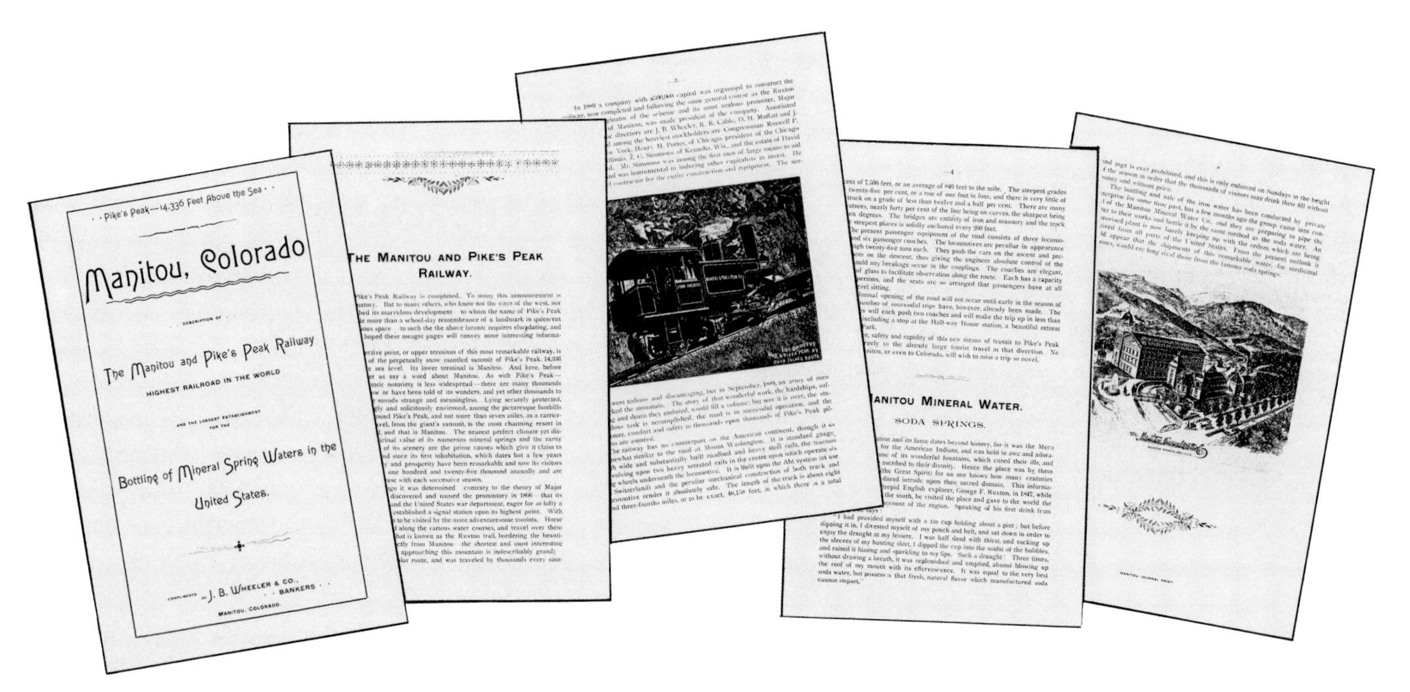

J. B. Wheeler & Co., bankers, Manitou, issued this booklet in 1890 to describe in detail the marvels of the Manitou & Pike's Peak Railway. Shown here are a few pages of the booklet which contain some beautiful line drawings of the Cog Road. Besides banking, Wheeler was a principal in R. H. Macy & Co., and vice-president of the Colorado Midland Railway. — MORRIS W. ABBOTT COLLECTION

sizes of rack bars, chairs and bolts.

There were seven switches, located only where the grade was no more than 12.5 percent, and they worked very satisfactorily. The original switches, complete with ties and bearing rails, were made in Johnstown, Pennsylvania, at a cost of $900 each, but the company later made several in its own shops for less than half that figure. There are four switches out on the line, all leading to the left into short spurs, at Minnehaha, Half Way House, Mountain View and Windy Point. Others are at the upper and lower termini.

Complete technical details of the track, rack, chairs, and roadbed construction may be found in the appendix section of this book.

During August and September Pike's Peak is a place of severe electrical disturbances, and these may have been unusually serious during the time of tracklaying, for Richardson records that several of the workmen "were badly shocked, one of them being confined to the hospital for a month in consequence." It was necessary to insulate wrench handles and other tools with lengths of rubber hose. However, these disturbances were not accompanied by lightning, and were probably what is known as St. Elmo's fire, for Richardson one evening saw the telegraph wire glowing so weirdly that it looked like a rope of fire.

Railway Age for January 18, 1890 carried the news that the M. & P.P.'s entire roadway would be lighted by electricity before the rail was laid, and a few months later announced that the sale of the road to the Rock Island had been reported. Neither occurred.

Finally, according to the *Manitou Springs Journal,* in July 1890 Zalmon G. Simmons, as general contractor, "turned the road over to its owners complete in every detail," upon which he and Mrs. Simmons left for their home in Kenosha, to return later in the summer. No doubt the ceremony, if any, was a simple one, since he was both general contractor and principal owner. Also, it seems that it was a bit premature, as tracklaying was not completed till October 20, and the last spike was not driven until October 22, with appropriate fanfare, amidst a group of officials and photographers.

According to the Interstate Commerce Commission Valuation Docket No. 749, Simmons received the entire stock issue as compensation for the building of the road. The same authority says that the road cost the corporation $500,000 of capital stock and another $500,000 represented by the general mortgage. What it had cost Simmons is not known, but it was all his money anyway.

PIKE'S PEAK

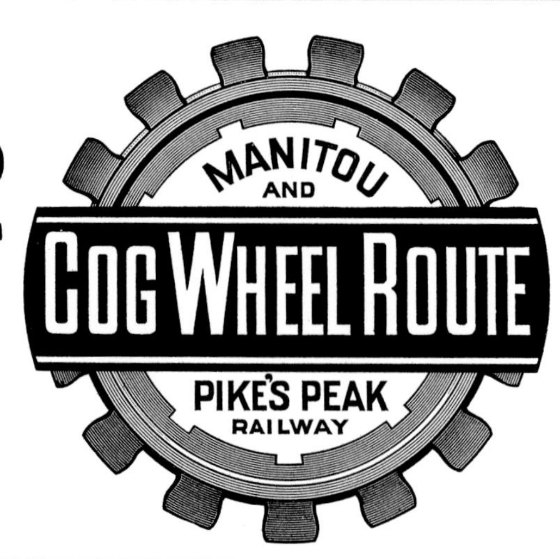

...Do Not Miss It...

The TRIP of a LIFE TIME

The Grandest Scenery on the Globe

ROUND TRIP IN 4 HOURS.

Low Rate Excursions for the N. E. A.

2 P. M. JULY 7, 9, 11, 13, 14, 15, 17, 19 & 21.

ASK PRINCIPAL RAILWAY TICKET AGENTS ABOUT IT

H. S. CABLE, Pres. and Mgr.
Manitou, Colo.

Cog Road poster issued about 1895. — MORRIS W. ABBOTT COLLECTION

4

EARLY OPERATIONS

THE LAST SPIKE was driven at 10 a.m. on October 22, 1890, with a certain amount of to-do. The *Denver Times* carried quite an account of the ceremony, under the date of October 25, and mentioned that the event was witnessed by "several of the officials and E. W. Irish of this city, who was employed to photograph the scene and other points of interest along the route." Unfortunately, no one has been able to locate any of these pictures. Irish, who was referred to in other articles as W. H. and W. E., was of the firm of Ogden & Irish of Denver, and was registered at the Cliff House in Manitou the previous day. The news-hawk who reported to the *Times* then succumbed to the effects of the altitude or the beauty of the scene, or something, and said that the road was "some 20 miles long," that the grades were from 8 to 25 "degrees", and that Chief Ouray, that noble Ute, had used Pike's Peak as a place for his signal fires to communicate with his braves hunting buffalo on the plains. The *Colorado Springs Gazette* devoted two lines to the event, in its "Manitou Springs News" notes — "The Pike's Peak cog road was completed yesterday."

A Baldwin Locomotive Works supervisor, C. D. Herman, had been in Manitou since May 1890 to assist in preparing the motive power for service, which he did with only indifferent success.

However, some trains other than work trains were run over part of the road in the summer of 1890. A test run was made as far as Artist's Glen on August 15, with the coach *Leadville,* and amongst the passengers were a number of general passenger agents, notably Shadrack K. Hooper of the Denver & Rio Grande. Although the brake test showed that the car could be stopped "within six inches," the ride was "not very smooth."

The cog road officially opened for business as far as the Half Way House on August 16 (or perhaps the 23rd), the first locomotive having arrived late in May and a grade prepared from the end of the Colorado Midland trestle to the cog road tracks to handle it. A regular schedule of two trains daily was inaugurated, one to leave Manitou at eight in the morning and starting back from the Half Way House at half after nine, the other leaving Manitou at three in the afternoon. Many passengers continued on to the top on horses from Palsgrove's Half Way House.

On August 22, a train carried a committee of citizens of Colorado Springs on the first leg of a tour of inspection of that city's water supply system. Messrs. Irving Howbert and William S. Jackson, both wealthy mine owners and later promoters of the Colorado Springs & Cripple Creek District Railway, were on this committee, which rode

Early photograph of a Cog Road train at Half Way House, possibly at the time this was end-of-track. Note the fireman of the *Manitou* has installed fringed padding on the sill of his window to cushion his left arm. — PIONEERS MUSEUM, COLORADO SPRINGS

the train as far as the Half Way House. They then took horses to Windy Point, cut down to Seven Lakes and returned homeward by way of the Bear Creek wagon road.

The 1891 season opened late, either because the snow was unusually deep or because they had not yet learned how best to remove it. On June 4 the first train ran as far as the Half Way House, the faithful horses taking some of the hardier souls (and their bodies) on to the summit.

Then came the dawn of The Big Day, and it was announced in the press that the first passenger train ever to ascend to the top of Pike's Peak would do so on June 29. A pride of officials, plus a gaggle of reporters and photographers, stood by, only to be put off a full day because the hardworking section crew had not been able to clear the rails all the way, and the best laid plans had to be relaid.

Came the dawn again, and the proud moment. The locomotive *John Hulbert* and the coach *Denver* rolled down to the loading platform of the ornate little depot and took aboard the following imposing aggregation:

M. & P. P. officials: Major John Hulbert, Zalmon G. Simmons, R. R. Cable, David H. Moffat, Jerome B. Wheeler and J. B. Glasser.

Manitou officials: Major and Mayor M. A. Leddy; trustees E. E. Nichols, H. F. Miller, E. P. Creighton, William Frizzell, Dr. Isaac Davis, D. L. Sterling; city treasurer F. E. Boynton; city clerk C. H. Frowine; city attorney Pearl S. King; police magistrate Homer B. Snyder; city physician H. M. Ogilbee.

Colorado Springs officials: Mayor Ira G. Sprague; aldermen S. J. Dunbar, W. R. Roby, D. W. Robbins, R. B. Hosick, J. A. Leech, F. L. Rouse, E. C. Bartlett; waterworks superintendent E. W. Frost; city clerk A. H. Corman; city engineer H. J. Reif; plumbing inspectors Deloz Durfee and F. A. Mangold; also S. H. Kinslee, James Doyle, Dr. E. C. Kimball, T. A. McMorris and marshal L. C. Dana. El Paso County commissioner David McShane joined the party by boarding the train at Ruxton Park or Mountain View.

There were others, including photographers George E. Mellen, J. G. Hiestand, S. E. Jones, O. R. Boynton, J. B. Palsgrove, F. E. Post and possibly also W. E. Irish. Newsmen included C. A. Lyman of the *Manitou Springs Journal,* G. Herbert

Even on the Manitou & Pike's Peak Railway, every operating railroad employee carries a time table different from the time table issued to the general public. This is Employees Time Table No. 1, effective August 20, 1890, and it shows two daily trains and one additional train on Sunday. The run of 2.63 miles to the Half Way House, end of operations at that time, was 50 minutes. — MORRIS W. ABBOTT COLLECTION

MANITOU AND PIKE'S PEAK RY.

TIME TABLE No. 1,

IN EFFECT ON AND AFTER AUGUST 20TH, 1890.

UP TRAINS				DOWN TRAINS		
No. 5 Sunday only	No. 3 Daily	No. 1 Daily		No. 2 Daily	No. 4 Daily	No. 6 Sunday only
p. m.	p. m.	a. m.		a. m.	p. m.	p. m.
12.30	3.00	8.30	.....MANITOU.....	10.20	5.20	2.35
1.20	3.50	9.20	HALF WAY HOUSE	9.45	4.45	2.00
p. m.	p. m.	a. m.		a. m.	p. m.	p. m.

Up trains have right of track against Down trains.
No. 4 will wait at Half Way House until Trail party arrives from Summit.

H. S. CABLE,
MANAGER.

This train, halted at the Half Way House for this photograph, contains many important people connected with the Cog Road. David H. Moffat is the whiskered gentleman wearing the top hat just to the left of the tree, while Thomas F. Richardson stands to the left of the overcoated man to the right of the tree. It is quite possible this is one of the two trains that were to have been the first to reach the summit the morning of June 30, 1891. Moffat was a passenger on one of those trains. — DENVER PUBLIC LIBRARY, WESTERN COLLECTION

The jaunty pilot of the *Pike's Peak* admires the scenery at the Half Way House in this early photograph. At this time the water tank had not been installed, the tracks were lined with planks, and many tree stumps remained. Photographer Hiestand's spare tripod was found lying around at the lower left. Behind the train is the north wall of Hell Gate, called Lion Rock. — CARL F. MATTHEWS COLLECTION

MANITOU AND PIKE'S PEAK RAILWAY.

Time Table No. 3   Tuesday June 30th 1891

Down Trains.					Distance from Summit		Distance from Manitou	Up Trains.				
Ex.	5	3.	4/1	1/1		Train		1/2	2/2	4	6	Ext.
Gamber	Ackley		Gamber	Ackley		Conductor		Gamber	Ackley		Ackley	Gamber
Mistler	Quinlan		Mistler	Quinlan		Engineer		Mistler	Quinlan		Quinlan	Mistler
J.H.	P.P.		J.H.	P.P.		Engine		J.H.	P.P.		P.P.	J.H.
9.34	5.49		from W Point	from Windy point	–	Summit	8.90			annulled	5.20	8.42
10.08	6.07			11.35	1.77	Saddle House	7.13				3.21	8.10
							N.P.	11.00	11.00			
11.06	6[illegible]		12.26	12.00	4.86	Mt View	4.04	9.25	9.30		2.17	6.42
11.20	6.56		12.42	12.08	6.27	H. W. House	2.63	9.13	9.19			3.57
11.36	7.00			12.18	7.10	Minnehaha	1.80	9.03	9.10		1.59	3.37
11.55	7.18 a.m.		1.17	12.38	8.90	Manitou	–	8.22 a.m.	8.37 a.m.		1.25 p.m.	3.00

Remarks: 1st + 2nd 2 stopped at Windy Point

No 6 delayed 1 hour and 33 minutes on account of rock on the track.

This original train sheet from the Manitou & Pike's Peak Railway collection shows when the first train reached the summit. We see that the first and second sections of train No. 2 reached Windy Point and were forced to return to Manitou. Train No. 4 was annulled, and train No. 6 became the first to make it all the way, though delayed an hour and 33 minutes for track clearing. This was followed by an extra train that left Manitou at 3:00 P.M. and returned at 11:55 P.M. — MANITOU & PIKE'S PEAK RAILWAY COLLECTION

Brown who represented several eastern papers, J. K. Burton of the *Pueblo Chieftain*, Bert Cassidy of the *Denver Republican*, and W. L. Wilder of the *Colorado Springs Gazette*.

At 8:22 a.m. the engineer whistled off and the train departed for the dizzy heights which not so many years earlier Lieutenant Pike felt might never be scaled by man. A reporter who had been over the road before said that there was little of the grinding and shaking that had been so objectionable the previous year. At 9:13 a.m. the train reached the Half Way House, above which "the 8 percent grade seemed almost level." The *Denver Times* representative wrote that "indeed the speed was that of a horse car. On nearly level ground it was as *fast* as a horse car, and on steep places it was as *slow* as a horse car." Water was taken often, through hoses, as the tanks were not yet functioning, and at each such stop pictures of the passengers were made by lensmen Mellen, Hiestand, Jones and Boynton.

A second train left the lower station soon after the first, carrying the Northwestern Kansas Editorial Association members and their wives. All went well until the first train was about to leave Windy Point, when it was learned that some large boulders had rolled down upon the track and the section men, though they had tackled the job in the early hours of the morning, had not been able to clear them off the track and could not open the road for some time to come. As the *Gazette* man put it, "There was a visible lengthening of faces as the news was announced," and we can be sure that the longest faces were those of Simmons and Hulbert. To make matters worse, the management had contracted to carry 60-odd excursionists to the summit that same afternoon.

Most of the passengers decided to return to Manitou with the trains, but some set out on foot for the summit, two terrible miles away. All of them eventually got down safely, but surely wiser. The *Gazette* reporter, being made of sterner stuff,

FIRST TRAIN TO THE SUMMIT

On the afternoon of June 30, 1891, the choir of the Highlands Christian Church of Denver assembled on the depot platform of the Cog Road. Little did they realize they would be the first passengers to reach the summit. In this scene the group on the depot platform pose for the photographer as they wait for the morning train to return, refuel and take them to the summit. — MRS. FRANK C. MARTIN COLLECTION

The first train to the summit stopped en route for photographs, or possibly the pause was to clear the track and the picture taking was incidental. In the scene at the left captured at Windy Point, the man wearing the high silk hat mounts the platform of the coach *Denver* and salutes the photographer, while the engine takes on water. (RIGHT) Above Windy Point the train stopped again. Passengers gaze off toward Seven Lakes, while a curious lad watches the photographer. — BOTH MRS. FRANK C. MARTIN COLLECTION

The first passenger train on the Manitou & Pike's Peak Railway has arrived at the summit of Pike's Peak. The members of the choir gather in front of the coach *Denver* and beside the Summit House for this memorable photograph. Track layers' tools lie alongside the track, and the heavy planks have not yet been spiked to the ties. There are many illustrations marked "First Train to the Summit," but this is the true first train to reach the summit of Pike's Peak. — MRS. FRANK C. MARTIN COLLECTION

An excellent study of the locomotive *Pike's Peak* standing below the Manitou depot. When first built, the first three cog engines had a large star on the plate attached to the smoke box. This was changed when the engines carried numbers rather than names. Note the inclined cylinders, sloping steam chest with an oil cup on top, and the "bootleg" stack. The locomotive did not have a pilot as the heavy piece of strap iron pushed against the coach, later replaced by a roller. — CHARLES E. FISHER COLLECTION

decided to see the thing through, so he sat down in the (then) log section house at the Saddle, ate his lunch and watched the progress of the work.

The afternoon excursion was of the choir of the Highlands Christian Church of Denver, with 60 or 65 people involved. They had left Denver by special train, so said the report, at 7:45 that morning. Arriving in Manitou at 11 o'clock, they had two hours to devote to the curio shops and to imbibing the odoriferous but supposedly healthful mineral waters before train time.

At 1:25 p.m., the locomotive *Pike's Peak* and the coach *Denver* took on the happy excursionists and headed up the hill, cylinder cocks open and all hands happy. The crew consisted of conductor P. B. Ackley, engineer Ed Quinlan, brakeman William Campbell, and fireman Homer Durham. They could not have had much more experience than the passengers. Arriving in due time at Windy Point, they cheered the men who had worked like granite-chewing beavers since 4 a.m., without a pause for refreshment, to clear the rocks away. "At 5:10 p.m. amid cheers from Superintendent Richardson and men, the train passed over the repaired track, and at 5:20 p.m. the train reached Summit, the first passenger car to reach it."

The day was a cloudy one, and by the time they had reached the top there was nothing left to do but head for home. In spite of the lack of sunshine, the lateness of the hour and the slowness of the lenses and films available, some of the photographers got pictures worth reproducing. Hiestand, who probably had the inside track with the management, was quoted as saying that he secured the only successful photograph of the party at the summit, but the one made by Post that is reproduced in this book casts considerable doubt on his claim. The whole party enjoyed a dinner at the company's expense at the Iron Spring Hotel upon their return to Manitou.

The gentleman in the high silk hat on the rear platform of the coach *Leadville* is none other than Zalmon G. Simmons, owner of the Cog Road. The train has stopped at the beginning of Son-of-a-Gun Hill, which appears to have been temporarily a water stop. Note the pipe and hose alongside the track. During the early era of railroading, each locomotive engineer cared for his engine with spit and polish. Many adorned the headlight with ornaments, like the antlers shown here on the *Manitou*. — STATE HISTORICAL SOCIETY OF COLORADO

Governor Rout's party of about 45 people made the trip "in two special trains." With him were state officials and their better halves, officers of the 7th Regiment U.S.A., and Captain F. A. Wadleigh of the D. & R.G., and others of importance. This was on July 11, 1891, and the train (one of them) was taken up by engineer Quinlan in 2 hours and 15 minutes and down in one hour 22 minutes, including all stops.

By this time the management felt secure in establishing regular timecard runs, and announced on July 18, 1891, that a series of moonlight trips would be made when the moon was full and bewitching, leaving Manitou at 5:15 p.m. and getting back about 10 o'clock in the evening.

Whether or not the moon had anything to do with it no one knows, but the first wedding to take place on Pike's Peak was celebrated on October 10, 1891, when A. B. Froman and Emma J. Michael, both of Colorado Springs, were married before a group of 60 guests, all of whom came up by special train.

Pike's Peak by Rail

MANITOU AND COG WHEEL ROUTE PIKE'S PEAK RAILWAY

The Manitou & Pike's Peak Railway

THE HIGHEST AND MOST WONDERFUL RAILWAY IN THE WORLD!

FOR INFORMATION AND TIME TABLES INQUIRE AT PRINCIPAL RAILROAD TICKET OFFICES OR ADDRESS

John Hulbert, PRESIDENT. H. S. Cable, MANAGER

MANITOU COLORADO.

COG WHEEL ROUTE TO PIKE'S PEAK

The Manitou & Pike's Peak Railway

...mpleted to the Summit of Pike's Peak, and the gold ...riven October 20th, 1890, after almost two years of ...ciably hard labor. The traveler who now makes ...t of the grand old mountain in comfort cannot con... ...e peril and hardship attending the survey, or the study devoted to the difficult problem by the ...neers and mechanics, or any of the many diffi... ...ntered in locating and grading the roadbed and ...ck. Camping out, climbing over the broken ...d with fallen timber and jagged rocks, the ...se cold, terrible snow storms, fearful winds, ...y of getting provisions, made this one of ...rtakings ever commenced.

...ummit of Pike's Peak has always been ...very one coming to Colorado. To this ...es, at a point starting from old Summit ...miles west of Manitou, a sort of an ...hacked out that led to within a short ...place. This was the original path... ...l was not very clearly established, ...d somewhat dangerous, only a few ...venturesome travelers availed ...1871-73 and 77 respectively, to ...d for shorter and more direct ...her trails were constructed. ...continually advancing, and ...still greater improvement in ...eak. During that year the ...le Canon, six miles above ...n miles in a zigzag path... ...the west side of the ...these routes, however, ...rney, never occupying ...ding to two or three. ...lists, foreseeing the ...e's Peak, organized ...e. Their idea was ...circuitous grade, ...enced and nearly ...owing to insuffi... ...se opinions as ...dertaking was ...oject, never... ...the advant... ...ccordingly

COG WHEEL ROUTE TO PIKE'S PEAK

on the 28th day of September, 1888, papers of incorporation for another organization entitled The Manitou & Pike's Peak Railway Company, were drawn up and filed with the proper authorities.

CAMERON'S CONE.

In two respects only does the Manitou & Pike's Peak railway differ to any great extent from ordinary railroads. The first and foremost of these is the very heavy grade that, in a few feet short of nine miles, makes an elevation of

Before the turn of the century, the time table was more than just a schedule of trains and the rates between points on the line. The time table was the billboard in brochure form which contained illustrations and descriptive data intended to lure the tourist. This time table and folder bearing no date is without doubt the first issue of the Manitou & Pike's Peak Railway. — MORRIS W. ABBOTT COLLECTION

Love having had its day, and winter approaching, the road closed for the season a week later, having carried 9,700 passengers that year. On the basis of that business and the knowledge that one engine could not handle two coaches, they ordered the fourth locomotive from Baldwin, and in 1892, "the conclave year," the road was blessed with 16,700 passengers. "The conclave" seems to have been a convention of the Knights Templar.

Another occasion of celebration was the operation of a very special train on September 12, 1896, to carry to the summit the guests of R. R. Cable attending the wedding of his son, Hiram S. Cable. The trainmen decorated the train in honor of the event. With conductor Haugg and engineer Mathews in charge, the special left Manitou at 2:30 p.m., spent 20 minutes at the top, and arrived again at the lower station at 5:29 p.m. Engine No. 3 powered the train, and the original train order sheet bears the notation "Clear and Pleasant."

SCIENTIFIC AMERICAN

A WEEKLY JOURNAL OF PRACTICAL INFORMATION, ART, SCIENCE, MECHANICS, CHEMISTRY, AND MANUFACTURES.

NEW YORK, JANUARY 24, 1891

UNDER THE CLIFFS.

NEARING THE SUMMIT OF PIKE'S PEAK.

GOING UP A STEEP SECTION.

THE PIKE'S PEAK RAILROAD LOCOMOTIVE.

INCLINED RAILROAD TO THE SUMMIT OF PIKE'S PEAK.

Engineering and scientific journals were quick to recognize the engineering and operating marvels of the Manitou & Pike's Peak Railway. The Cog Road was the lead article in *Scientific American* for January 24, 1891. Many of the line drawings featured in this publication were used on posters and in Cog Road time tables and literature of the time. —DONALD DUKE COLLECTION

Harry Standley was one of many famous photographers to capture the Colorado scene. He photographed many of the breathtaking views of the Cog Road during the late years of steam. In this 1930 era view, engine No. 6 works a train at the Saddle. Just to the left of the engine a cement storage shed once stood during and after construction. As late as the early 1900's, hardened cloth sacks of cement could be found lying about. To the right, it is possible to look out over the plains and down into a spot called the Crater, which it never was, because the Peak was never a volcano. — BERT WARD COLLECTION

5

THE STEAM LOCOMOTIVES

IN HIS paper, Richardson went into considerable detail as to how the cog engines differed in appearance from conventional locomotives, but the illustrations here make it unnecessary to say much on that score.

An order had been placed with the Baldwin Locomotive Works at Philadelphia for three Abt system locomotives, which were to weigh 26 tons each with coal and water. The bearing frames were so inclined that the boilers were level when they stood on a 16 percent grade, which was the average of the road. Water was carried in two tanks, one on either side of the boiler, and a bunker or bin at the rear of the cab held about a ton of coal.

Each engine had three axles, the two forward ones rigidly fastened to the frame, the rear one furnished with a radius bar. An inside frame fastened to the forward axles carried three double pinions or cog wheels, which were made of hammered crucible steel with a tensile strength of 100,000 lbs. per square inch, the teeth being cut from the solid disk. Thus the cogs were in the form of a ring or tire, and these were fastened to centers so as to allow about one-sixteenth inch play, since excessive wear on the teeth would have resulted had they been rigidly fastened to or shrunk on the centers. Hence, if the rack rail is slightly out of adjustment, the pinions accommodate themselves to it. The pinions of first No. 4, for instance, were so arranged that for every 1.2 inches of forward motion of the engine a different tooth became fully engaged with the rack rail, while other teeth were in partial contact simultaneously. The rigid wheelbase of the engines was six feet eight inches, total wheelbase 11 feet two inches.

The cylinders were 17 by 20 inches, and their power was transmitted to a main drum whose teeth drove two rear cog wheels, the forward cog wheel being connected to the next one by side rods.

These engines were designed to push two cars weighing 21 tons up a grade of 25 percent at three miles per hour, and to maintain a speed of eight miles per hour on the lightest grades, but they were unable to do so. They also developed other troubles, including frequent breakage of the inside frame. These three were unnumbered, but were named *John Hulbert, Manitou* and *Pike's Peak*, and in that order were later numbered 1, 2 and 3.

On the evening of June 10, 1892, a re-christening ceremony was held on the M. & P.P., and the engine until then named *Manitou* was renamed *T. F. Richardson*, in honor of the construction engineer. The *Manitou Springs Journal* of the next day reported that Richardson was in Chicago and

The rugged nature of Engelmann Canyon practically all the way from the Cog depot and shops at Manitou to Minnehaha, makes it easier to understand what Richardson meant when he said the upper portion of the road toward the summit was easier to grade and build. In this illustration, No. 2 and a coach pause by Hanging Rock which is partially obscured by smoke. A section of water pipe appears at the lower right, the first to carry pure mountain water down to the lowlanders in Colorado Springs. Ruxton Creek is at the right as well, but invisible amongst the rocks. —DR. L. L. WILLIAMS COLLECTION

MANITOU & PIKES PEAK RY.
2
No 2

In a classic pose, the engineer of the *John Hulbert* complete with long spouted oil can, oils around while the locomotive rests at the summit. The old Summit House has yet to receive its two-story north end, and the steel observation tower was to come much later. The whole top of Pike's Peak is covered with rocks like those pictured, and larger, but in the few and scanty patches of soil grow myriads of Alpine plants, many of them almost microscopic gems, grasses, mosses and lichens. — CARL F. MATHEWS COLLECTION

consequently unable to attend, but being informed of the event, sent a basket of champagne to aid in the ritual. The *Journal* claimed inability to report more fully on the goings-on for the reason that, up to press time, its representative had not been seen or heard from, and some others who were present were a bit hazy as to the details of the program.

The locomotives' names and also the numbers, either alone or in combination, were used for a time. Photographs have not come to light showing Richardson's name on the cab, but at least one shows the figure 2 on a locomotive also bearing the name *Pike's Peak,* although *Manitou* was definitely No. 2.

An Interstate Commerce Commission valuation docket is authority for the statement that the M. & P.P. estimated in 1918 that the three engines had originally cost $54,817, the six coaches $17,450, and work equipment (presumably two flat cars) $1,600.

In 1930 Samuel L. Vauclain's autobiography appeared under the title *Steaming Up.* In it he tells of troubles with the Pike's Peak engines not hinted at in the press. As mentioned before, The Baldwin

Locomotive Works had sent an expert out with the original engines to get them running smoothly, — a man who had had experience on the Corcovado road at Rio de Janeiro, which had a 33 percent grade. He did not succeed on the Pike's Peak road, and even a second engineer had to wire Philadelphia for help. Vauclain himself was sent out, being then plant superintendent, with the twofold purpose of making the locomotives work right, and collecting for them.

He found the three engines all out of service and with parts missing or broken. His account of what ensued proves that he knew his locomotives and that he did not suffer from an excess of modesty. Omitting his description of what the Cog Road "superintendent of motive power" (whoever that was) said and did, and in what words Vauclain told-him-a-thing-or-two, one is expected to believe that nobody there knew even the rudiments of running a steam locomotive. *Steaming Up* does not explain why Baldwin had to send an important and busy official out to do a job that two of its experts had failed to accomplish.

At any rate, Vauclain wrote that they had removed the injector from the locomotive and thrown

The *Manitou* on the siding at the Half Way House is one of three locomotives delivered to the new Cog Road by the Baldwin Locomotive Works. The builder's construction No. 10919 is quite legible in the center of the Baldwin plate attached to the smoke box. — STATE HISTORICAL SOCIETY OF COLORADO (BELOW) A Baldwin Locomotive Works builder's portrait of the *Pike's Peak* as it looked when outshopped at the Philadelphia plant in May 1890. Note how the water tanks were designed to make room for the valve gear. — MORRIS W. ABBOTT COLLECTION

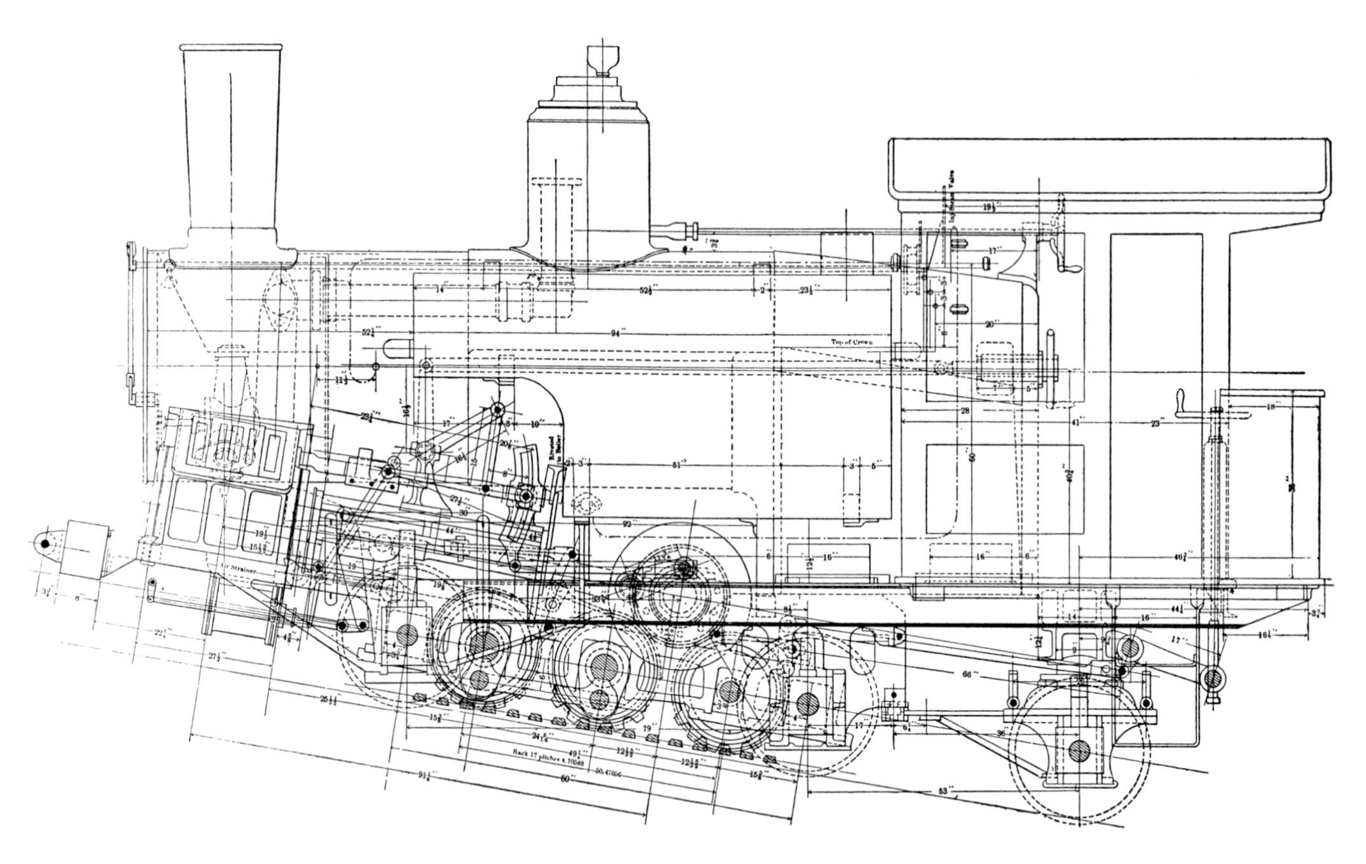

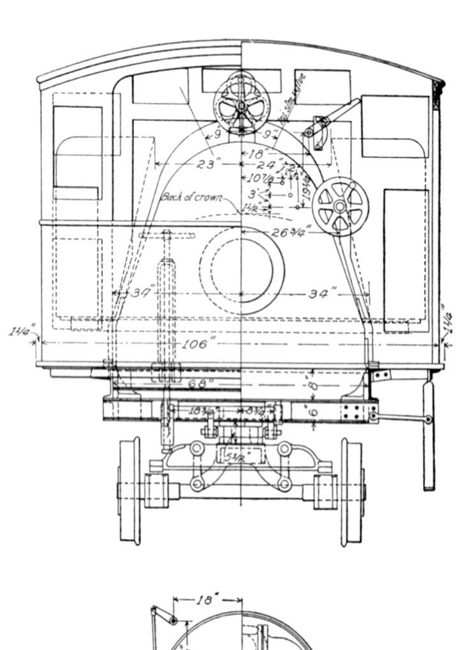

As soon as the Manitou & Pike's Peak Railway cog locomotives were in operation, the mechanical and trade journals filled their pages with details of this novel design of motive power. These drawings appeared in the February 7, 1891 issue of *The Railway Review*, and they also appeared in *Scientific American*, *The Locomotive Engineer* and *The Railroad Gazette*. The side elevation of the Abt rack locomotive is shown above. The boiler is set so that the tubes will be horizontal when the engine is upon a 16 percent grade. (LEFT) Cross-section and rear elevation of the locomotive showing the screw type throttle rather than the lever as seen in most steam engine cabs. (LOWER) A cross-section drawing of the cylinders as the locomotives were originally built. This type of cylinder was not entirely satisfactory because of the disagreeable vibrations they set up. The Vauclain system of compounding relieved this problem. —DONALD DUKE COLLECTION

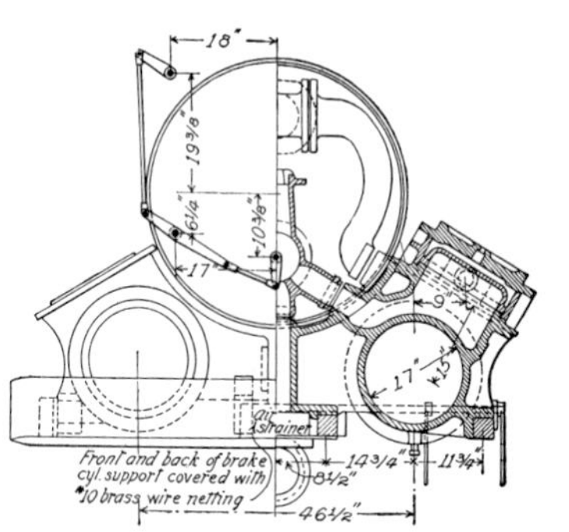

it down the bank. After it was re-installed, he found by trying the gauge cocks that the boiler was so full that the water nearly ran out of the whistle. After getting the water level down to normal, he was able to get one engine to work and took it out on the line. Then he got the other two to operate, hired new crews (for he had fired men right and left), and demanded payment for the three engines.

The president refused to pay, saying that they were dangerous coming down hill. Taking the official along, Vauclain and crew headed for the top, admired the scenery and started down. Vauclain's description of the president's emotions and efforts to jump are probably exaggerated, but he did get his check for $70,000 (remember that the M. & P.P. in 1918 thought they had cost $54,817), but not until he had threatened to lock up the locomotives if they were not paid for at once.

Whom did Vauclain mean when he wrote of "the president"? Probably Major Hulbert, for he is credited with using the words "your damned engines," and Simmons would not have said that. Who "the superintendent of motive power" could have been must remain a mystery, as no reference has been found to such an official, nor even to a master mechanic before 1893. The whole ancedote sounds less than convincing.

Close-up of the front driving axle of locomotive No. 2 showing the double cog wheel, the central rack-rail teeth, and the corrugated brake drums. —MORRIS W. ABBOTT (BELOW) Locomotive No. 3 stops for water at the Half Way House. The depot-post office is as it was when first built. The left one-third was the post office, while the rest of the space was given over to the sale of souvenirs and soda pop. The water tank on the right is not what one considers a railroad water tank when compared to main line railroad standards. —W. H. APPLEGATE COLLECTION

Requiring an additional locomotive, the company ordered a fourth engine from Baldwin for delivery in 1892, and radical changes were made in its design. This carried road number 4, and was a Vauclain compound, the first three having been simple. The inside frame was done away with, as was the main drum, and power was delivered directly, by means of rocking beams and cranks, to the two (instead of three) cog wheels, which were fastened to the axles of the bearing wheels. This engine was first No. 4, known to its friends as "Little 4," and was never named officially.

No. 4 proved to be a decided improvement both as to fuel consumption and running time, reducing the latter from 2 hours 25 minutes up-bound and 2 hours down, to 2 hours upward. Coal consumption dropped from about one and one-quarter ton to less than a ton per trip.

Richardson described the braking system of No. 4 this way: "The cylinders of the engine are used as air brakes when coming down the mountain, the valve gear being reversed. Thus the air sucked in by the pistons at each stroke is stored in the steam pipes, and after a few revolutions of the wheels, the pressure of this air would stop the pistons unless means were provided for letting it off. This is done by means of a pipe leading to the cab, with a suitable valve controlled by the engineer. The wider this valve is opened, the faster is the descent, but if the valve is closed, the engine stops almost immediately. In addition to this, the engines are provided with a steam brake, controlled by the engineer and working on similar corrugated collars on the rear pinions. Either of these last two brakes was sufficient to control the train, the screw brake being generally used to make stops at stations."

Locomotive No. 4 was built by Baldwin in May 1892 and had cylinders 9 and 15 by 22 inches. In 1938 Baldwin's records were somewhat sketchy as regards this engine and carried the notation "Destroyed." And destroyed it was, for it broke a rod on one side and ran away on August 30, 1896. Details of this affair will be mentioned later.

Before No. 4 ran away, this locomotive's superiority over the first three locomotives was so evi-

On the oposite page, a Heistand photograph of first locomotive No. 4, from which many thousands of post cards were made and sold on the summit. — COLORADO SPRINGS PUBLIC LIBRARY (RIGHT) After first No. 4 met a sad end, second No. 4 was also built by the Baldwin Locomotive Works and is shown here rolling down into the Manitou depot. At the left of this scene is the stub end of the trolley tracks on the north side of the creek. These tracks were later moved across the creek. — R. H. KINDIG COLLECTION

Baldwin Locomotive Works builder's illustration of first No. 4, better known to the men of the Cog Road as "Little 4." This engine built in May 1892 had lightweight rods, and this later led to her undoing. Heavier rods were then installed on all the other locomotives. — MORRIS W. ABBOTT COLLECTION

The *John Hulbert* soon after its conversion to Vauclain compound. The locomotive also features a new straight stack, plain rods, and a front number plate bearing No. 1 in addition to the name on the side of the cab. — MORRIS W. ABBOTT COLLECTION

dent that the older engines were shipped back to Baldwin in Philadelphia for rebuilding, returning to Manitou in time for the 1893 season, but now as Vauclain compounds with cylinders 10 and 15 by 22 inches, boiler pressure 180 lbs. Not only was the change made from simple to compound, but the whole train of power was altered to match that of No. 4. *Railroad Gazette* gave as one reason for the rebuilding the fact that, as originally built, the engines developed disagreeable vibrations.

Some time before they were rebuilt the original three engines sported road numbers on bronze plates on the smoke boxes, where previously had been plates showing a large star, occasionally just visible in early photographs.

The road had, therefore, four effective engines from 1893 through most of 1896, then only three until the delivery early in 1897 of second No. 4, which had the same dimensions as Nos. 1, 2 and 3.

The locomotive *Pike's Peak* on the shop tracks with the Manitou depot below. Before the first three locomotives were rebuilt into Vauclain compounds, the smoke boxes held the bronze Baldwin Locomotive Works plate with a polished star. — OTTO C. PERRY COLLECTION

Second No. 4 at the summit on July 22, 1937. She was rebuilt in 1912, got new tanks in 1924 in addition to a new coal bunker. This locomotive was a heavier and stronger engine than "Little 4," and she was the last steamer to operate on the line. This steamer now rests on her laurels at the Colorado Railroad Museum at Golden, Colorado. — RICHARD B. JACKSON (BELOW) Another scene of second No. 4 taken from the steel observation tower atop the old summit house. The old searchlight used to stand near the corner of the fence to the right of second No. 4. Seven Lakes (Reservoirs Nos. 4 and 5) are visible in the upper right of this scene. — R. H. KINDIG

No. 5 was built in 1901 and was put through her paces late in July of that year, having recently arrived from Philadelphia. The *Denver Times* reported that the tests were witnessed by 500 people half a mile above Manitou, and if this were true they must have been very congenial folk, for there isn't much standing room. "The engine was turned loose with nobody on board except E. F. McKay [newspaper reporter?], who was there by request of Manager Sells to testify to the fact that there was no one on board to control the brakes. The engine ran wild until a speed exceeding 25 m.p.h. had been attained, which was a matter of comparatively few seconds. This speed and the jolting of the machine over the cog caused the coal to roll out of the bunker and the roadbed was strewn with it. The automatic water brake attachments became operative, however, and in the course of a couple of rail lengths the powerful little locomotive came to a standstill." A coach was tested separately, to show how efficient were the hand brakes.

No. 6 was also built by Baldwin and began life as an oil burner in June 1906. It was, like the others, a Vauclain compound, with cylinders 10 and 15 by 24 inches, however. It weighed 30 tons, carried 600 gallons of water and 325 of fuel oil. The oil burner used was of a type favored by the Southern Pacific, but oil as fuel was in the experimental stage and one season of it was enough for the Cog Road. By 1907 the bunker carried coal, the same as the others. For many years, No. 6 was always the last out, which would suggest that it may have steamed poorly or had gremlins of some sort to plague the crew.

Under a rolling cloud of smoke and cinders, locomotive No. 6 with its coach churns up the Big Hill, where the gradient reaches 25 percent. In the background rises Mt. Almagre (Old Baldy in earlier days) to an elevation of 12,349 feet above sea level. This photograph, made about 1930 by the late Harry Standley, was chosen as the subject of the Howard Fogg watercolor painting that accompanies this volume. — JOHN FETLER COLLECTION

Locomotive No. 6, built by Baldwin in June 1906, was decidedly different from any of its predecessors, in that it had a distinctive rod arrangement and burned oil, the tanks being under the cab on both sides. — MORRIS W. ABBOTT COLLECTION

As can be seen clearly in Baldwin Locomotive Works photographs, the rod arrangement differed materially from that of the others, with the rocking beam's main bearing near its center instead of bottom, and it had three instead of two pinions, all drivers. The oil tanks were under the cab windows. No. 6 was rebuilt in 1912 along with the older five engines, so that at the last it resembled them. Being larger and heavier than the others, it was familiarly referred to by the crews as "he," instead of the customary "she," and was known to several generations of employees as "Old Jimmy Hix."

In July 1901 Samuel M. Vauclain and Mrs. Vauclain were guests of the Cog Road and made the trip with No. 5 propelling, which he praised highly. Vauclain became a good friend of William H. McKay and often visited him in later years whenever he came to Colorado.

In the accompanying Baldwin photograph of No. 5, note the polished disk about half way between the forward axles and partially obscured by the slanting rod. This was part of a device designed to apply brakes automatically if excessive speeds were reached, in which event a centrifugal mechanism behind the disk would cause a moveable arm to actuate a trigger mechanism (just above the disk), which would cause the spring (at right of disk but indistinct in the photograph) to contract and set in motion, through connecting levers, some sort of brake. This does not appear on

Baldwin built No. 5 with the rod arrangement adopted in the 1892 rebuilding, but added an automatic speed control feature which evidently did not work out as expected. — MORRIS W. ABBOTT COLLECTION

Enginehouse activity at Manitou during August 1941 with No. 3 and No. 5 on the job. In this scene No. 5 is spotted alongside the coal pocket. The shop track and the coach shed at the extreme left. — R. H. KINDIG (LEFT) Surging over cog rails, No. 2 pushes its load of sightseers toward the Peak as it moves just above the Manitou shops. The track at the right leads down into the shops. — R. H. KINDIG COLLECTION

any of the other locomotives nor in action pictures of No. 5, so one may assume that it was deemed either unsatisfactory or unnecessary, or both. This was probably the automatic brake mechanism referred to in the foregoing newspaper account of the tests.

In 1923 four locomotives were equipped with new water tanks, four tanks made by Baldwin and four in the Manitou shops, without the offset or recessed lower front corner, which had once been made necessary by the valve mechanism of the original single expansion engines. Master Mechanic McKay later raised these tanks eight inches, so that the engineer could have easier access for oiling and inspection.

No. 2 was for some years the "old reliable," when for some reason Master Mechanic Jones was not able to keep his power in condition. Herman (Herm) Gosling must have been more than an engineer, for he kept No. 2 going when the others were failing on almost every trip. He must have spent many an hour working on her and probably wouldn't let anybody else touch her with a ten-foot slicebar. When No. 2 was finally retired about 1939, she was said to have made 12,000 round trips, and Gosling had been her engineer for 32 years.

The rolling stock got so bad that delays were frequent and costly. The writer can recall days when it required three engines to get one coach up and back. In 1919, for instance, they sometimes killed disabled engines and left them on sidings along the way until they had time to bring them down. All this changed after McKay took over.

Access to the engine house and shops could be had only from the lower or depot end, which meant that cripples had to be taken first to the depot and then pushed or hauled uphill for repairs. They finally built a special track down into the shop from above, which not only made it easier but kept the tourists from seeing disabled engines limping in for surgery.

The rebuilding of 1912 was done in the company's shops, new parts having been made mostly by Baldwin from M. & P.P. plans.

About 40 years ago, Herm Gosling halted the 3 Spot on a work extra not far below Minnehaha, with Ted Wiegand firing for him. At this point the old Ruxton burro trail crossed the line from left to right. Harry Standley, who made this picture, was more than a photographer. In addition to being a member of the Ad-Am-An Club, he climbed all of the more than 50 peaks in Colorado that exceed 14,000 feet in elevation. — BERT WARD COLLECTION

6

EARLY COACHES AND FREIGHT CARS

TO BEGIN operations, six passenger coaches were ordered and built by the Wason Manufacturing Company of Springfield, Massachusetts. It was expected that "each engine will have power enough to handle two loaded cars," and two coaches would constitute a train. As first constructed each coach had a roller at either end, to make contact with the engine or the other car or both.

The Wason coaches were shipped to Manitou, complete with wheels, on flat cars. The first two arrived via the Colorado Midland Railway, and were in that line's Iron Springs Yard on August 16, 1890. These were named *Leadville* and *Colorado Springs.* A "shoo-fly" track had been laid to bring them from the Midland track to the M. & P.P. track just below the depot.

The coaches were 43 feet long (though Richardson said 41 feet), eight and one-half feet wide, and had a capacity of 50 passengers. A tiny open-hopper "necessary" occupied the rear righthand section. At first they were four wheeled affairs, with carrying wheels, one double cog wheel and two corrugated brake drums on each of the two axles. The bearing wheels were free to turn on the axles. Both front and rear platforms had two brake wheels, one connected to each axle, so that both could be set from either end. In practice the brakeman stood at the right front brake wheel when upbound, and at the right lower brake wheel when descending, where he actually assisted the engineer in controlling the speed of the train, applying or releasing the brake as the grade demanded.

The coach windows had plenty of glass, and the doors did too, and were hung on rollers instead of hinges. The seats were rather narrow and close-coupled, and originally were upholstered in "old gold plush," which later was replaced with the ordinary red plush common on railroads.

The exteriors of the cars were handsomely finished in dark Pullman green, with much ornate striping in gold leaf and colors around the doors and at the corner posts, even on the step risers. Swinging iron platform gates were present at both ends, but later disappeared, as passengers were inclined to sit on the platforms whenever possible, contrary to the rules. By the time the train had reached Windy Point, however, the cold had usually driven them inside.

On account of the cold weather, the conductors were permitted to add to their probably meager incomes by renting overcoats to the thoughtless and shivering tourists at two bits a throw. Each conductor had his own collection of secondhand coats of all sizes, patterns and colors, which he stored in the depot and carried out to the train before each trip.

On the siding at the Half Way House, we see the engine *Manitou* with coach *Denver*, but the train is perhaps secondary in interest to the cast of characters. Besides the crew, we have four gents wearing bowlers, one of them a flat-top. Another carries a shotgun at the ready, one might be a Victorian hippie, another is a white-bearded pedestrian. The flatcar, barely visible at the right, bears evidence of lettering on its side, the only such example found to date. — STATE HISTORICAL SOCIETY OF COLORADO

MANITOU & PIKES
AK
DENVER

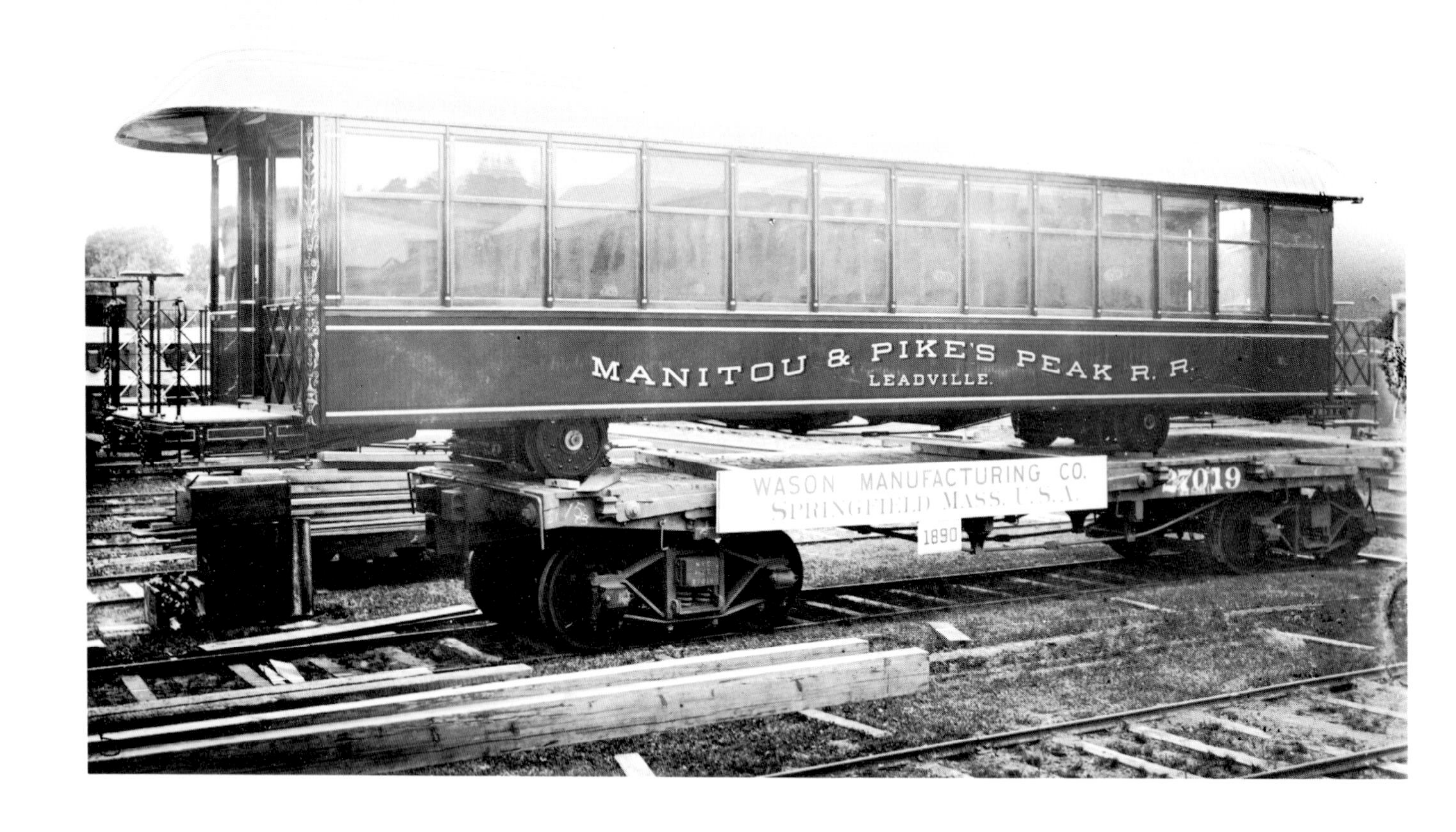

A very rare photograph of the coach *Leadville*, loaded on New York Central flatcar No. 27019 (with link-and-pin coupler) ready to leave the Wason factory at Springfield, Massachusetts, in 1890. This view clearly shows the lettering on the side with the erroneous initials R.R. instead of RY. When new the coach had striping and especially fancy ornamentation on the corner posts. (RIGHT) This rare and water damaged glass plate print is of the interior of the *Leadville*. It shows the old-fashioned roll-over seats with their plush covering. The rear sliding door bears the words "Wason Manfg. Co., Builders, Springfield, Mass." There is a row of ventilators along the center line of the roof, and a single oil lamp just ahead of the toilet section at the far left.
— BOTH DUKE-MIDDLETON COLLECTION

The use of only four wheels per coach soon proved to be unsatisfactory, as the wheelbase was too long (20 feet 6 inches), and in consequence the cars were reluctant to take the curves well. These gave way in a few years to four-wheeled trucks which had the cog wheels between the two axles, the four carrying wheels being independent of the cog wheels. These trucks are said to have been made and installed by the Colorado & Southern Railway, but this can be questioned, for the reason that they were in use before the C. & S. came into being. Early photographs show what appear to be bolt heads or nuts on the wheels, which may have been patent "paper wheels."

In addition to the first two coaches, the later arrivals were named *Cripple Creek, Aspen, Denver* and *Salida,* after Colorado cities and towns. This gave the road six coaches, all named. At an undetermined date, somewhat later, five of these coaches were numbered 101 through 105, and the names discontinued. The sixth was set on the ground just below the shops, its wheels removed, and is still in use as a storage shed. Unfortunately for the historian it is not known which coach was

Engine *Pike's Peak* eases coach *Salida* gently down Son-of-a-Gun Hill. In this J. G. Hiestand time exposure print, note that the coach still carried the incorrect initials R.R. instead of RY., as the Manitou & Pike's Peak was always a *Railway.* — CARL F. MATHEWS COLLECTION

These illustrations are two snares for the unwary. At the left, an artist portrays a cog train pushing two cars through Hell Gate, which was never done. (ABOVE) A pure fake, for this engine was built by Baldwin in 1888 and was No. 7 of the Estrado Principe de Graõ Pará of Brazil. Both views are from a Denver & Rio Grande Railroad promotional piece entitled *The Story of Manitou* published in 1892. — BOTH MORRIS W. ABBOTT COLLECTION

retired from service and not numbered. When the coaches were first painted, the sign painter erred, as he lettered the car sides with the abbreviation "R.R." instead of "RY."

The statement that the original intention had been to have one engine push two cars is borne out by the fact that six coaches were ordered for three locomotives. A pamphlet issued by the Denver & Rio Grande in 1892, when the cog road had been operating for perhaps two years, shows an artist's conception of a two-coach train on the M. & P.P., and a line cut of a rack locomotive carrying the numeral 1 and *PIKE'S PEAK* in large letters on its tank. Actually that locomotive had been built by Baldwin in 1888 for the Estrado de Ferro Principe de Graõ Pará of Brazil, was numbered 7 and lettered "E. F. P. G. P." It bore little resemblance to the Pike's Peak engines.

The late Harrison J. Holt, onetime president of the M. & P. P. and still earlier chief clerk to President Sells, said that when they tested an engine by loading two coaches with rails to a weight equal to that of 50 passengers, the second coach buckled, and they never actually tried to run two-car trains at all.

Only No. 104 remains of the original six, sitting alone in the coach shed at Manitou, with peeling aluminum paint and inartistic lettering. Lately it has been used for storing spare parts for the new Swiss cars.

Coach No. 106, like its locomotive counterpart, differed in design from that of its predecessors. It was delivered in July 1906 by the American Car Company of St. Louis (later taken over by J. G. Brill Co.) and was described by *Railroad Gazette* as being a Brill semi-convertible type with arched roof. It was 41 feet, 4 inches over crown pieces, 33 feet 4 inches over end panels, with a three-foot front platform and five-foot rear platform where l.c.l. freight could be carried. "The rear dashboard is made with an opening in the middle, with a slide therein, to permit passage from car to car when desired," which is indeed odd, since two-car operation had been proven impossible, unless they expected No. 6 to outpush its predecessors, which it did not. The seats were plush upholstered, the ceiling painted deep green, the interior finish was cherry, and green silk "Pantasote" curtains (meaning shades) topped off the decor. The front platform was vestibuled.

This coach was considerably heavier than the others, just as No. 6 was heavier than the earlier engines, and was not used unless all others were in service. It would be rolled out now and then for a small private party, such as Otto Kahn's. After the advent of diesel power and before 1944, No. 106 was set out at Mountain View siding, its trucks removed, and used as a bunkhouse. As it occupied too much of the siding, it was reduced in length by amputating the front end. There it sits today. One of the other coaches was for a time at Minnehaha siding, and another was cannibalized to build a longer flat car, which was later scrapped.

Coach No. 102 was bought by engineer and Mrs. Frank Smith in 1948, with the idea of making a hamburger drive-in. Instead the Smiths sold it to John Paddock of Colorado Springs, who in turn sold it William Gosch, who used it as an office in

A rare and excellent photograph of the seldom used coach No. 106 with locomotive No. 3. Here the train is about to drop down to the depot for a load of passengers. This coach was rarely used because of its excessive weight and due to the vestibuled front end which hindered the passengers' view ahead. —STATE HISTORICAL SOCIETY OF COLORADO (BELOW) The remains of coach No. 106 parked on the Mountain View siding in 1940. Later the upper or front end was scrapped in order to shorten it and take less room on the siding. — JOSEPH SCHICK

his junk yard. Late in 1949 or early 1950 a fire in the yard finished its long career.

The original order placed with Wason included two flat cars, which were delivered. At least there were two such cars on the line for many years, and lacking other information we can assume that these were the originals Wason delivered. Their car numbers, if any, remain unknown today. One of the flat cars was customarily left at the lower end of track just below the depot, the other at Minnehaha. One or both were rebuilt with steel underframes, and an additional and longer one was built using the frame from a scrapped coach. Today there is only one flat car on hand, equipped in the winter of 1967-1968 with a steel dump bed and hydraulic lift to speed up the unloading of snow.

A report hard to credit was mentioned in one publication, to the effect that two observation cars had been included in the original order, in addition to six coaches and two flats. The *Colorado Springs Gazette* for June 14, 1890, announced the arrival of two flat cars and a *hand car!* In later years a four-wheeled affair was sometimes pushed up by the work car, but it is obvious that a hand car was of no value on the Manitou & Pike's Peak Railway.

At the mouth of Engelmann Canyon, close to the famous Ute Iron Spring, are the Manitou depot, shops, and operating headquarters of the Manitou & Pike's Peak Railway. In this superb William H. Jackson classic illustration, of 1890 vintage, may be seen the facilities of the Cog Road. At the lower right, are the shops, engine house and car shed, while down the rails toward the center of the view is the Cog Road depot. Directly above the depot and to the left is the famous Ute Iron Springs Pavilion. Barely visible just above the Pavilion is a dark line which is the curving trestle of the Colorado Midland Railway. — STATE HISTORICAL SOCIETY OF COLORADO

7

ALONG THE LINE

WHEN A train was about to depart from Manitou, the locomotive slowly waddled down from the engine house and stopped just below the depot. The steamers made a lot of smoke, so a metal smokestack was presently erected to carry it up and away from the passenger platform, and the engineer would spot the engine stack right under it. Then a brakeman would let a coach roll down, and a grand rush ensued to be first on board. In later years the tide was slowed somewhat by pipe railings, but in earlier times it was every man for himself, and the hindermost got the rear seats.

Having loaded the first train to capacity, instead of running it out on the road, they would sometimes drop the second one down, load it and send it out first, to the disgust of those who had fought a good fight and expected to get started ahead of all others.

Spurting steam and water from its cylinder cocks for a few hundred yards, the engine would huff and puff, gently on the easy grade, out across Ruxton Creek, past the shops, and soon it was hard at work.

The route of the Cog Road is interesting every foot of the way. The passenger has his choice of geology, flora, perhaps some fauna, and plain and fancy scenery aplenty. Engelmann Canyon, named for the abundance of Engelmann spruce that grow in it, is a narrow one with steeply sloping sides. Huge boulders of granite have tumbled down from the heights, in a few places bridging over Ruxton Creek which flows down from the eastern slope of Pike's Peak. It was named for the intrepid young English explorer of Mexico and the United States in the days before much was known about things west of the Mississippi River.

In earlier years Colorado Springs got much of its water from Ruxton Creek at a point not far above Manitou, but now it takes it farther up, bringing it down through a pipeline from Ruxton Park to Mount Manitou and thence to an electric power plant (the Hydro plant) and into the mains.

There are some interesting rock formations in Engelmann Canyon, especially for those with active imaginations—Elephant Rock, Hanging Rock, the Ace of Diamonds, Henry Ford's First Car, Gog and Magog, the Lizard Rock, and others. A slightly less steep section is called Butterworth Flat and appears on recent timetables, though there was never anything there to see, nor an identifying sign, and it was never even a flag stop. However, it is a good place for climbers to pause for the breath that refreshes, though most of them don't need any special place for that.

A welcome sight along the way on a hot day was a spot known as Shady Spring, where enterprising

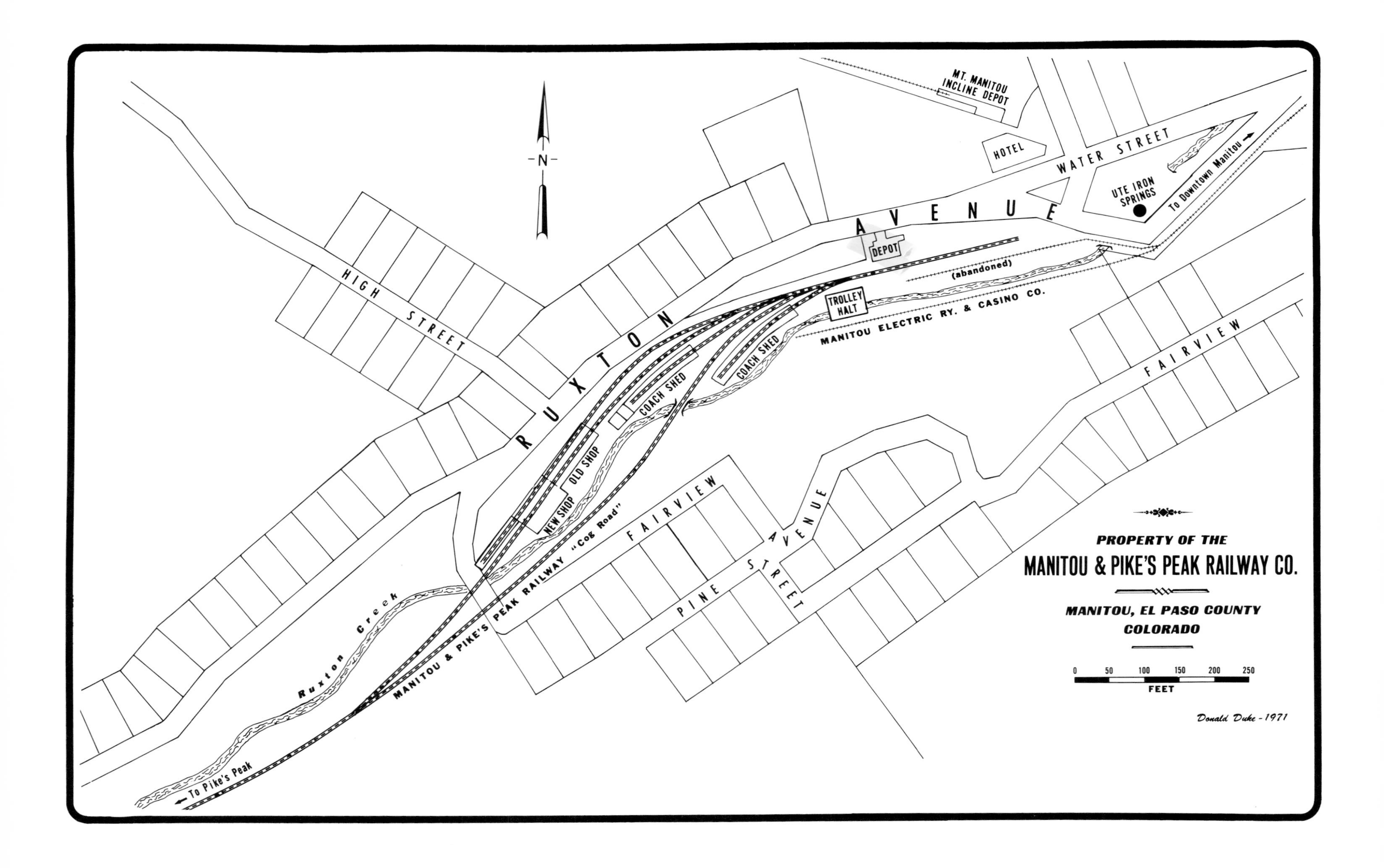
PROPERTY OF THE
MANITOU & PIKE'S PEAK RAILWAY CO.
MANITOU, EL PASO COUNTY
COLORADO
0
50
100
150
200
250
FEET
Donald Duke - 1971
N
MT. MANITOU INCLINE DEPOT
HOTEL
WATER STREET
UTE IRON SPRINGS
To Downtown Manitou
RUXTON AVENUE
DEPOT
(abandoned)
TROLLEY HALT
MANITOU ELECTRIC RY. & CASINO CO.
HIGH STREET
COACH SHED
COACH SHED
OLD SHOP
NEW SHOP
MANITOU & PIKE'S PEAK RAILWAY "Cog Road"
FAIRVIEW
FAIRVIEW
AVENUE
PINE STREET
Ruxton Creek
To Pike's Peak

DOWN BY THE DEPOT

On the opposite page a map showing the physical plant of the Cog Road in relation to the other facilities located in Engelmann Canyon. At one time the owners of the Manitou & Pike's Peak Railway planned quite an extensive real estate tract surrounding the railway. Note how the trolley tracks of The Manitou Electric Railway and Casino Company were moved across Ruxton Creek shortly after the Cog Road opened. — MANITOU & PIKE'S PEAK RAILWAY COLLECTION (RIGHT) The upper level of the depot at Manitou, where passengers arrived by hack, now by car. (BELOW) Early trackside view of the depot with No. 1 ready to start its climb to the summit. At this time the trolley tracks had not been moved across Ruxton Creek, the lunch room had not been built, nor the smoke pipe installed to carry off the smoke while the train loaded at the depot. — BOTH STATE HISTORICAL SOCIETY OF COLORADO

As passenger business expanded, a lunch room was added to the depot complex in 1905. This facility may be seen to the right of the depot in this scene. In the background are the ruins of the Iron Springs Hotel, and the gash in the hillside above the depot is the route of the present Mt. Manitou Incline Railway, then a tramway. — STEWARTS COMMERCIAL PHOTOGRAPHERS (RIGHT) Passenger level photograph of the depot. Note how the trees have grown since the above photograph was made in 1905 and the 1938 date of this scene and note the stack for carrying off engine smoke. — RICHARD B. JACKSON (BELOW) Under a rolling cloud of smoke and cinders, a train leaves the Manitou depot for the summit. In the background, one of the new diesel trains is being unloaded. — BERT WARD

The Manitou & Pike's Peak Railway established its shops, engine house, and general operating headquarters in Manitou along Ruxton Creek, just a few yards from its depot. While the Cog Road lacks the familiar turntable and smokey roundhouse of large railroads, its shop facilities and engine house are just as efficient. At the right, No. 4 is in the engine house about to back down a few yards to take on water and coal. The other track is the shop track, while the long building is the coach shed. — RICHARD B. JACKSON (CENTER) No. 1 has just spotted its empty coach at the coach shed and is drifting down to the switch preparatory to running up to the engine house. Note the chime whistle which was home made of copper pipes. — R. H. KINDIG (LOWER) With Magog Rock looking down from the mountain top ahead, engine No. 3 starts up the main line with coach No. 101 in this 1938 photograph. — RICHARD B. JACKSON

The camera just catches a glimpse of No. 4 a hundred yards or so above the shops. From here on it is hard work all the way to the summit. — BERT WARD

MT
MANITOU PARK
SCENIC INCLINE RY.
MT MANITOU
SCENIC INCLINE
MT MANITOU PARK

Mt. MANITOU INCLINE

Longest and highest railway of its kind in the world, the Mt. Manitou Scenic Incline Railway offers magnificent panoramic views as it rises nearly 3,000 feet in one and one-quarter mile, and leads to the hundreds of acres of rugged and beautiful Mt. Manitou Park at its summit. (OPPOSITE PAGE) In its early years, the cable road looked like this. The big building at the left is a hotel which later burned to the ground. The Cog Road depot is just out of the picture to the left of the hotel. — STEWARTS COMMERCIAL PHOTOGRAPHERS The three folders at the right advertised the famous funicular over the years, which is owned and operated by the proprietors of the Cog Road. — DONALD DUKE COLLECTION (BELOW) For years the Mt. Manitou Incline used open cars like this, which gave unlimited vision, but decidely limited protection against the frequent summer showers. This 1919 view shows the safety cable that passes through a clutch under the car. — MALLORY HOPE FERRELL COLLECTION

One of the steepest grades on the line is encountered soon after the trains leave the Manitou depot. The flat glen by the depot merges into a rugged and narrow defile called Engelmann Canyon. Here the trains hug the left hand wall of the canyon beneath high peaks of solid rock. On the right, the gulch carries the splashing waters of Ruxton Creek as it races down the mountain. The illustration on the left shows engine No. 2 working hard as it moves its coach in Engelmann Canyon, and the worst is yet to come. — R. H. KINDIG COLLECTION (BELOW) A bit farther up the line in the vicinity of Shady Spring, Magog Rock surveys the scene from the skyline. Its companion rock, Gog, is out of view to the left. The reader will immediately recognize these names from Ezekiel Chapter 38 or Revelation Chapter 20: 7-8. — MORRIS W. ABBOTT COLLECTION

ENGELMANN CANYON

Tired hikers bound for the summit of Pike's Peak slaked their thirsts with soda pop from the tent refreshment stand, while relaxed passengers listen to locomotive No. 5 blast through Shady Spring about 1915. — R. H. KINDIG COLLECTION (LEFT) In this 1891 Hiestand photograph, Hanging Rock (above the locomotive stack) seemed to have a precarious perch, as the *Pike's Peak* chuffed past it, but the rock is still hanging there. — MIKE KOCH COLLECTION (BELOW) This train is passing Rose Emma Falls. As the creek has almost no water in it today except after a heavy rain, nobody notices it now, nor recalls who Rose Emma was. — MORRIS W. ABBOTT COLLECTION

young folks used to set up shop each summer, dispensing cold soda pop to panting tourists. Artist's Glen, not far below Minnehaha, is a narrow opening on the left of the train where one can get a brief glimpse of Cameron's Cone, a 10,700 foot mountain that looks high from here but from farther along looks like the proverbial anthill.

A long whistle announced that the train was approaching the first station stop, Minnehaha, which has a Minnehaha Falls looking rather anemic now because most of Ruxton's water has been diverted into a pipe far up on the mountainside. This was for years a small but attractive summer resort colony, most of the people coming from such far eastern states as Nebraska. At one time it served as headquarters for a group of botanists conducting the Pike's Peak Alpine Laboratory, whose interests lay in the flora of the high country. Across the creek on the left a number of rustic cottages adorned the hillside, while a little farther up and on the right side of the track stood the water tank and a frame section house. A stub siding long enough for two trains and a flat car takes off to the left, as do all the sidings on the line.

MINNEHAHA

Minnehaha was the first stop out of Manitou. At one time it was a quaint hamlet of rustic cottages snuggled in a tiny park. The region took its name from Minnehaha Falls, whose foaming waters once filled the air with melody. (LEFT) The train here winds its way out of Engelmann Canyon as it approaches Minnehaha, between rocks of impressive magnitude. The caption on the reverse of this old Hiestand print taken in 1891 reads, "From Phantom Curve, A Glimpse of the Plains." Due to the limitations of the film in those days, the plains are hardly visible. — MORRIS W. ABBOTT COLLECTION (BELOW) This was the summer colony of Minnehaha, showing Minnehaha Falls while Ruxton still flowed with its pristine volume. The cabin ahead of the train was the first there, owned by C. J. Phelps of Schuyler, Nebraska. The Alpine Laboratory later had its headquarters here, studying the flora at high altitudes. — DENVER PUBLIC LIBRARY, WESTERN COLLECTION (LOWER LEFT) Diesel train No. 8 and steamer No. 6 meet at Minnehaha on August 4, 1940. The station-looking structure on the right is a frame section house which by that time was no longer in use. — R. H. KINDIG

SON - OF - A - GUN HILL

One illusion on the Manitou & Pike's Peak Railway that excites comment is the grade. Every inch of the road is up; yet when approaching a moderate grade from a steeper grade, the passenger declares the track must be on a down grade. The grade at Son-of-a-Gun Hill is perfectly described. In the scene below, the abandoned plant of the Pike's Peak Power Co. as it looked about 1907. The plant was powered by the fall of water down Son-of-a-Gun Hill, the pipe running into the plant through the small shed at the center. — MRS. C. C. MCREYNOLDS (LOWER) This 1891 Hiestand photo of the *Pike's Peak* appears to be at the top of Son-of-a-Gun Hill. — STATE HISTORICAL SOCIETY OF COLORADO

After a few hundred yards of comparatively level track the train curves to the right around a large boulder to whose side clings Lizard Rock. Opposite this boulder there once stood a two-story frame building that housed the Pike's Peak Power Company's generating plant. The power was furnished by the fall of water through the pipe that followed the railway. This pipe shows in some old photographs of washouts. In the early years of the century this was only an empty shell, with some broken lightning arresters, fuse boxes, and what had been the penstock. Here begins what is generally called the first 25 percent grade on the line, Son-of-a-Gun Hill, though Richardson's profile shows two stretches that steep above Shady Spring.

HALF WAY HOUSE

Half Way House, which was far from halfway to the summit, was a rustic mountain hotel surrounded by a grove of stately spruce, and towering above it, the pinnacled rocks of Hell Gate. (RIGHT) The train is smoking up to the water tank at the Half Way House, the brakeman ready to set the hand brake, after which he will climb the ladder and hold open the valve till the tanks are filled. The fireman remained in the cab, while the engineer "oiled around." — STEWARTS COMMERCIAL PHOTOGRAPHERS (BELOW) This is how Half Way House looked before the depot was built, which stood back in the trees to the left. The south side of Hell Gate looms at the top, just left of center. — CARL F. MATHEWS COLLECTION

Working manfully and noisily, the engine conquers the grade and proceeds past a large gravel slide toward the Half Way House, passing without mention the Two Fools Mine, so christened by its discouraged owners. Here the train crosses two more short bridges, and there are no more higher up; only a culvert or two.

Then a short stretch of 12-15 percent grade to the site of the Half Way House and its post office and depot, a water tank (all now gone) and the second spur siding. The depot was a small frame building that stood between the main and the siding, possibly 12 by 20 feet, half of which was closed in and the other half an open platform merely roofed over. This was a shelter for tourists, whilst the rear or uphill half served as ticket office, refreshment stand and post office. The only refreshments available were Crackerjack, chewing gum and cold pop, the last standing in a shallow tank of water piped in from Ruxton Creek. The brands of gum in those days were Yucatan (the best seller), California Fruit, Beeman's Pepsin and Black Jack. Post cards enjoyed a good sale, and occasionally local mineral specimens could be had, such as amazonite, smoky and clear quartz crystals and iron pyrites.

A toboggan rider poses at the Half Way House depot in the early 1900's. A pipe from Ruxton Creek running under the track feeds the water tank. — TUTT LIBRARY, COLORADO COLLEGE (BELOW) A post card with the Half Way, Colorado, cancellation and the Summit House imprint.

The author captured this rare view of No. 6 passing the Half Way House on July 10, 1910, with a box camera. — MORRIS W. ABBOTT

The post office was established in 1896 and operated only four months of the year as a "star route," and mail came up six days a week from Manitou on a mule, but the office had its own name, "Half Way, Colorado." The incoming mail was always light, but because of the many post cards mailed from there (often including those sent down from the summit house) the outgoing pouch could be heavy. Money orders were sold now and then.

While it cannot be said that every man's hand was against the tourist, it was true that every man's palm was outstretched then as now in a tourist-supported community. Accustomed to paying double for nearly everything and having learned that prices increase directly in proportion to the rise in elevation, tourists were known to approach

The Half Way House, the popular hostelry, as it looked in the early 1900's. The small building at the left was a curio stand, the one with the sign was the lunch counter for burro party members and hikers. In back of the hotel, the burro stable. Accommodations were far from luxurious, board and room costing $10 per week when this Hiestand picture was taken, and some weeks it was worth it. — STEWARTS COMMERCIAL PHOTOGRAPHERS

During 1910, a Manitou to Pike's Peak burro party poses at the Half Way House. —AL WARWICK (BELOW) Half Way House, about 1916, after a light snowfall. — MRS. C. C. MCREYNOLDS

the post office window and respectfully engage in the following exchange with the clerk on duty.

"Is this a post office?" (The sign said it was.)

"Yes."

"A government post office?"

"Yes."

"Do you sell stamps?"

"Yes."

"How much are they?"

The property there had originally been Booth's ranch and was bought about 1882 by Thomas T. Palsgrove, who intended running cattle in the high country. There was a one-room log cabin on the property where South Ruxton and Ruxton Creeks come together, and right in front of it passed the Pike's Peak trail built by the Army Signal Corps as its "new" or Ruxton trail, with a single telegraph wire following it. Being a hospitable cuss, Tom Palsgrove would pass out cups of hot coffee to the cold and weary hikers of the era. When this finally got to be too much of a good thing, he set up a lunch stand and went into business. The cows took care of themselves anyway. This naturally led to the addition of a few rooms, and he had a hotel of sorts, which was about 1884. He also had a daughter born that year, named her Mary and then named a nearby mountain for her. She was living in Colorado Springs in 1971, Mrs. Mary Palsgrove Hoe.

There were other Palsgrove brothers, and John B. Palsgrove took over the running of the hotel later on. He and his wife agreed to disagree, and she continued with it and was accidentally electrocuted on August 1, 1907, the evening of the author's first day in the hotel. That night a special train came up about 11 o'clock to get her body.

After her death the place was run for a time by some relatives, but was taken over about 1910 by William H. Harris, who made numerous needed improvements. The property had before that been sold to a group of Nebraskans who eventually sold out to the City of Colorado Springs. Vandals were blamed for a fire that damaged the building in January 1922, and it was never repaired. At last it was razed in 1926 and some of its lumber was used in building a camp for men working on the Big Tooth Dam above Dark Canyon on South Ruxton Creek.

In its palmy days amongst the spruces it had perhaps 15 rooms in addition to a large main room and a dining room, each with a large stone fireplace, and a hot, crowded kitchen. No running water, of course, except a pipe into the pantry from the creek above, which served for drinking as well as dish washing, laundering, and keeping food cool. Flies were ever a problem, and the presence of the burro barn nearby was no help in combatting them. The burros, however, made good disposers of garbage.

On some recent maps of the area this place is designated "Midway," which is simply an error, as it was never so called by anybody at any time. Why call it the Half Way House, when it was only a third of the way up? Probably because Tom Palsgrove liked the name.

Only a few hundred yards above the Half Way House, Tom Palsgrove laid out a town site which he called Ruxton Park, where Sheep Creek runs into Ruxton. He sold a few lots, but not many, and as they were laid out without regard to the nature of the terrain, some of them were more perpendicular than horizontal. In the early 1900's the City of Colorado Springs built a settler or settling basin there, it being an intake for a pipeline that runs to Mount Manitou, where it descends sharply to Manitou. In Ruxton Park were several log cabins which Palsgrove had built for vacationing people, and later on houses were erected for the caretakers of the properties of the city and the power company.

RUXTON PARK

Ruxton Park, with Hell Gate in the background. This is a very early William H. Jackson photograph, as evidenced by the planks spiked to the ties, the wood chips, and the keg of spikes. The intake for the Colorado Springs Water System was later built where the burro stands patiently. — STATE HISTORICAL SOCIETY OF COLORADO

Official photographer Hiestand captured this breathtaking scene from Lion Rock (north wall of Hell Gate), and it shows Castle Thunder (the opposite wall), to the left of which stands Mt. Mary. Mt. Almagre appears in the distance, with Mt. Wilson to the right. The right foreground shows a peak bound train with locomotive No. 3 stopped at Ruxton Park for this photograph, while to the left of the train note a sign offering lots in Ruxton Park from $25 to $200. — MORRIS W. ABBOTT COLLECTION

A local burro party, not equipped for the Peak trip, pauses on the old Ruxton trail to Pike's Peak on a busy day in Ruxton Park in the late 1890's. Pilot Knob appears above the track in the distance. — STATE HISTORICAL SOCIETY OF COLORADO (BELOW) Both guardian rocks of Hell Gate loom up behind this train at Ruxton Park, before 1920. — MRS. C. C. MCREYNOLDS

MOUNTAIN VIEW

This panorama was made shortly after the completion of the Cog Road, and includes 3.5 miles of track within the scope of the lens. Photographed from Pilot Knob, between Ruxton Park and Mountain View, it shows the Big Hill leading around the shoulder of Sachett Mountain. One of the construction camps occupied an area just to the left of the train. — DENVER PUBLIC LIBRARY, WESTERN COLLECTION

From Ruxton Park to (Old) Mountain View the grade varies from eight to about 10 percent which, after what had passed, was as nothing, and the old steam trains seemed actually to speed along. On the way, Pilot Knob (earlier called Sheep Rocks) rises to divide the watershed of Ruxton Creek from that of Lion Creek, which latter the Cog Road follows. Here for the first time the passengers get a view of the mountain they have been heading for all the time, and here William H. Jackson, "picture maker of the Old West," made a panoramic picture of the peak that has been repeated by many photographers since.

At (Old) Mountain View stood a small red building that may once have been a section house but for many years housed the *Pike's Peak Daily News.* A little farther along was a siding and water tank called "Gulch Tank" because it was in Lion Gulch. Some years later the building was moved up to where the siding and tank stood, which is known today as Mountain View.

The *Pike's Peak Daily News* was published almost from the beginning. As it appeared every day the trains ran, it probably was entitled to call itself a daily. Beginning in June 1891 it was published, till the line closed for the season, by Manville Lindsay, who called it "The Most Elevated Publication on Earth." Just how the volumes were numbered and who owned what are hard to determine today. In the writer's youth, Tom Wilson was the proprietor and his daughter, Mrs. Helen Wilson Stewart, says he began publishing it in 1893. The issue of May 26, 1899, is Vol. 3, No. 27, and Grace T. Wilson was listed as its publisher. In 1905 the publisher was C. E. Tschudi, and the issue dated August 27 was Volume 9, Number 175. There were seven trains up to the Peak that day. Volume 17, Number 99 was dated August 19, 1913, the same C. E. Tschudi was listed as manager of the *Pike's Peak Daily News.* On this particular day there were five trains bound for the Peak in the morning alone, and no doubt about three scheduled for the afternoon run.

PIKE'S PEAK DAILY NEWS

THE ONLY CHALYBEATE SPRINGS IN MANITOU

THE FAMOUS IRON SPRINGS of MANITOU

JUST BELOW COG DEPOT

Good Pictures Perpetuate the Pleasure of Your Sight-Seeing Trips

THE D. Y. BUTCHER DRUG CO.

COLORADO SPRINGS, COLORADO

THE JEWELER YOU CAN TRUST

Watches, Diamonds, Souvenir Spoons, Native Stones, Mounted and Unmounted

Expert Repairing

THE JOHNSON JEWELRY CO.

cRae Restaurant

Private Dining Rooms

The Largest Restaurant in the City

e Finest and Most Sanitary Kitchen in the West

COLORADO SPRINGS

For an

celled Panoramic

w of Manitou,

he Plains

ountain

e Railway

Half Fare, 40c

Pike's Peak Daily News.

SMALL PAY FOR PREACHERS

A front cover and an inside spread of the *Pike's Peak Daily News*, the latter including the names and addresses of the Cog Road passengers of that day. — MORRIS W. ABBOTT COLLECTION (BELOW) Publication office of the *Pike's Peak Daily News* at Old Mountain View. This building was later moved across the track. The Summit House is a mere speck directly above the central telegraph pole. The train, with engine No. 3, is on the siding. — STATE HISTORICAL SOCIETY OF COLORADO

In later years the "official" group pictures were taken at Mountain View while the engine took on water. The author (holding hat) and his wife are seated on the platform, the date September 3, 1923. — STEWART BROTHERS (BELOW) Locomotive No. 5 takes water at Mountain View in 1941. The shell of retired coach No. 106 is on the left. — R. H. KINDIG

The paper was an eight-page affair about the size of a modern tabloid newspaper. The front cover was flamboyant to say the least, and to see it is to appreciate the advances made in color printing since those days. It featured a wasp-waisted, long-skirted female equipped with field glasses and engaged in admiring the view of Pike's Peak, while some astonished Rocky Mountain sheep gaze at her. In one version of the cover a male companion with shoulders three feet broad and wearing a stiff straw hat is also present. In the distance two or three cog trains wend their ways upwards, scaling the heights, behind which the sun rises (or sets) in splendor. Everest in all its glory was not so arrayed.

Inside, the whole thing was preprinted, with the sole exception of the third page which carried the names of the day's travelers to the summit. Some of this was called boiler plate in printers' talk, which meant miscellaneous information included to fill space, some local advertisements, together with a rather good description and history of the road up to that time. The most distressing feature, however, was a poem of about 200 lines entitled "The Legend of Lake Moraine," whose author modestly declined credit. It related in the best Victorian manner and in the meter of Longfellow's "Hiawatha" the tragedy of Kula, daughter of Chief Kokoma, and her sad and fatal affair with one Don Ireno, a gay caballero. At the end they both drowned in Lake Moraine, but that was before the Colorado Springs Health Department promulgated its regulations against pollution of the watershed.

The idea of the paper, of course, was to sell it to the tourists, without whom one did not eat regularly in the Pike's Peak area. A representative of the publication would board the first train at Manitou and pass around slips on which the passengers were asked to write their names and addresses. The reporter would drop off at Minnehaha and do the same on the second train, and leave all the slips at Mountain View. Thereupon the manager-publisher-compositor-pressman-devil would proceed to set the names in type and run off enough copies on an old "kick press" while the trains were going to the top and back. By the time they arrived on their way down, he had the papers ready to take on board and sell for two bits each.

The last steam passenger run to the summit of Pike's Peak was made September 3, 1958, with locomotive No. 4 and coach No. 104, shown here at Mountain View. — R. H. KINDIG

TIMBERLINE

Edging up sheltered slopes, stands of Engelmann spruce and subalpine fir lose size perceptibly as they approach timber line on Pike's Peak. In this latitude of the United States, trees seldom survive above 11,500 feet. This is caused by lack of moisture and frost-free growing time. Trees are not only dwarfed by the arid cold as they approach timber line, but also deformed by fierce prevailing winds. (RIGHT) This is Grecian Bend, above Mountain View and near the start of the Big Hill to timber line. From here to Windy Point the fireman was kept busy heaving coal into the firebox, and occasionally it was necessary to stop and build up steam pressure in order to go on. — DONALD DUKE COLLECTION (BELOW) Timber line on the Big Hill. At the left grow the stunted, gnarled spruce trees typical of the elevation, blown and twisted by continual winds. All around, rocks and more rocks. Ahead, through a shallow cut and around a curve to the right is Windy Point. Here the grade is close to 25 percent, the elevation nearly 12,000 feet. — GERALD M. BEST

Diesel-electric locomotive No. 8 with coach No. 11 pauses going down the Big Hill to let some of the passengers stretch their legs. — MANITOU & PIKE'S PEAK RAILWAY

Mountain View used to be a water stop, but more recently has been a photograph stop, after which the train begins a long and steep climb, swings around Grecian Bend (named for the stylish appearance of vertebral curvature produced in Victorian ladies by the wearing of a bustle) and into the Big Hill, where the grade just misses being 25 percent to Windy Point.

Here the track rounds the shoulder of Sachett Mountain, which is itself a shoulder of Pike's Peak, through a cut and past the old stone section house. This also was a water stop, and the siding remains. Here lived John B. Taggart, section foreman, with his family and hardy crew of trackmen. He had been with the construction crew, and stayed on almost until his death in 1935. The original section house, however, had been a slab affair a little farther up, at the Saddle. For many years a steam-driven pump some distance below on the barren slope to the west furnished water for the locomotives. Its remains can still be seen there. It is possible that the first water tank was at the Saddle.

The flora above timberline is alpine, and amongst the small flowers that grow there is the Pike's Peak or alpine forget-me-not (*Mertensia alpina*). In earlier days a girl would board the train at Windy Point and ride on up to the summit, selling these little blue flowers for 25 cents a bunch.

WINDY POINT

The *Pike's Peak*, with coach *Colorado Springs*, takes water through a hose above the Saddle in 1891. The engines were using more fuel than had been expected, hence the boards to increase the capacity of the coal bunker. — STATE HISTORICAL SOCIETY OF COLORADO (BELOW) On a cold day, No. 2 takes water for the last climb at Windy Point tank. — DR. L. L. WILLIAMS COLLECTION

Smoking up the Big Hill, above timber line and not far below Windy Point, with a wonderful view of Lake Moraine far below. This is a semi-artificial lake used as a reservoir of the Colorado Springs Water System. Ruxton Creek flows from it and down to Ruxton Park, where most of the water is conducted by pipe to Mt. Manitou and down to a power plant near the Cog Road depot. — BERT WARD COLLECTION

Those who have never seen the desolation above timber line can scarcely appreciate or understand it, but the picture above will help. The train has just left the Saddle, and a chilling wind is blowing the smoke across the rocks and out over the Crater. Even the sound of the locomotive's exhaust seems to blow away. The old Summit House with its observation tower shows faintly on the skyline near the right edge of the picture. —STEWARTS COMMERCIAL PHOTOGRAPHERS

THE SADDLE

The Rocky Mountain Railroad Club excursion of August 27, 1939, with locomotive No. 3 and coach No. 101 near the Saddle. This was the first of three such steam trips arranged by the club for its members.—R. H. KINDIG (BELOW) Back in the days of four-wheeled coaches, this train stands where there is a view back toward Windy Point. The mountain in the distance at the right is a shoulder of Mt. Almagre. —MORRIS W. ABBOTT COLLECTION

Boulders, boulders and more boulders! That is what the summit of Pike's Peak is like and it can't be expressed any better than this picturesque scene. This is also one of the many photographs captioned "First Passenger Train on Summit of Pike's Peak," but actually made in 1893. This illustration shows locomotive No. 3 with coach *Denver* waiting for the return to Manitou. —RICHARD B. JACKSON COLLECTION

THE SUMMIT

A moderate 10-11 percent grade brings the train to the Saddle, where a brief glimpse of the plains can be had. From this point begins the last climb, with grades from 16 to 24.4 percent, and finally the summit is reached. Here the tracks fan out to provide space for at least six trains at one time. The summit house is to the left or west of the railway, and the indescribable view of the plains to the right or east. Bottomless Pit, which seems almost that, is to the north. Far to the south the Sangre de Cristo Range is usually visible. The Cripple Creek mining district, about as inactive as a mining camp can be and still live, is in plain view, and at night the lights of Denver and Pueblo are clearly visible.

The summit house, the original of course, began life as a squatty affair with very thick stone walls for the protection of the U. S. Army Signal Service residents. It was built in 1882, and after that project was abandoned it was vacant for a time, but was reactivated when the Cog Road was built, as its upper terminus. On May 10, 1890, the Secretary of the Interior, through the Land Office, granted an easement of 5.52 acres of land on the top of the mountain to Zalmon G. Simmons for such terminal purposes.

In May 1891 Messrs. Weir & Rupp were engaged in remodeling the summit house for use as a hotel for tourists, with accommodations for 15 guests, a lunch counter and a curio stand. "A competent chef will be engaged and only fresh food (no canned) will be served."

The *Manitou Springs Journal* poked fun at Rupp in this manner: "D. H. Rupp returned yesterday from the summit house . . . and claims he can make light biscuits, but one of his guests declared that the one he ate was so heavy it tired his horse coming down. Rupp later brought down some of his biscuits and distributed them amongst friends, who will have them cut and polished as souvenirs."

The locomotive *John Hulbert* and train at the old Summit House. The structure was built in 1882 as a weather station, then later abandoned. It was reactivated when the Cog Road was built, and made an ideal upper terminus. — RICHARD B. JACKSON COLLECTION

The Summit House in the very late 1890's. Atop the tower is a telescope whose use was included in the 25 cent fee for ascending. Note the photographer on the platform working under his black focusing cloth in order to adjust his large view camera. This photograph was made by the famous photographer William H. Jackson, and was taken prior to 1900. A large thermometer and a Western Union sign adorn the stone wall, and a frame of specimen photographs obtainable inside. — STATE HISTORICAL SOCIETY OF COLORADO

Before 1900 a steel tower was added to the north or two story end of the summit house, above the hotel rooms, and of course there was the usual charge of 25 cents for the privilege of climbing a little higher. It did enable one to see over portions of the summit which obscured the views in some directions. The house also contained a Western Union telegraph office ("Send a telegram home from the highest telegraph office in the world!"), though in later years messages were accepted there but sent over the wires from Colorado Springs. Of course the place was lined with souvenirs for eager tourists and food was dispensed at what were then terrific prices — like 10 cents for a cup of coffee.

When the author's family spent a night there about 1908, in order to be on hand for the sunrise without having to get up and catch the sunrise train, it was a cold night and the sleeping rooms were unheated, though there was one stove in the hall outside the rooms. The furnishings were Spartan, — an iron bed, a chair, a washstand with pitcher and bowl, and of course the important earthenware receptacle under each bed, for the "necessary" was downstairs, out the front door, across the tracks, over the rocks through the cold wind and possibly snow. (It was a cloudy morning and we never did see the sunrise.)

In those days they had an unusually capable colored chef, and he did himself proud that night. It wasn't often they had overnight guests, and for that occasion he served us a delicious and beautifully prepared planked whitefish! We did not disappoint him, and left mighty little of it. About two o'clock in the morning each and every one of us became violently ill. Before we departed on the first train down to the Half Way House, we were informed that this was likely to happen. We had been enjoying ourselves so much, the chef didn't want to spoil our pleasure by warning us against

WORLD

Cornerstone of the old Summit House. — MORRIS W. ABBOTT (LEFT) "Mayor and Town Council" reads the original caption of this 1891 photograph. The "mayor" is in the middle and obviously intends to maintain law and order. — PROCTOR W. NICHOLS COLLECTION

eating a heavy meal before retiring at that high altitude. This same chef, according to legend, preferred to spend his summers up there because it was a good place to stay away from John Barleycorn and get paid for doing so. He was referred to by some as the Mayor of Pike's Peak, and on occasion would pose for pictures wearing his Prince Albert.

Sanitary facilities were always a problem, as there is no water there, and cesspools, septic tanks and sewers are out of the question. In fact, it became the highest offense of its kind in America. This, and the simple fact that a summit house that could take care of the tourists who came up the mountain in 1895 just couldn't accommodate the quarter-million or more who now visit the place annually, led to its replacement.

Finally in 1964 a new summit house was opened with a flourish on June 15. It was built by the City of Colorado Springs at a cost of just over $440,000, which is a lot of money for a shelter, but the tourists deserve it. Actually, the structure was in use as soon as the automobile road was opened on April 28. The building had to be designed and built

A typical group of tourists on the tenth train of the day up the Peak on August 19, 1913. The author is standing nearest the camera, in the center of this view, showing his grandfather the sights. He is also wearing a Cog Road button in his lapel, expressing his early interest in the railway. — MORRIS W. ABBOTT COLLECTION

The new Summit House, opened in 1964, is a great improvement over the old structure, but by no means as photogenic. Old timers miss the stone work and the tower. The Summit House is used by both railway and auto road visitors. —STEWARTS COMMERCIAL PHOTOGRAPHERS

to stand winds of up to 200 miles per hour (they have been measured at 178 m.p.h.) and temperatures as low as 65 degrees below zero, Fahrenheit. From test borings it was learned that the summit includes layers of disintegrated granite interspersed with ice, technically known as lenses, which borings showed to be of various colors, ranging from white to sky-blue and rust red to black. Because of this it was necessary to remove gravel and ice to a depth of ten feet and then haul gravel up from about four miles below. This was compacted to a depth of six feet over the building area, and upon this was placed the steel foundation, also affording an insulating barrier that will, it is hoped, prevent the heat of the building from melting the natural ice and upsetting the *status quo ante.* A three-inch layer of styrofoam was laid atop the gravel for further insulation, and large I-beams encased in poured concrete form the foundation. (The old summit house had settled so that the doors and windows often became inoperable.)

The heating system, which is all overhead, uses oil as fuel and is filled with antifreeze solution. Because no power lines reach the summit, the new building has its own electric generating system.

The west wall, facing away from Colorado Springs and against the prevailing winds, is of large granite boulders found in profusion at the site. The other three walls are of precast aggregate stone made in Denver. Glass areas have been kept to a minimum, though there are enough to afford adequate views, and rolling steel shutters cover them in winter. Lightning protection has been installed, grounded in the ice lenses.

In the summit house's 11,692 square feet are two large public rest rooms, a large curio room, lobby and information desk, concession stand for light refreshments (seating 85), a small office and dispatcher's room for the Cog Road, manager's office, Highway Patrol office, photographic darkroom and sales room, a large kitchen, dishwashing room, storage facilities, walk-in refrigerator and employees' dining room. There are also sleeping quarters for 22 employees, small rooms for the manager and assistant manager, and one for the U. S. Forest Service radio equipment.

Although there are as yet no telephone wires to the summit, the building has telephone booths, useful for doodling. Presumably this lack will be corrected.

The new structure was built northwest of the old summit house. Local people with historical interest in the Pike's Peak region had hoped that the original part could be preserved, but it was demolished, except that the east or front wall is being used as a retaining wall for the parking area, its empty window and door openings mutely protesting.

In return for the right to use the building in perpetuity and a guarantee of no rail competition, the M. & P.P. gave up all but half an acre of its original 5.52 acre easement. In April 1969 the press reported that the City of Colorado Springs had placed a contract with a Connecticut firm to install a sewage ultrafiltration plant on Pike's Peak to permit recycling and limited reuse of the scant water supply, to reduce the cost of trucking water up from below.

The little one is a miniature cog train powered by an automobile engine, built in Manitou to carry passengers from the Broadmoor Hotel to the Broadmoor Zoo in Colorado Springs. In the front seat are Spencer Penrose (left) and master mechanic McKay. Engine No. 5 and coach No. 101, with employees as passengers, show the comparative size. — WILLIAM H. MCKAY COLLECTION

8

REJUVENATION

IN 1925 the ownership of the Manitou & Pike's Peak Railway passed from the Simmons family to that of Spencer Penrose, owner of, among other things in the area, the Broadmoor Hotel complex and the Pike's Peak Auto Highway Company. It is said that Penrose approached Zalmon G. Simmons, Jr., saying that neither the railway nor the auto road was making money, and that either he would buy Simmons out or Simmons could buy him out, after which they could be combined in some manner so that tourists could go up one way and come back the other.

The local newspapers carried the news of an impending change when, on June 19, 1925 they quoted Spencer Penrose as saying that the consolidation of the M. & P.P. with the Pike's Peak Auto Highway Company might be an accomplished fact by the first of July, and he pointed out, though no reasons were given in the press, how it would be of great benefit to the community. He said that negotiations were under way with the owner of the cog road, "Zed G. Simmons of St. Louis," but were not completed.

On July 25, less than a week later, the highway company became owner of all of the stock of the Cog Road, the Crystal Park Highway and the Manitou Electric Railway & Casino Company. The reputed price was $50,000 — lock, stock, barrel and deficit. Penrose appears to have received in the deal an unexpected and unexplained asset, of all things: $100 par value of stock in the National Chautauqua Association.

Within a few days F. C. Matthews, traffic manager of the Midland Terminal Railway, the Pike's Peak Auto Highway Co., etc., took over the same duties for the Cog Road and subsidiaries. It was announced that the Midland Terminal shops would thereafter repair the Manitou & Pike's Peak rolling stock.

The bankrupt Crystal Park highway had been taken over by the Cog Road in 1919, while the street car line was from the beginning a Cog Road baby, to the extent that it was organized, built and operated by the same men who ran the Cog Road.

The new officers elected or appointed after the change of ownership of the Cog Road were:

President	Spencer Penrose
Vice-President	Charles L. Tutt
Secretary and Comptroller	E. S. Hartwell
Treasurer	A. S. Gill
General Manager	J. J. Cogan
Master Mechanic	Wm. H. McKay

Directors: Penrose, Tutt, A. E. Carlton, W. A. Otis, and F. M. P. Taylor.

Those familiar with Colorado railroad lore will recognize several of these men as associates of

The colorful and widely diversified ventures of Spencer Penrose (left) created an exciting chapter in the history of the Pike's Peak region. A frequent partner in business ventures was Charles L. Tutt (right) a boyhood friend from Philadelphia. — BROADMOOR HOTEL

At the right, a book of commutation tickets good on the *Dinky*, issued to Mrs. W. S. Crosby (sister of Cog Road engineer Gosling) and signed by H. J. Holt, manager of the street car line and president of the Cog Road. (BELOW) The *Dinky* street car in front of the Iron Springs Pavilion just below the Cog depot. The trolley tracks were later moved across the creek to the south side. — DENVER PUBLIC LIBRARY, WESTERN COLLECTION

The toll gate on the old carriage road running from Cascade to the summit of Pike's Peak. — STEWARTS COMMERCIAL PHOTOGRAPHERS (RIGHT) This old William H. Jackson photograph is of the "Ws" on the carriage road, with several carriages descending. The present auto highway follows the old road for the most part. — DENVER PUBLIC LIBRARY, WESTERN COLLECTION

Penrose in the Pike's Peak and Cripple Creek regions. Penrose remained president until succeeded in 1940 by Charles L. Tutt, whose son, William Thayer Tutt now occupies the chair at the head of the table. The June 1971 issue of the *Official Guide of the Railways of the United States* lists the officers of the Manitou & Pike's Peak Railway Co. as follows:

President	William Thayer Tutt
Vice-President	Russell T. Tutt
Vice-President	Gunnar Alenius
General Manager	Martin R. Frick
Traffic Manager	David C. Pierce
Secretary-Treasurer	R. J. Montgomery
Auditor	Kenneth E. Hutchings

After three years of discussion amongst the presiding elders, Penrose ("Speck" to his friends), Tutt and McKay, it was decided that the Cog Road had to progress or die. Accordingly, McKay began work on a gasoline-powered railcar which led, in a few years time, to dieselization and salvation. The 1930's were not exactly a time of good tourist business. It is not hard to understand why some-

The gasoline-powered rail car No. 7 ushered in the new era of transition from steam to diesel-electric power on the Cog Road. This illustration shows the car on a trial run up Engelmann Canyon in 1938. — MANITOU & PIKE'S PEAK RAILWAY

thing had to be done, and certainly no money was being made maintaining a fleet of obsolescent and aging locomotives. To be sure, Penrose had plenty of money, but he could see no good reason for throwing it away.

The first step toward modernization was the *Streamliner*, for in those days everything that moved had to be "streamlined." It was a 24-passenger affair costing $17,000 and was assembled at the Manitou shops, being the first self-propelled car to operate on the road. As the front end more or less resembled the nose of the Burlington's *Zephyr*, it was even referred to as a Zephyr-type. The aluminum body was made in Denver and the car was at first powered by a General Motors 175 horsepower 1,200 r.p.m. engine.

On Sunday June 14, 1938, a test run of the chassis was made with 14 men aboard. The trip to Mountain View was accomplished in 15 minutes less time than the steam trains required for the same run, and everything worked to perfection. Two days later seven men took the new car all the way to the summit and No. 7 exceeded the management's expectations as to performance. At last the Cog Road had a car that could be operated economically when patronage was less than half a train load, and this was more often than not.

When traffic was light, as it was when No. 7 was designed and built, this small vehicle enabled the road to keep going. Not many passengers were in sight on the summit this day. — SANBORN (BELOW) This is how No. 7 looked in 1955, after a Cadillac motor had been installed. Rail car is on the main line near the Manitou depot. — MORRIS W. ABBOTT

Rail car No. 7 standing in a deep snowdrift in Windy Point cut, just two and one-half miles from the summit of Pike's Peak. — MANITOU & PIKE'S PEAK RAILWAY

Over the next few years the *Streamliner's* power plant was altered from time to time. Lastly No. 7 received a Cadillac V-8, 4,300 r.p.m. engine. With newer equipment now available, its future appears very dim, and presently it is in storage, with no power plant at all.

While gas car No. 7 was still in its infancy, the management determined to go ahead with plans for a diesel-electric train. In 1938 a contingent of engineers from the General Electric Company, headed by Robert W. Barrell of that firm's Transportation Engineering Department, descended upon Manitou and conferred at great length with Master Mechanic McKay and W. R. Jackson, M. E.; General Motors and Westinghouse Airbrake Company sent representatives, too. Barrell, while in the region, visited Scott Auto Body Company of Denver to discuss details of the proposed coach.

Diesel train No. 8, the first of the diesel-electrics, is shown here propelling a trainload of Rocky Mountain Railroad Club members to the summit on August 27, 1939, the first year of its operation. Seven Lakes and the plains are visible in the distance. — R. H. KINDIG (LEFT) The power plant of No. 8, looking downward toward the rear of the locomotive. — GATES RUBBER CO. (RIGHT) No. 8 detrains passengers at its new loading platform at the summit. — GERALD M. BEST

The M. & P.P. now has five diesel-electric locomotives, numbered 8 through 12, which are substantially alike, the main difference being that No. 8 is powered by three General Motors diesel engines (model 6-71), while the rest each have two Cummins diesels (model NHBIS-600). The reason for the change from GM to Cummins diesels was that the M. & P.P. wanted to reduce the number of power plants from three to two without reducing the horsepower. Simulated altitude tests by GE indicated that the two Cummins engines at 2,100 r.p.m. would produce the required power at 14,000 feet of elevation.

At first it was expected that three locomotives would be ordered, but only one was bought before World War II, which postponed further buying. The order for the engine was placed with GM through the Electric Equipment & Engineering Company of Denver.

All of the diesel-electrics have the same traction motors, GE's type GE-1204, a bus and small locomotive 600 volt DC series traction motor designed for rigid mounting to the locomotive frame and for driving through a driveshaft with double universal joints. This shaft is connected to a double reduction (15.65 to 1) gear box mounted on the axle and driving the axle on which the rack gear is tightly mounted.

No. 8 has three such motors, two on one axle and one on the other. Nos. 9, 10, 11 and 12 each have four traction motors, two on each axle. This was done because three motors would not work well on two generators, nor four motors on three generators.

As with the steam trains, the engines are not coupled to the cars but push them. Three types of braking are provided — electric, air and hand. The first of these normally provides all the braking effect required on the down trip and is obtained by positioning the controller handles to connect the motors across sections of a braking rheostat. The air and hand brakes act independently on the same set of corrugated cast steel brake drums, the brake shoes having lands that fit into the grooves of the drums. There is one brake drum bolted to each side of each rack or pinion gear, and since there are two such cog wheels, one on each axle, there are four brake drums on each locomotive. The brake rigging of each axle is independent of the other, and in the case of the hand brakes there are two completely independent hand brake systems, each with its own hand brake wheel and acting on one axle set of brakes.

The engineer controls the air brake by an air brake valve, Westinghouse Air Brake Company's M-36 self-lapping, straight air type. Normally this brake is used only for bringing the train to a dead stop, after maximum electric braking has been applied. An emergency application of the air brake because of train parting or because of action by one of the train crew results in an emergency application on both locomotive and car. Magnetic brakes were discussed at one stage, but not adopted.

A novel and probably unique feature of these locomotives is their ability to operate the entire down trip of nearly nine miles entirely on gravity power. The engines are ordinarily shut down upon reaching the summit and not started again until ready to leave Manitou depot and start uphill again. One air compressor and one battery-charging auxiliary (37 volt) generator are axle driven, the latter supplying electricity for train lighting, control operation and battery charging.

Originally the electric brake resistors of No. 8 were located inside the cab and below the windows at the uphill side, it being supposed that natural ventilation would take care of the heat. This proved not to be the case in descending, and in actual use the cab temperature approached 160 degrees Fahrenheit. This was remedied by installing a partition of heat-resisting glass across the cab. When No. 9 was built, however, the braking resistors were placed on the roof of the cab, and this was done also with Nos. 10 and 11.

"Springtime in the Rockies." After a short snowstorm, passengers aboard No. 9 mingle with snow shovelers at the summit of Pike's Peak. Note the glass in the roof which improved the visibility from the new diesel-electric trains. — BOB MCINTYRE

No. 8 was undoubtedly the first diesel-electric rack locomotive and the first diesel-electric to reach as high an elevation as Pike's Peak. The first trip to the summit was made on July 12, 1939, with GE engineer Barrell at the controls. (Barrell became Senior Engineer of GE's Export and Industrial Locomotive Engineering at Erie, and most of the data on locomotives Nos. 8 through 11 are from him.)

The management arranged a special run of No. 8 on July 14, 1939, for about 50 invited guests, who were shepherded by conductor Ben Kirk and engineer Joe Cox. The party included M. & P.P. officials and their wives, GE and GM engineers, local celebrity and ex-railroader Bill Crosby and Mrs. Crosby (sister of the late engineer Herm Gosling). The next night the train, lit up like a Mississippi River show boat, was on exhibition at the Manitou depot. Regular runs started on Sunday, July 16, 1939, and the $70,000 gamble began to pay off right from the start.

The passenger unit has a capacity of 52 and was built to Manitou & Pike's Peak Railway specifications by the Winter-Weiss Company of Denver, riding on trucks furnished by the road. Where the old coach windows were difficult to raise after being once lowered into the car body, the new ones operate like automobile windows. Unlike the later coaches, this first one does not have glass extending into the roof section. Entrance is through a door at the rear or lower end, on the right hand side, which avoids the use of a view-obscuring door at the front end. Lighting is by electricity, where the old coaches had no illumination, though an oil headlight might be placed on the front platform on night trips, pointing ahead.

Diesel-electric No. 10 backs down from the engine house and will pause below the switch. The coach at the left will roll down to make the complete train. — MALLORY HOPE FERRELL COLLECTION

Diesel-electric locomotive No. 11 just outside the engine house in Manitou during May 1955. The building behind the engine is the hydro-electric power plant through which passes the water brought down by pipeline from Ruxton Park via Mt. Manitou. — MORRIS W. ABBOTT

Both power and coach units were painted and lettered by Dinty Moore of Colorado Springs, aluminum with red and black lettering.

No. 9 came along in 1947 and Nos. 10 and 11 were delivered in March 1950, bringing the stable to four steam trains, one gas car and four diesel-electric trains, with a total carrying capacity of about 330. In practice the steamers and gas car were brought out only when their use was unavoidable.

No. 12 was built in the company's own Manitou shops and trial tested in the fall of 1955. It was built without the benefit of blueprints and was ready for service early in the 1956 season. Credit for its construction has been given to General Foreman Charles B. O'Brien by Master Mechanic McKay. Following the general pattern of the earlier diesel-electrics, No. 12 nevertheless has important differences. It is powered by two 330 horsepower (at 2,100 r.p.m.) General Motors Series 110 diesels. Four General Electric traction motors were used. The coach, as with the other diesel trains, was built by Winter-Weiss of Denver.

The next development was the acquisition of two handsome rail cars designed and built in Switzerland. The Swiss, having had a great deal of experience with mountain railroading, designed an ideal cog train. These self-propelled passenger cars, each with a seating capacity of about 80, were ordered in 1960 and delivered late in 1963, having travelled by water from Hamburg to Houston and thence on flat cars to Colorado Springs.

Before the Swiss Locomotive & Machine Works (S.L.M.) shipped the new rail cars Nos. 14 and 15, they were tested with good results on the line of the Arth-Rigibahn in Switzerland, where the maximum gradient is 20 percent. This road climbs Mt. Rigi and uses the Riggenbach rack system. The train in this view is No. 14 during the trial runs, with Riggenbach cog wheels installed for the tests. — SWISS LOCOMOTIVE & MACHINE WORKS

These Swiss cars carry road numbers 14 and 15, and were built in Winterthur by the Swiss Locomotive & Machine Works (Schweizerische Lokomotiv- und Maschinenfabrik), with electrical equipment by Brown, Boveri & Co. of Baden, Switzerland.

With the exception of the controls and the heat dissipating grids, all equipment is located underneath the car bodies. Each car had two 8-cylinder air-cooled SLM diesel engines of 220 horsepower (at 1,600 r.p.m.), which were direct-coupled to the generators which powered the two traction motors. Each motor drove one axle of each truck, and the motors were in series and synchronized through the rack rail. For braking downhill the motors operated as excited generators. The placing of the power plant below deck made it necessary to mount the traction motors longitudinally, with transmission through double reduction gears, and hydraulic control of the mechanical brakes takes the place of rodding. There is also a band brake acting on brake drums. If an excessive speed devel-

As surely as Colorado tops the nation with its 52 peaks that tower above 14,000 feet, so also does it top the nation in early fall color. With aspen trees turning a bright golden color, diesel rail car No. 15 passes through Ruxton Park on one of the trial trips to the summit of Pike's Peak. — SWISS LOCOMOTIVE & MACHINE WORKS

These twins are the last two diesel trains received by the Cog Road from the Swiss Locomotive & Machine Works. Here they await the return trip on the morning of August 23, 1971. Note the removeable panel (with road number on it), which Nos. 14 and 15 do not have. — MORRIS W. ABBOTT

No. 15, with which No. 14 is identical, is pictured here discharging passengers at the summit. These railcars can be operated by a single operator, but for greater safety a two-man crew is on board, one trainman is continually at a brake wheel. — MORRIS W. ABBOTT COLLECTION

ops while descending, the brakes are applied automatically, which reduces the possibility of a runaway.

These cars have a typically clean, Swiss style about them. They are almost 52 feet long and are painted a striking red, with chrome cog wheel insignia fore and aft on each side. The interior walls are decorated with an olive green and white vinyl covering, and the floors have inlaid linoleum. The unupholstered, contour-moulded seats are a far cry from the old, narrow, plush "roll-over" seats of the original coaches. There is a control stand at each end, and the cars are equipped with a public address system. The windows are extra large, affording the passengers an unobstructed view at all times. In common with the older diesel-electrics on the road, there is constant short wave radio communication with the dispatcher's office and the summit house.

Before these rail cars were shipped from the factory in Winterthur, they were tested on the Arth-Rigi Railway, where the grades are almost as steep as the 25 percent maximum on the Pike's Peak road, though the elevation is less. The new diesel units originally were powered by air cooled diesel engines. As these engines did not perform as expected at the higher altitude, it was decided, after a first period of operation, to replace them by a water cooled engine type — that is, Cummins six-cylinder horizontal engine.

Nos. 16 and 17, identical with Nos. 14 and 15, and similarly powered, were put into service in mid-summer 1968. All four are now giving excellent and continuous service to the Manitou & Pike's Peak Railway. Although each car could be handled by one man, a two-man crew is used for the sake of greater safety.

It will be noticed that, out of respect for the powers of evil, there is no No. 13 on the road. After all, why ask for trouble?

Today most of the passenger equipment has been repainted to match the Swiss cars, and a vast improvement it is.

The early procedure was for section hands either to walk to work and back, if a work extra were not needed, or, if the distance were great, to ride up on the back platform and cab of the first passenger train in the days of steam. This meant getting a late start on the job and sometimes an early quitting time, which the help doubtless enjoyed. Davy Jones, for many years master mechanic of the line, did try to build a gasoline powered work car that would fill the bill, but with little success. He built one that got up as far as Ruxton Park (about 3 miles) and no farther. A press report in November 1903 quoted Jones as saying that the new car would carry four men to the top in 40 minutes and would have 48 horsepower. The only place it reached was the scrap heap.

Many years later, when internal combustion engines had been greatly improved, it remained for W. H. McKay to design and build a successful work car. By then the road was owned by the Pike's Peak Auto Highway Company, which owned and operated a fleet of powerful Pierce-Arrow cars for hauling tourists about the region. McKay wangled an engine, frame and various parts of a Pierce from the parent company, put a cog axle under each end, and installed an experimental gear box from the Ford Motor Company, giving the car a ratio of 14.5 to 1. Propulsion is only through the front or upper axle, but there are brakes on both.

This rail car is No. 20 and made its first trip in 1934. It is still in use whenever needed, which is often, as nobody now lives in the section houses and all hands are carried up to work from Manitou. The Pierce-Arrow engine has long since gone to its reward, and a General Motors 707 engine is in its place, removed from gas car No. 7.

Work car No. 20 at the summit in 1934, while it was still powered by a Pierce-Arrow motor, with Boyce Motometer on the radiator cap. Master mechanic McKay is second from the left of the two men standing on the ground. The gentleman directly above McKay, with his hands in his pockets, is Charles L. Tutt, president of the Cog Road. — WILLIAM H. MCKAY COLLECTION

The section gang is unloading new ties along a stretch of track near Windy Point. By this time the Pierce-Arrow engine had been replaced with a General Motors 707 engine from rail car No. 7. — MANITOU & PIKE'S PEAK RAILWAY

This was the old way of bucking snow on the Cog Road. The locomotive, with a flatcar bucker plow on the front, would make a run with the plow into a drift, thus automatically loading the car with snow. It then dropped down hill to a clear space, where men shoveled it off. In this 1905 scene, the telegraph poles seem to stalk across the snowy mountainside. — GRANT G. SIMMONS, SR., COLLECTION

9

SNOW

ANOTHER McKay first was a rotary snowplow designed by him and built in the company shops in Manitou Springs. At one time they had had in mind buying from the narrow gauge Rio Grande Southern what remained of its rotary plow No. 2, which had never been quite the same after a watchman let the water in its boiler run low, resulting in an explosion on a siding at Vance Junction, Colorado. The boiler of No. 3 was eligible too, but instead it was scrapped and the steam rotary plow idea abandoned.

After a number of discouraging difficulties had been overcome by the trial-and-error method, McKay, over a period of several years, produced in 1953 a successful diesel-powered rotary. It is self-propelled, equipped with two General Motors Series 110 275 horsepower diesel power plants, one for propulsion and the other to operate the 8-foot, 12-bladed wheel at 200 r.p.m. In the spring of 1964, for example, the heavy snowfall of the previous winter had been cleared out by April 24, though snow and ice to a depth in places of 12 feet were encountered.

The M. & P.P. simply shuts up shop when winter comes to the mountains, which is usually late in October. In the first years of operation, when snow removal was as yet an unlearned art, the line opened later in the spring than today. It was sometimes late June before operation all the way to the summit began. It didn't always pay to remove the snow too early in the season, for when they did, crews sometimes had to repeat their labors several times. In fact, some repetition is considered normal. In 1904 the road was opened on April 15, and the previous year on March 28. This was a mistake, however, for soon thereafter a seven-foot snowfall closed the road again for six weeks.

For many years, in fact until the rotary came along, snow removal was accomplished with a flat car, a plow arrangement improvised for it, and a crew of hardy shovellers all bundled up against the cold and the glare of the sun. A wedge plow was never even tried, probably because you never get up enough speed to ram a drift properly on a 25 percent grade.

One of the two 4-wheeled flat cars was used for snow removal, and it was usually parked at Minnehaha when not in use. At the front or uphill end was attached a steel inclined plane or plowpoint that could be raised or lowered by means of a lever made from a piece of a rail, which extended back over the bed of the flat car. When a drift was approached, the plane was lowered to the level of the top of the rail, and the engineer proceeded to ram the drift. The plane would run under the snow, which would pile up on the car, whereupon

Plowing snow on Pike's Peak above the Saddle. The shovelers are bundled up against the cold and the glare of the sun off the snow. — STEWARTS COMMERCIAL PHOTOGRAPHERS (LEFT) These snow-birds (shovelers) have raised the plow point (which when plowing is lowered to the railheads) and are about to head for home from Windy Point. — HAROLD J. SEELY COLLECTION (LOWER) Locomotive No. 6, with flatcar-snowplow, has a load of snow to be shoveled off by the gang waiting below. —CARL F. MATHEWS COLLECTION

Grey skies to the east, and plenty of snow to shovel at Windy Point. Cameron's Cone, the mountain in the center of this scene, is a mere 10,600 feet above sea level. — MRS. C. C. MCREYNOLDS (BELOW) On May 10, 1955, three loads of snow cleared out Windy Point cut, but a week later there was a 14-foot drift here. — G. B. HIBBARD

the engineer would back down to a clear place and the men would shovel the snow off to one side of the track. Then they would have another go at it, again and again, until the track was clear. Lee Jamison, who worked on the snow trains for many years, said that the jolt when the plow finally stalled was so bad that it nearly derailed the engine.

This was slow work and required a lot of manpower. As the years passed and fewer men cared to shovel snow above timberline regardless of the compensation, it was then that McKay built No. 21, the rotary snowplow.

The snow clearance in the spring of 1900 was a real job, and it took all of April and until May 25 to clear the line. It was said to have cost $10,000, which would take a sizeable bite out of the profits, if any. As far down as three miles from the summit, perhaps as much as a mile below Windy Point, drifts as deep as 30 feet were encountered, and these were tightly compacted. The quantity of snow removed was estimated to be 2.6 million cubic feet. In digging trenches along the track to allow the coaches to clear on the curves, it required three men, one at track level, one halfway up on a snow shelf, and a third man on top of the drift. Each load of snow on the old flat car plow weighed 8 to 13 tons.

After changes were made as need dictated, rotary No. 21 has solved much of the snow problem. In photographs of the rotary in action, a diesel-electric locomotive is usually in evidence. This is used not only to get the plow to the scene of action more quickly than its own power plant could, and descend faster, but also to lessen the danger of a runaway in case the rotary should climb the rack rail if the icing is bad. The additional engine in such cases could block and slow the rotary's descent.

Perfection did not come easily nor all at once for the rotary, and the old method had its supporters in the years of transition. The late G. B. "Perk" Hibbard wrote about it as follows in the fall of 1955:

"Three years now and she has been a dismal flop. Opened the road last spring well enough, simply because there wasn't any snow. Had to take along snipes to pick ice, though, after she derailed and got all four wheels on the ground when she ran up on ice at 13,000 cut. Then this spring she sailed gaily off to open the road in two or three hours, as there was scarcely any snow again this year. But when she hit the hard packed stuff in Windy Cut, she washed out; wouldn't shove in far enough for the rotor blades to cut, and when they tried to force her, the front end lifted out of the rack and began jumping up and down. That put too much strain on the gear box and it stripped. So that was that. Next day we went up with No. 5 and the old flat car and plow point, which we had been assured we would never have to take out again, and we opened the road with it in three hours. Only three loads out of Windy Cut and two or three from there to Summit, one of the easiest openings we had ever had.

A derailment of the coach *Salida*, on the last hill below the summit. In the early days the coaches had only four wheels and trouble resulted. In this scene some men are struggling with the front end of the coach to get it back on the track. — DENVER PUBLIC LIBRARY, WESTERN COLLECTION (BELOW) A bit of "cheesecake," wherein a lovely girl in the cab waves at a frigid photographer. Old No. 6, youngest of the steamers, was scrapped in 1955. —JOHN FETLER COLLECTION

"... One year we made it through in passenger time. Then we operated trains about a week or ten days and everything was going quite peacefully. Then it began snowing the night of May 17 and kept it up all of the next day and night. The plow point was parked at Minny, and we took off with the flat car and engine No. 5 to pick it up, little suspecting how much snow we really had up there. The snow began to lay on below Butterworth Flat and fast increased in depth from there on. By the time we reached Alpine Bridge (just below Minnehaha) we were pushing snow ahead of the flat, and barely made it to Minny without derailing. Twenty inches there. We shovelled out the switch, ran in and hooked onto the point, then derailed backing out with it, and had a hell of a time getting rerailed again. Got on the main finally, dropped the plow and rolled along plowing it off as far as Ruxton, where we had to hang the plow and shovel off the crossing. Twenty-eight inches of snow on the level at Ruxton, and still coming down.

"On our way again, slowly rolling along, and the snow increasingly deeper, soon up level with the car. Over three feet on the level at Mountain View, and we couldn't tell where the switch ball was, with the result that the plow rammed it and tore up the switch and derailed us again. Well, we got the car back again, shovelled out the switch and made temporary repairs so we could cross it. Hung the plow and crossed, dropped it again and on up to the tank for water, then started on.

"The snow was so deep that there wasn't any place for the plow to shove it aside, and it was dry and sugary and rolled around the point and back under the car and engine, so we had to flounder through, with the danger of derailing at any moment. Got to Mile 5 and shoved in and stalled. When we tried to back out we broke the big log chain tying the car and engine together. Patched it up and tried again, with the same result. And again and again, till finally it held and the engine pulled the car out.

"I'd had a big plenty by then, and there was no sense in trying to go on, with it still snowing hard and everyone wet and frozen, and no chain to yank the car back out when we stalled. So I told our new manager the-hell-with-it, and hung the plow and we went back to town.

"Well, he being new and anxious to get the road open of course, he finally persuaded Ed [Weller] to try the rotary on only one gear box, so they took

Diesel-electric locomotive working with the flatcar-snowplow above Windy Point on May 10, 1970. —COLORADO RAILROAD MUSEUM (BELOW) A group of hardy Kiwanians obviously enjoying the snow in Windy Point cut on May 14, 1923, en route to the summit of Pike's Peak. — PROCTOR W. NICHOLS COLLECTION

Snow clearance was hard and slow work. As the years passed, fewer and fewer of the men wished to brave the cold on Pike's Peak. Rotary snowplow No. 21 was built to solve this dilemma. In this scene, shop foreman Edward B. Weller stands beside the rotary near the Manitou shops. This shows how the machine looked in May 1953. — STANLEY J. PAYNE (RIGHT) The lower end of No. 21, rotary snowplow, at Manitou. The roller is useful because the plow is ordinarily pushed to the job by a locomotive. — MORRIS W. ABBOTT

Something seems to be amiss with the Rotary at Mountain View. Quite often a large piece of wood or a rock could be drawn in by the blades and cause the operator to stop the motors. Here a group of trainmen check out the situation. Coach No. 106 may be seen at the right. — MANITOU & PIKE'S PEAK RAILWAY

Here is a spectacular view of the rotary snowplow in action. The rotary is almost out of sight in this deep drift on the Big Hill in April 1964. It took nine days to reach the summit, with drifts and ice up to 12 feet deep. — BOB MCINTYRE

her up with a diesel behind her, and the old crate worked fine in the sugary snow, went right up to Grecian [Bend] by evening. So things looked promising once again. Took her up the next day and she performed nicely on up to timberline through some lighter drifts, really heaved it over the bank! But it was a different story later when she hit the big drifts below Windy Cut, which were wind packed and tough. Same things again there, and out went the remaining gears, so she was done. So-o-o, out came the old standby again next day, and to make a long story shorter, we battled the snow with the old plow every day for the next two weeks.

"In the meantime they had obtained a new set of gears for No. 21 and installed 'em, and brought her up and tried her again. Same old story, — OK in the lighter drifts, but when she hit the deep wall in Windy Cut she stalled and began jumping up and down and battering the racks. So to save ripping out the gears, they gave it up, and we battled our way through the cut with the old plow, with discouraging delays, spending several days on two occasions just getting back to the cut after high winds blew everything level full again.

"But at last we broke through the cut, 14 feet at the deepest, and plowed on through to above the Saddle. By then they had worked the rotary over again, and wanted to try her, so up she went and we followed with the old reliable just in case, and waited at Windy. She did pretty well for a short way, then hit hard packed snow again, and as usual went to stamping up and down on top of the rack and broke and bent three of them.

"So that ended that for the day. We robbed Windy siding of three racks and went up and got 'em in, and continued with the old hog and sheer plow next day. Deep drifts and very hard packed around Mile 8, and we made very slow progress, though steady. The big shots grew anxious again and sent the rotary up for another try, but she wouldn't cut it, and we finished with the oldtimer again. It was open for a couple of days, and then a gale drifted the cuts full again above Windy. They sent the rotary up again and she did pretty well in the new stuff, only they had to cut away so much of the hood and stack that she threw most of the snow back on the track behind her and couldn't even come back down over where she had been. We had to follow with the old plow and clean up, but anyway, she held together and

The old flat-car bucker plow was fine at combating ice and tightly packed snow which gave the rotary a bad time. A new and decidedly modern plow was designed in 1967-1968. This new plow was similar to the old flatcar bucker plow, but did away with the shoveling off of the snow, employing a hydraulic platform lift. Here snow is being cleared out from under the tilting bed of the snow plow. When it is tipped to an angle of 45 degrees, the snow slides off the waxed surface of the steel bed. — TOM DANIELS (BELOW) This hydraulic-powered arrangement has saved countless hours of hand shoveling, by dumping its load of snow which simply falls off. — MANITOU & PIKE'S PEAK RAILWAY

These two scenes show the flatcar-snowplow as it reposes with retired engine No. 5 at the end of track near the Manitou depot. The view above shows how the point is lowered to scoop up the snow, while at the right a view looking at the plow head-on. — BOTH MALLORY HOPE FERRELL

churned through to the top, and that was the only time she ever really has been of much help to us.

"Well, they got another set of gears for her this summer and installed them and made some alterations in the hood, etc., and are waiting for the first good snow to take her up for another trip; so that is the situation at present. Personally, I have my doubts that she will ever prove a success in snow that has packed and frozen all winter, unless they figure out some sort of augers at the lower corners to chop up the snow and ice so she can move ahead without humping up and getting on top of the rack.

"Our new manager doesn't think much of her either. Says that if it weren't for the fact that she has cost the company about 75 grand, so they've *got* to make her work now, he would have one of the old hogs put up in top shape to do the ramming, and have a steam lift installed on the flat car to tilt the bed and dump the load instead of men having to shovel it off each time, and we would open the road a danged sight faster than the rotary ever will."

When crews went up to plow out the road in the spring of 1959, they found that 18 inches of ice had formed across the track above Windy Point, which No. 21 could not remove. It was necessary to fire up No. 4 again and put her to work with the old flat car plow. That was the last time that steam power was used on the Manitou & Pike's Peak Railway. It was because of the ice that the management had kept No. 4 as long as they did.

Because of the superiority of the old plow in combating ice and tightly packed snow, a new and decidedly modern plow was designed in 1967-68. One of the shortcomings of the old plow was that it required so much hand labor in shovelling the snow off of the flat car. This led, logically, to the idea of a self-cleaning plow.

Accordingly, a steel skeleton-frame bed was built and topped with a smooth steel plate, which can be tilted by hydraulic power to an angle of 45 degrees. To discourage sticking of the snow to the tilting bed or plate, the skier's practice of waxing is used. This worked well, but there still remained the necessity of dropping down hill, sometimes a considerable distance, to find a place where there was enough clear space on the left side. To solve this problem, they added what has been christened the side-plow. This is a blade similar to a highway snowplow or bulldozer blade. It is mounted at the upper end, left side, of the flatbed, in such a way that about three-quarters of it can be extended out past the side of the plow. This blade then serves to push the snow already discarded farther away, making room for additional dumping. Thus manpower, fuel and time are saved.

Snowfalls in 1969 lasted late and then began early in the fall. On June 28, the plow worked in drifts 5 to 7 feet deep, and on October 10 a three-foot snowfall closed the road for the season, the earliest in many a year. The average October snowfall on the peak is about nine inches, but in 1969 it reached about 70 inches at Ruxton Park and at the summit.

Diesel-electric train No. 8 at the summit of Pike's Peak, 14,110 feet above sea level. While there are higher peaks in Colorado, there is no accessible elevation on earth that affords so extended a range of vision as that from the summit of Pike's Peak. This photograph was taken from end-of-track looking back toward the old Summit House. —GERALD M. BEST

10

A LITTLE OF EVERYTHING

RAILS, TIES, LOCOMOTIVES, cars, freight, passengers, profits, and losses, are all things railroads are made of. When you add a rack rail and a climb of almost a mile and a half in nine miles of track, something different emerges, and this is why the Manitou & Pike's Peak Railway is unique.

Besides these, there are a number of less important and downright unimportant matters that contribute to the charm of the Cog Road — the battles with snow, the toboggans, the doper, and other details that memory and curiosity have brought to light.

One of the tales told in the Simmons family is about five deaf people who made the trip to the summit on the cog road, and were astonished to find that they could hear! It happened that Simmons was there at that time, and they were so overcome with emotion that they kissed his hand. The story ends there, and one wonders if they were not sorely disappointed to find themselves again stone deaf when they returned to Manitou.

WHAT EVER BECAME OF . . . .?

"The old order changeth, yielding place to new," and the old steam locomotives have disappeared from the active list these many years.

No. 1, once named for Major Hulbert, was moved from Cheyenne Mtn. to Cheyenne Mtn. Zoo, near Colorado Springs in 1971. No. 2 which was first named *Manitou,* but briefly was the *T. F. Richardson,* was donated to the City of Manitou Springs, and rests now on a concrete base across from the city hall. Her low-pressure cylinders carry plates indicating that she was Baldwin compound No. 342. No. 3, erstwhile *Pike's Peak,* was cannibalized for parts, and second No. 4 seems to have a cylinder that once belonged to No. 3.

Towards the end of the steam era, No. 4 was kept on hand and in condition to be used in emergencies, such as bucking snow, which could be done only with considerable inconvenience, due to the lack of watering facilities above Manitou, not to mention a dearth of experienced steam engineers. Her left low-pressure cylinder carries a Baldwin plate saying she is Vauclain compound No. 722, whilst the other one says she is No. 343. Obviously some shuffling of parts took place. Second 4 was donated by the M. & P.P. to the Colorado Railroad Museum of Golden, Colorado, in October 1968, where she rests on a section of 16 percent gradient track, — cold but operable.

No. 5 has been assigned a place of honor just below the Manitou cog station. Her interior has

Veteran locomotive No. 1, erstwhile *John Hulbert* and now over 80 years of age, takes it easy on Cheyenne Mountain near Colorado Springs. It has since been removed to the Cheyenne Mountain Zoo. — R. H. KINDIG

Engine No. 2, once named *Manitou*, was given to the City of Manitou Springs and now rests across from the City Hall. — GERALD M. BEST (BELOW) The late Brough J. Taggart, longtime station agent of the Cog Road at Manitou, stands beside old No. 5 just below the depot. — BOB MCINTYRE

President William Thayer Tutt and general manager Martin R. Frick watch the loading of No. 4 on a low-bed trailer for delivery to the Colorado Railroad Museum, September 30, 1968. — BOB MCINTYRE

a burned crown sheet and some other complaints, thus rendering her *hors de combat.* However the engine is intended only as a monument to the steam era on the Manitou & Pike's Peak Railway. Before she was placed on her throne, No. 5 received a new axle, having donated one to No. 8 back in 1942 when the latter had need of replacement in wartime.

No. 6, so altered in rebuilding as to resemble only slightly its original self, was scrapped. Its number plate is on loan by the author to the Colorado Railroad Museum, as is No. 3's whistle.

The Rocky Mountain Railroad Club of Denver operated three steam-powered excursions for its members, in 1939 with No. 3, 1940 with No. 6, and 1941 with No. 5. The last steam passenger train ran in September 1958, when a group made the trip ahead of No. 4, at which time author M. C. Poor recorded the sounds that no longer echo from the rocks of Ruxton Canyon and the Big Hill. At his behest so many crossing whistles were blown that the train had to halt once to get up enough steam to go on. And there are no crossings on the line.

This post card wins the prize for fakery. The train was painted in by an artist, who did very well, except that he has the train charging furiously *downhill* toward a complacent burro party, at the lower edge of Ruxton Park. — MORRIS W. ABBOTT COLLECTION

This post card justifies the use of the word "phony" if anything does. The lettering is not that used on the Cog Road coaches, it is not in the center of the side of the car, and it says "R.R." instead of "RY." Parts of a letter S and numeral 3 show at the left and right, the windows and roof are not of a Cog Road coach, and other details, too! — KENNETH G. BROOKS COLLECTION

DOUBLE-TRACKING AND ELECTRIFICATION

There were flurries in the local press every now and then, reporting or rumoring plans to double-track or electrify the Cog Road, or both. Some of these may have been President Sells' way of getting free publicity, and he was always being credited with having fantastic plans for the road.

In March 1904 the *Colorado Springs Gazette* carried an article saying that Sells had spent several months in the East "discussing electrification plans with greatest experts in the United States," and went on to say that two trolley wires would be used, the current would come up from Manitou on one such trolley wire, pass through the motors and return on the other wire. No ground would be used, "as the huge potential in the ground on Pike's Peak would burn out the motors." The poles would carry "lightning rods to attract electricity from the air, and transmit it through the four rails of the Cog Road to a power house in Manitou where it will be transformed and converted and stored for use." Continuing, "It is a big proposition and will cost a big lot of money. One estimate places the cost of plants and poles at $250,000. It is the purpose of the Cog Road to get their plans in shape to electrify the road for the next year if possible, or at all events the year after that."

The *Denver Republican* the previous month had printed a somewhat similar account, but quoted Harrison J. Holt (president after Sells) as not being as optimistic. He said that electrification had been considered for years, but the problem was no nearer solution than before. It spoke of the great amount of static electricity in the air at high elevations and said that if one holds up a moistened forefinger, blue sparks will appear at the tip, "while the finger will sing like a telegraph pole when the current is humming along the wires. No shock is experienced, however." The article went on to say that if storage batteries were used they would require a second car to carry them.

In the *Colorado Springs Gazette* of July 25, 1907, Sells, the reporters' ever-ready help in time of news shortage, denied that he had discussed the use of electricity, but admitted that it would be fine if it could be used.

In spite of all this, in early 1909 Sells was reported to have announced that the M. & P.P. would install an electric third rail and double track the line at a cost of $750,000, and that Z. G. Simmons, owner of the road, would arrive from Kenosha the next week for his semi-annual inspection trip. Work was to start in the fall, and "engineers everywhere" were even then studying the road preparatory to bidding, as contracts would be let within a month. It was said that fares might be reduced as much as 50 percent. Then, in the July 30, 1909 issue of the *Gazette,* Sells did an about-face and denied that there were any plans to double track or electrify.

CONVERSION TO OIL FUEL

As early as 1902 the press reported that the cog road would convert its five locomotives to burn crude oil, and Master Mechanic Jones spent two days in Denver in April of that year conferring with the superintendent of motive power of the Colorado & Southern. The superintendent was credited with being an expert on the subject, having been the first to so equip a standard locomotive on any of the southwestern lines when he was superintendent of motive power for the Gulf, Colorado & Santa Fe. Beaumont oil would be used, and was to be brought to Manitou in tank cars via the Colorado & Southern. Nothing came of that, either.

WINTER OPERATION

In December 1937, Spencer Penrose was quoted in the press as saying that the M. & P.P. would run all winter to take skiers to the 12,000 foot level with, perhaps, a cable tow the remaining two miles to the summit. A large shelter was to be built at Windy Point, and "Count Phillipe de Pret, a ski expert brought to the United States by Mr. Penrose, has laid out what he claims to be the world's longest ski course, starting from the summit of Pike's Peak and winding about 20 miles to the base of the mountain."

THREATS OF COMPETITION

On more than one occasion competing railroads to the summit of Pike's Peak were proposed, but none ever got past the planning or conversational stage. As early as June 14, 1891, the *Rocky Mountain News* of Denver reported a plan to revive the idea of a railroad via Bear Creek, Crystal Park, Lake Moraine, etc., substantially the route of the ill-fated Pike's Peak Railway & Improvement Company's line promoted by Professor Kerr. Emphasis was placed on the profits to accrue from the exploitation of resort sites, stone quarries, mineral deposits and scenery. This seems to have been backed by a Colonel H. S. Ervay, who waxed eloquent on the subject to the Colorado Springs correspondent of the *News.*

Two Colorado Springs papers, the *Evening Mail* and the *Telegraph,* carried stories in August and September 1901 of the filing of incorporation papers of the Seven Lakes & Pike's Peak Railroad Company, to build a standard gauge adhesion railroad from Clyde (about 25 miles from Colorado Springs on the Colorado Springs & Cripple Creek District Railway), which would be 11 to 15 miles in length. It was a pet scheme of Colonel Apponyi, who owned land in the area of Seven Lakes. C. W. Sells' comment to the reporters on this subject was that "the M. & P.P. has never paid a dividend and at times has failed to pay interest on its bonds."

The *Denver Post* of April 10, 1903 mentioned a cog road to be constructed from Victor (near Cripple Creek) to the top of Pike's Peak, there to connect with the M. & P.P. The *Colorado Springs Gazette* announced on April 17 of that year that C. W. Sells had released the news that the M. & P. P. would extend 18 miles to Cripple Creek "as soon as conditions warrant."

In April 1907 the news burst out of a line projected from Manitou to Crystal Park. Although no mention was made of Pike's Peak, there is enough mystery about it to warrant a few lines here. The Manitou & Crystal Park Railway Company, the paper said, had made a deal with Colonel Lewis Ginger of Colorado Springs to use his patented device for mountain climbing, and the road would be built that same season. He would receive $10,000 for the use of his invention, which was not described, "for elevating cars up the mountainside, and extensive tests made by the engineers of the Manitou company have satisfied them that it will be entirely successful on their line." There was an incline railway or funicular up to a shoulder of Red Mountain above Manitou at one time, but it involved nothing new and did not operate very many years.

One of the more recent projects was described in some detail in the Denver and Colorado Springs papers on November 12, 1911. This was to be a 32,000 foot long aerial tramway to carry passengers from Manitou over the hills and far away to the summit of Pike's Peak, in cars carrying five or six persons each. None other than Alderman "Bathhouse John" Coughlin of Chicago backed the organization of the Pike's Peak Aerial Tramway Company in the fall of 1910, in association with A.

The Colorado Midland Railway trestle crossing Engelmann Canyon in Manitou. The Cog Road depot is up the canyon, near the center of the illustration. The early Manitou & Pike's Peak Railway cars and engines were unloaded near the house at the far right while the Midland was in operation. — MORRIS W. ABBOTT COLLECTION

E. Norton (president of the First National Securities & Savings Bank of Denver), W. H. Colburn of Colorado Springs, his son Walter Colburn, Dr. F. R. Coffman, Harry A. Lindsley (Denver attorney), J. Mignolet (Belgian consul), E. C. Healy and Ed Yoxall (cattleman and capitalist). Norton, who had an office in Colorado Springs, was said to have bought the patent rights and rights-of-way for $90,000, including land in Manitou at Ruxton and Manitou Avenues, and was about to put in a 250-foot "moveable stairway" and a 500-foot elevated sidewalk to connect with the main depot. The peak evidently falling short of Mr. Norton's idea of what a mountain should be, he would build a 200-foot observation tower thereon, and a hotel with a capacity of no less than 400 guests.

The cable would carry, at a rate of 500 feet per minute, 40 cars ascending and as many descending. Thus they planned to transport up to 210 passengers an hour or 2,100 in a day. The time from bottom to top, or vice versa, would be one hour and four minutes. A safety factor of six to one was planned as far as the cable was concerned, and the whole thing was to be ready for operation by the first of June 1912. There appear to be no further references to the matter.

TOBOGGANING ON PIKE'S PEAK

The idea did not originate on the M. & P.P., but before long employees and others were taking advantage of the law of gravity to speed the down trip. The vehicle used was called a toboggan or go-devil, and a moderately good one could be made by any handyman with a few pieces of wood, a few bolts, a few feet of strap iron and a hunk of rubber. More elaborate and safer ones were made of iron in the Manitou shops and used by employees with or without the knowledge of the management. It is likely that the brass (officials) chose not to notice them. At any rate, many a train pulled out of the lower station with a toboggan on the back platform, in company with an employee who wanted to get back in a hurry, or a City of Colorado Springs caretaker who had used his to get down quickly for a shopping trip.

The original type consisted of a seat for the rider, perhaps two and a half feet long and 8 or 10 inches wide, which rested upon the rack rail.

Cleats on the under side of the seat, between and on both sides of the rack bars, kept it in position. Arms extended outward to each running rail to keep the thing from tipping sideways, and one of these (in the case of the wooden toboggans) had a piece of rubber on its under side that could be pressed down upon the top of the rail by the rider's leaning that way, to act as a brake. The shop-made ones had pipe arms and a clasp brake that was operated by one or two upright levers, which slowed the vehicle by squeezing the rack rail from the sides. These were safer, perhaps, but too heavy to carry uphill. The wooden ones could be carried or pushed up by the use of a long stick.

If not properly controlled, these toboggans would simply try to go into orbit, and a grave danger was that one might run into a rack rail whose teeth had bent inward by a fallen rock or had been battered by use, in which case the toboggan would slow down abruptly, and the rider, being subject to Newton's law of motion, would tend to continue in a straight line until, with dire results, his flight was affected by an external force.

It was necessary to stop and portage around all the switches on the way down, as the rack rail was not continuously double at these points.

In recent years the toboggan has been simplified. It now runs on the standard rail and has ball bearings underneath, and is much lighter and smaller, making it easier to carry up the hill. At one time in recent years it was standard practice for an employee to ride up on the first train in morning and afternoon and then down on a "scooter," to inspect the track.

Other things have sometimes been tried as substitutes for a regular toboggan. Gandy dancers

On the opposite page, the photographer captioned this "Mile a Minute" scooter. Actually this serious young man and his toboggan are resting a few yards above the Half Way House switch. —STEWARTS COMMERCIAL PHOTOGRAPHERS (RIGHT) A modern scooter runs on the standard rail, and this employee was following a down train very closely, back in 1940. —GERALD M. BEST

were observed riding down on their shovels, and considerable skill was required to keep from falling off. It was also possible to ride down on a flat rock, at least on the steeper grades, but it wasn't easy either.

Back in 1905 a waiter from the Iron Springs Hotel in Manitou tried to slide down seated on a quart bottle, whose contents he may have sampled. The bottle gave up after about 20 feet, and a piece of glass severed an artery in his leg. This happened near the Half Way House, and his friends managed to get him to the lower station alive, but he died before the horse-drawn ambulance could get there from Colorado Springs.

One fatal toboggan accident was reported in the press in October 1911. George DeWalt, a machinist employed by the road, died on the 27th from concussion of the brain suffered two days before. The coroner's jury found that he was "violently thrown from a toboggan upon which he was riding . . . from the summit of Pike's Peak" and that "he was riding said toboggan at his own risk and against the express orders of his employers."

The unofficial record for the fastest toboggan descent may be the trip reported to have been made by J. G. Hiestand, photographer and concessionaire at the Summit House and owner of the Ute Iron Spring pavilion, etc. In November 1898 the *Railway and Engineering Review*, without mentioning the name of the intrepid speedster, stated that the descent had been made in 11 minutes for the 8.9 miles, including the time required to carry around the four switches. The average descent was given as 844.8 feet per mile. Based on that time, and allowing 30 seconds for carrying around the switches, the average speed must have been about 50 miles per hour. The following account casts some doubt on the 11-minute time.

G. B. "Perk" Hibbard, late gandy dancer (section man) on the Cog Road, wrote this about toboggans in 1955: "Yes, I recognize the old-style toboggan in the picture of the snipe riding one just below the summit . . . There used to be one lying around in our tool house for several years after I first went to work over there, that was Dave Jones' personal buggy. Finally it was scrapped. Any sort of toboggan riding was frowned on at that time. We weren't allowed to have any, so we rode rocks and balanced ourselves with a shovel held across the rack. We crossed our feet on the rail ahead and squeezed our heels together for a brake. Brough (Taggart) would let us do that, but old John, his father, wouldn't permit it. However, if he ever noticed that practically every snipe on the road had the insides of his heels worn down, he ignored it.

"Later, after John passed away and Brough took over, and before we got motorized, every snipe had his personally built toboggan for business as well as pleasure. We would work below Minny (the only section house used by then) mornings, then catch a train with our toboggans and ride up to another job for the rest of the day, and then all ride home of an evening.

"By then the teeth of the racks rails were becoming so battered that a rack toboggan was too dangerous. The center guide would catch in tight spots and spill you, and that was a danged good way to get killed easily. The new type were T-rail toboggans, and to make them roll faster and surely, we used the ball bearings from auto rear axles, with sideguards to keep them on the rail and a balance arm with a steel sled riding on the top of the rack. How fast they will go depends entirely on how much guts or foolishness you have.

"I'm sure some one will eventually try to beat Dave Jones' record. As the story goes, he made it from the top to bottom in 14 minutes, stopping and walking around four switches . . . That's really traveling.

"I've often heard the oldtimers tell about how they carried a bar of laundry soap and when they hit 'the flats' and began to slow down, they would just reach down and touch the soap to the top of the rack and, ZOOP!, away they would go again."

THE DOPER

Steam locomotives during their later years each carried a five-gallon tank of lubricant on its pilot beam, which applied oil to the rack rail in order to lessen the wear on the rack and the cog wheels. That had not always been the practice, however. In earlier days it was customary to apply a tar-like substance manually to the uphill surface of each rack tooth. Whatever this substance was, it hardened rather quickly, was thought to be beneficial, but was expensive to apply.

A man known along the line as "the doper" would start out from Manitou equipped with a bucket of "dope" and a long handled brush. Dipping the brush into the dope, he would proceed to inch his way upward, dabbing each cog with the dope brush. The mills of the gods are not as slow as the doper, who could feel the breeze kicked up by the snails rushing past him. To make matters worse, his progress was impeded by the hardening qualities of the dope, so that he had to stop every few hundred yards, build a fire and reheat it until its consistency was such that he could resume his climb. This also gave him an opportunity to stoke up his pipe and enjoy its fragrance. In later years the doper carried a charcoal heater.

The trip to the summit took him about 30 days, as he would ride up to work on the first morning train and come down on the last one in the afternoon. When he had doped all the cogs to the top, he would start again at the bottom, and so on, *ad infinitum*. The doper in the writer's youth was a whiskery gent known as John to the summer folk. He usually appeared as if he had slept in the company coal dock each evening.

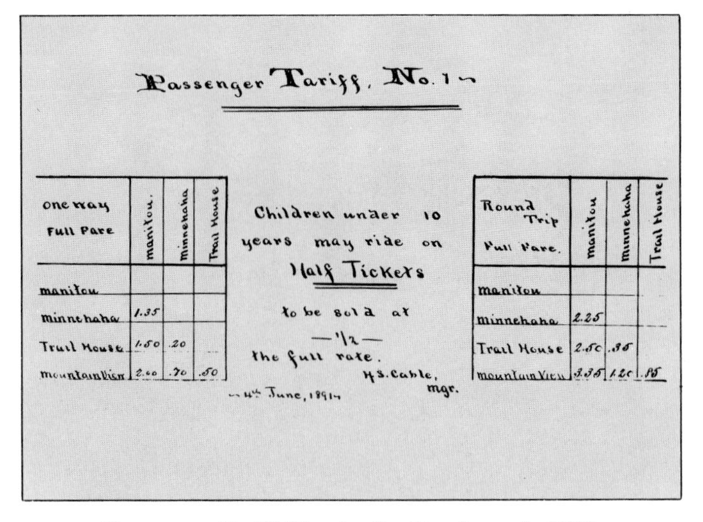

Passenger Tariff, No. 1

One way Full Fare	Manitou.	Minnehaha	Trail House
Manitou			
Minnehaha	1.35		
Trail House	1.50	.20	
Mountain View	2.00	.70	.50

Children under 10 years may ride on Half Tickets to be sold at —1/2— the full rate.

H. S. Cable, mgr.

4th June, 1891

Round Trip Full Fare.	Manitou	Minnehaha	Trail House
Manitou			
Minnehaha	2.25		
Trail House	2.50	.35	
Mountain View	3.35	1.20	.85

Passenger Tariff No. 1 effective June 4, 1891, shows service only as far as Mountain View.
— MORRIS W. ABBOTT COLLECTION

EARLY TIMETABLES AND TARIFFS

The earliest passenger tariff available is a hand-lettered schedule dated June 4, 1891, No. 1. It shows one-way and round trip fares only between Manitou and Mountain View and intermediate points, although the line had by then reached the summit. On the other hand, timetable No. 1 was dated August 20, 1890, almost a year earlier, but read only to the Half Way (or Trail) House.

Passenger Tariff No. 4 appeared May 1, 1892. The round trip fare between Manitou and the summit of Pike's Peak was $5.00 and a ten-trip commutation ticket on "Form C" was authorized between Manitou and points other than the summit. No. 5 followed on July 15, 1894, with essentially the same fares. So much for the very early ones.

Freight Tariff No. 1 was issued May 1, 1892, giving rates for LCL freight (Less-Than-Carload) at 50 cents per 100 lbs. to all points except the summit, which was one dollar. A minimum carlot of 15,000 lbs. could be shipped up to Minnehaha at 20 cents per 100 lbs., to Half Way House for 21 cents, to Mountain View for 22 cents, and 45 cents all the way to the top. LCL freight had to be such that it could be carried on the rear platforms of the coaches. Tariff No. 2 appeared a year later and included a 90 cent rate to Windy Point, lowered the minimum carlot to 10,000 lbs., increased the carlot rates to 30 cents, 33 cents, 35 cents, 62 cents and 67.5 cents to Minnehaha, Half Way House, Mountain View, Windy Point and Summit respectively.

The coming of the diesel-electrics brought reductions in running times, and for a while the

Pike's Peak by Rail.

Time Table No. 17.

IN EFFECT JUNE 23, 1894.
SUBJECT TO CHANGE WITHOUT NOTICE.

14,147 Feet — MANITOU AND PIKE'S PEAK RAILWAY — COG WHEEL ROUTE — Above Sea Level.

The Highest and Most Wonderful Railway in the World.

TRAINS FOR THE

Summit of Pike's Peak

LEAVE MANITOU.	RETURN ARRIVE MANITOU.
Daily, 8:55 a. m.	1:00 p. m.
" 2:00 p. m.	6:00 p. m.

Giving ample time to view the Grandest Scenery on the Globe. Stop-over privileges allowed.

DO NOT MISS IT.

FOR DESCRIPTIVE MATTER AND INFORMATION ADDRESS
H. S. CABLE, MANAGER,
MANITOU, COLO.

DISTANCES
ON M. & P. P. RY.

	MILES
Summit (Pike's Peak)	
Saddle House	1.77
Windy Point	2.25
Timber Line	2.87
Mountain View	4.86
Half-Way House	6.27
Minnehaha	7.06
Manitou	8.90

ELEVATIONS
ABOVE SEA LEVEL.

		FEET
Pike's Peak,	(M. & P. P. Ry.)	14,147
Saddle House,	"	12,502
Windy Point,	"	12,233
Timber Line,	"	11,578
Mountain View,	"	9,705
Half Way House,	"	8,913
Minnehaha,	"	8,400
Manitou,	"	6,629
Mt. Washington, N. H. (Mt. W. R. R.)		6,293
Rigi, Switzerland, (Arth Rigi R. R.)		5,832
Pilatus, Switzerland, (Pilatus R. R.)		6,963
Jung Frau, Switzerland		13,667
Denver, Colorado		5,314
Colorado Springs, Colorado		5,915
Pueblo, Colorado		4,400

Public Time Table No. 17, dated June 23, 1894, when Pike's Peak was thought to be 37 feet higher than modern surveys make it. Although only two trains are indicated, the Cog Road ran extras as long as they had passengers to go and equipment to handle them. — MORRIS W. ABBOTT COLLECTION

timetables showed times for steam and diesel-electric trains separately during the transition period. The only other changes were the dropping of the names of the Half Way House and Saddle House, which latter had not existed for many years before the former disappeared.

The only ones who know why Butterworth Flat appeared in the timetables in the first place have joined their ancestors, as there never was even a signboard there to identify it. Yet it still appears on some modern maps. Many of the public timetables issued before the present issue carried along an error that somebody injected into it more than 40 years ago. The elevation of Ruxton Park was given as 9,705 feet, which actually was that of (Old) Mountain View. There is a United States Geological Survey bench mark at the top of the Hell Gate hill (meaning at the lower edge of Ruxton Park) indicating an altitude of 9,010 feet.

TRAFFIC AND PROFITS

Passenger traffic has necessarily been the lifeblood of the Manitou & Pike's Peak Railway, with no commuters to either help or hinder it. Reference is made to Poor's *Manual of Railroads* between the years 1890 through 1940 which shows the figures furnished by the management, who declined to release any figures for the years prior to the one ended June 30, 1894, and for the fiscal year 1896-97.

All of the stock and bonds of the M. & P. P. have been owned since 1925 by the Pike's Peak Auto

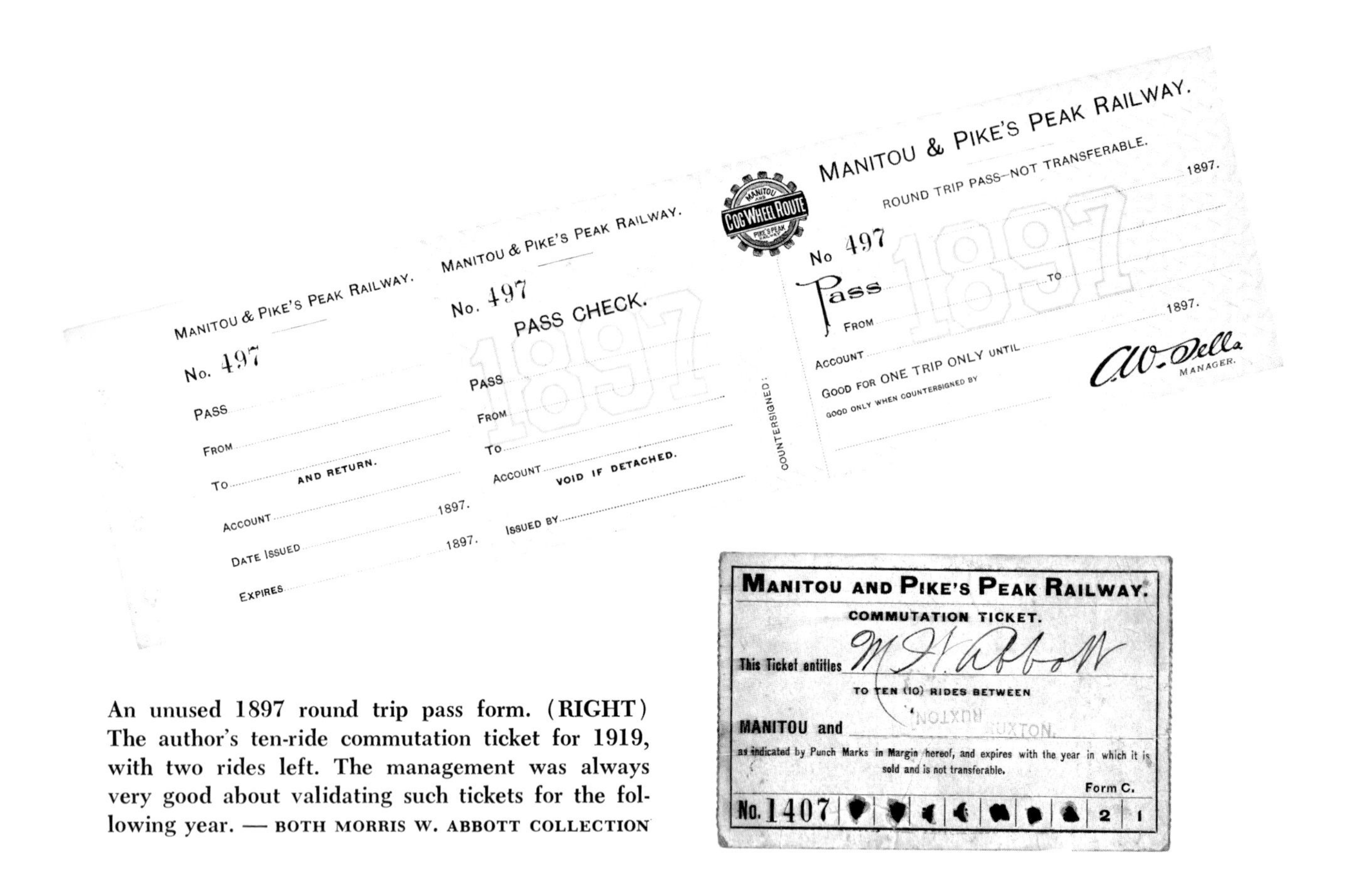
MANITOU & PIKE'S PEAK RAILWAY.
No. 497
PASS
FROM
TO AND RETURN.
ACCOUNT
DATE ISSUED 1897.
EXPIRES 1897.

MANITOU & PIKE'S PEAK RAILWAY.
No. 497
PASS CHECK.
1897
PASS
FROM
TO
ACCOUNT
VOID IF DETACHED.
ISSUED BY

COUNTERSIGNED:

MANITOU & PIKE'S PEAK RAILWAY.
COG WHEEL ROUTE
ROUND TRIP PASS—NOT TRANSFERABLE.
1897.
No 497
1897
Pass
FROM
TO
ACCOUNT
GOOD FOR ONE TRIP ONLY UNTIL 1897.
GOOD ONLY WHEN COUNTERSIGNED BY
MANAGER.

MANITOU AND PIKE'S PEAK RAILWAY.
COMMUTATION TICKET.
This Ticket entitles M. H. Abbott
TO TEN (10) RIDES BETWEEN
MANITOU and RUXTON.
as indicated by Punch Marks in Margin hereof, and expires with the year in which it is sold and is not transferable.
Form C.
No. 1407 2 1

An unused 1897 round trip pass form. (RIGHT) The author's ten-ride commutation ticket for 1919, with two rides left. The management was always very good about validating such tickets for the following year. — BOTH MORRIS W. ABBOTT COLLECTION

Highway Company, which is itself a closely held corporation.

A perusal of the figures will at least convince the reader that there are probably easier ways of getting rich than operating a cog railway. The road paid a 40 percent dividend in 1913 and 10 percent in 1915, and none before or since those years. Recent years have shown operating profits. For the earlier years some figures are available as to the number of passengers carried, train miles, passenger miles and freight miles, and we shall look at the passengers-carried figures briefly. The opening year was a short season and 9,700 passengers were carried. The following year (1892) was referred to as "the conclave year" and the number of persons carried rose to 16,700, the peak day coming in August, when 625 people made the trip. That meant at least 13 trains, based on a coach capacity of 50 persons, and this was accomplished with four locomotives.

According to Poor's *Manual,* passenger traffic for the years 1907-16 ranged from 37,582 in 1915 as a low to 69,159 the next year as a high, the fiscal year in those days ending June 30. The next three years were poor indeed, but some of the blame may be placed on the wretched condition of the motive power. For the years 1917, 1918 and 1919, the figures are 22,704, 20,230 and 19,940 passengers respectively.

Freight traffic some years was, for a summer tourist carrier, rather good, especially when the City of Colorado Springs was building something on the watershed. In 1891 a pipeline was built up Ruxton Creek from Manitou to bring water down from a higher intake less subject to pollution than the one just above Manitou. Later on pipe was hauled up for use at Lake Moraine and other reservoirs, and when it was decided to build a settler and intake at Ruxton Park there must have been a considerable freight business, though for some reason it is not reflected in the figures in Poor's *Manual* for those years. The Mt. Manitou Incline Railway, now also owned by the interests that control the Cog Road, operates where there had been a tramway constructed to haul pipe up for the line from Ruxton Park to Mt. Manitou.

Freight revenues also took a decided jump upward when the Big Tooth dam and reservoir were built on South Ruxton Creek, a mile or so upstream from the site of the Half Way House, and were high for the years 1924-30 inclusive. Ordinarily they were only a few hundred dollars per annum.

Annual passes of four eras of the Manitou & Pike's Peak Railway. The 1892 pass with the signature of Jno. Hulbert, the 1895 issue signed by H. S. Cable, the 1904 pass signed by C. W. Sells, and the 1935-6-7 issue with the printed signature of F. C. Matthews. The last pass bears the emblem that was used for a few years instead of the cog wheel. — ALL MORRIS W. ABBOTT COLLECTION

THE BOOK OF RULES

The company adopted *Rules and Regulations, Code No. 1* effective the first of May 1892, commonly called by railroaders the Book of Rules. It was obviously patterned after the rules of a standard railway (perhaps the Rock Island), which makes a few of the regulations sound absurd. For instance, Rule 38 reads, "A train overtaking another train of the same or superior class, disabled so that it cannot move, will run around it, assuming the rights and taking the orders of the disabled train, to the next telegraph office which is open, where it will report to the manager. The disabled train will assume the rights of the last train passing it, till the next telegraph office is reached." Unless the train became "disabled so that it cannot move" while standing on a siding (all four M. & P. P. switches are spurs, which dead-end), another train would have had a rough time running around it. As there were no telegraph offices at all along the line, that would also complicate matters.

Rule 65 provided for telegraph operators (who did not exist) to display red signals when they had train orders to deliver. Actually dispatching was done by the company's telephone line, which was a "party line" with code rings for each of the several stations, as follows:

1 Ring	Manitou dispatcher
2 Rings	Minnehaha section house
3 Rings	Half Way House
4 Rings	Mountain View
5 Rings	Windy Point section house
6 Rings	Summit House
1 Long + 1 Short	Manitou shops

All daylight trains were reported to the dispatcher simply by calling him and announcing, for example, "Third train passed Half Way House." It was advisable to avoid using the telephone line during a thunderstorm, with the lightning arrester snapping merrily on the wall nearby. Dispatching today is by radio, directly between the dispatcher and the train in operation.

MANITOU AND PIKE'S PEAK RAILWAY.

Employes' Time Table No. 24. In Effect June 30th, 1897.

COG WHEEL ROUTE — MANITOU AND PIKE'S PEAK RAILWAY

DOWN TRAINS											UP TRAINS									
27 SUNSET SPECIAL	25 Daily	23 Daily	21 Daily	19 Daily	17 Daily	15 Daily	13 Daily	11 Daily	Miles	STATIONS	Elevation	12 Daily	14 Daily	16 Daily	18 Daily	20 Daily	22 Daily	24 Daily	26 Daily	28 SUNSET SPECIAL
p. m.	p. m.	p. m.	p. m.	p. m.	a. m.	a. m.	a. m.	a. m.				a. m.	a. m.	a. m.	a. m.	p. m.	p. m	p. m.	p. m.	p. m.
7.50	3.20	3.05	2.50	2.36	10.20	10.05	9.50	9.36	......	SUMMIT	14,200	8.50	9.05	9.20	9.35	1.50	2.05	2.20	2.35	7.05
......	......	......	......	......	......	......	......	......	1.77	1.77 SADDLE HOUSE	12,555	......	......	......	......	......	......	......	......	......
8.12	3.42	3.27	3.12	2.58	10.42	10.27	10.12	9.58	2.25	0.48 WINDY POINT	12,286	8.26	8.41	8.56	9.11	1.26	1.41	1.56	2.11	6.41
......	......	......	......	......	......	......	......	......	4.28	2.03 GULCH TANK	10,120	......	..	......	......	......	......	......	......	......
8 39	4.09	3.54	3.39	3.25	11.09	10.54	10.39	10.25	4.86	0.58 MOUNTAIN VIEW	9,752	7.56	8.11	8.26	8.41	12.56	1.11	1.26	1.41	6.11
s8.53	s4.23	s4.08	s3.53	s3.39	s11.23	s11.08	s10.53	s10.39	6.27	1.41 HALF-WAY HOUSE	8,960	s7.42	s7.57	s8.12	s8.27	s12.42	s12.57	s1.12	s1.27	s5.57
9.01	4.31	4.16	4.01	3.47	11.31	11.16	11.01	10.47	7.06	0.79 MINNEHAHA	8,447	7.33	7.48	8.03	8.18	12.33	12.48	1.03	1.18	5.48
......	......	......	......	......	......	......	......	......	7.74	0.68 BUTTERWORTH FLAT	7,793	......	......	......	......	......	......	......	......	......
9.18 p. m.	4.48 p. m.	4.33 p. m.	4.18 p. m.	4.04 p. m.	11.48 a. m.	11.33 a. m.	11.18 a. m.	11.04 a. m.	8.90	1.16 MANITOU	6,676	7.15 a. m.	7.30 a. m.	7.45 a. m.	8.00 a. m.	12.15 p. m.	12.30 p. m.	12.45 p. m.	1.00 p. m.	5.30 p. m.

Trains Nos. 11, 13, 15 and 17 have right of track over
" " 20, 22, 24 and 26.

C. W. SELLS,
Manager.

Employees' Time Table No. 24 of June 30, 1897. It lists eight regular trains daily and a Sunset Special. A few years later the sunset trains were rare, but regular Sunrise Specials operated Wednesday mornings, leaving Manitou about 2:30 A.M. — STATE HISTORICAL SOCIETY OF COLORADO

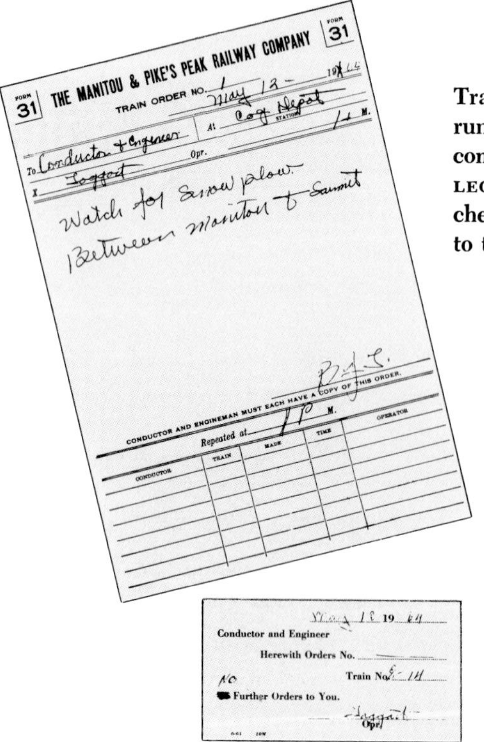

FORM 31 THE MANITOU & PIKE'S PEAK RAILWAY COMPANY FORM 31

TRAIN ORDER NO. 1 May 12 1964

To Conductor + Engineer At Cog Depot Station 1 M.

X Taggart Opr.

Watch for Snow plow
Between Manitou + Summit

CONDUCTOR AND ENGINEMAN MUST EACH HAVE A COPY OF THIS ORDER.

Repeated at 1 P M.

CONDUCTOR	TRAIN	MADE	TIME	OPERATOR

May 12 1964

Conductor and Engineer

Herewith Orders No.

No Train No. 5-14

Further Orders to You.

Taggart Opr.

Train Order issued to engineer Frank Smith for the first run of Swiss rail car No. 14 on May 12, 1964, and the accompanying Clearance Card. — MORRIS W. ABBOTT COLLECTION (BELOW) Master mechanic William H. McKay checks with the dispatcher at the summit. The stairs led to the tower of the old Summit House. — RONALD BROWN

COG ROAD LITERATURE

Reproduced here are examples of the promotional literature issued by the Manitou & Pike's Peak Railway. The brochures above cover a range of time from the turn-of-the-century to 1930. (BELOW) The literature begins with 1944 and covers the transition period from steam to diesel-electric motive power, ending with a modern day folder showing the new Swiss built train. — ALL DONALD DUKE COLLECTION

MISHAPS

It would be difficult, if not impossible, to find a railroad anywhere with an accident record to approach the excellence of the Manitou & Pike's Peak Railway. There has never been a serious injury to a passenger riding in or on one of its trains, though actually one passenger was killed by a train, under peculiar circumstances.

It happened on the Fourth of July 1892. A number of the passengers were standing on the front platform of the coach at the summit, waiting for the car door to be unlocked for the return trip. A family group from Chicago had made the trip together, and the father thought it would be a fine thing to take a "snapshot" of the family, grouped around the front platform. They lined up, but unfortunately the engineer, unaware of what was going on out of his range of vision, released the engine brake to drop the train down to the loading platform. The locomotive had been standing for almost an hour, and enough steam had leaked into the cylinders from the lubricator to cause the engine to lunge forward a few feet, and in so doing it knocked down and fatally injured six-year old Freddie Morrill. A coroner's jury heard a considerable number of witnesses, and exonerated the carrier from all blame for the accident. In the more than three-quarters of a century since then, no fatalities have occurred, — an enviable record.

The first death after operation began was that of W. H. Tucker, brakeman on a freight train engaged in carrying a flat car load of iron pipe destined to Lake Moraine in November 1891. He released the brake, which on a Cog Road flat car is only at the lower end, to drop the car down to where the locomotive stood. Tucker allowed the car to pick up too much speed, so that it collided with the engine. He fell between them and died of internal injuries.

Fortunately other accidents involved only damage to equipment rather than injuries to personnel. The first was the runaway of the original No. 4, which ended its brief career. On August 30, 1896, No. 4 was used to power a special train carrying distinguished British railwaymen, including General Manager Harrison and Superintendent Turnbull of the London & Northwestern Railway.

About a quarter mile below Artist's Glen both

This interesting episode took place, probably in the early 1900's, at Artists' Glen. The huge boulder made quite a dent in the right-of-way and no doubt in the net profits for the year. — GRANT G. SIMMONS, SR., COLLECTION

A cloudburst in the higher places can wreak havoc below, as it did here about 1913, below Minnehaha. Note the exposed water pipe of the City of Colorado Springs. — MRS. C. C. MCREYNOLDS

connecting rods and one side rod broke almost simultaneously, knocking out the left cylinder head, according to the letter Manager Sells wrote to Simmons a few days later. He went on to say "The Eng'r and fireman applied the steam and hand brakes but the broken rods would strike the ends of the ties and lift the Engine, with cogs, out of the rack rails thereby rendering the brake application ineffective. The Engine held the track, momentarily losing and regaining the rack, without acquiring any remarkable speed until some of the machinery, evidently, dropped under the cogs, on the sharp curve just above Shady Springs, causing it to take a lunge when it spread the tee rail, entirely throwing the Cogs out of the rack rail and leaving the Engine at the mercy of gravitation."

Then No. 4 left the right-of-way at what must have been a very high rate of speed, for Sells said that it jumped over a boulder 25 feet high and turned a complete somersault. The boiler and trucks landed four or five rail lengths from the take-off point. Sells said, "the tanks and other parts were so widely spread around that their location is hard to account for."

The crew, meaning engineer Harry Jones and his substitute fireman, jumped in time to avoid serious injury. The coach was stopped instantly by the brakeman on the rear platform and there were no injuries. A boy hiker was cut about the face by flying gravel, and no doubt the engineer and fireman would have preferred more gentle landings.

Most of "Little 4" was removed, for the understandable reason that it was poor public relations to have the wreck lying exposed to view, but the boiler remained where it landed until a scrap drive during World War II, when it was hauled out as part of a training program for Army engineers from Camp Carson, and the scrap was used to advance the cause of the war effort. Before that the section crew would shovel gravel over it now and then to hide it from the public's sight. This engine was built rather too lightly, and its failure resulted in heavier, fluted rods being used on all the locomotives.

No. 5 ran away on June 15, 1919, near Butterworth Flat and was badly damaged, the coach of course being stopped immediately and without incident. The engine, however, had broken a pinion and proceeded to demolish the rack rail, shearing off bolt heads and laying the rack bars neatly on either side of center. Gathering speed, it left the track and landed on a large rock at Shady Spring. Having done their duty, the crew had jumped at the start of the affair, so spectators were puzzled when they heard a cry from under the engine, "Get me out! Get me out!" Investigation brought to light a boy hiker, almost buried under a pile of coal, but otherwise unhurt.

August 24, 1935, engine No. 3 was running as the third section, skippered by conductor Tom Connell, with engineer Lee Jamison and fireman Bill James. There was a bad piece of track at the lower end of the Diamond Rock curve that had settled and had too much elevation. The first two sections of the passenger train passed over this section safely, although the cog wheels did climb the rack, but dropped back again. The second section's brakeman was left at the spot to warn the third section of the condition. Jamison slowed down, but the engine climbed the rack and headed down grade rapidly. A main axle broke when both enginemen jammed the brakes on, and No. 5 "headed for the barn." Both enginemen jumped, James spread-eagled on the gravel slide to avoid rolling back onto the track, and Jamison into the wild raspberry bushes on the creek side, not stopping to pick any berries. As usual, the coach was brought to a stop without difficulty or injuries, but No. 3 sheared off the rack teeth, bent rails and generally wrecked the right-of-way, topping it off by rolling over a low bank at Butterworth curve, between the track and the creek.

Here was another accident the railway did not wish to advertise to the riding public, so the company built a shed over the remains, after having

W R E C K of No.5

The Manitou & Pike's Peak Railway has a fantastic safety record, but once in a while an accident did happen. On June 15, 1919, No. 5 ran away near Butterworth Flat, gathered speed and finally left the track at Shady Spring. The coach stopped immediately, but the engine had a broken pinion and proceeded to demolish the rack rail. In the scene above, passengers walk down past the wreck of No. 5 to the relief train waiting below. — MRS. C. C. MCREYNOLDS (LEFT) This broken pinion or cog wheel is thought to have caused No. 5 to break loose. (LOWER LEFT) No. 5 very neatly laid the rack bars aside. The stranded coach waits above. (BELOW) The wreck of No. 5 with fireman Ted Weigand standing on the left main rod. — ALL LEE D. JAMISON

removed some parts to the Manitou shops. There, at trackside, No. 3 finished the season. This accident explains why, in later photographs, No. 3 has a modern, sleek, all-metal cab. After being rebuilt, she steamed well, but continually damaged the rack, to the disgust of the track gang. In 1955 her boiler was sold for scrap and her other parts bequeathed to her sisters.

Service was resumed the second morning, the section crew having worked around the clock to get the track back into proper shape again. There were no casualties, but one crew member's trousers were so badly damaged that the company felt constrained to replace them, an example of paternalism.

A happening that could have injured a number of persons took place in August 1901. On the down trip, a brakeman on the rear platform of the old steam train customarily helped control the speed by applying and releasing the hand brake on the coach, depending on the grade. This particular day an inexperienced brakeman applied the brakes with such vigor as to stop the car completely. He then stopped thinking, released the brakes and let the coach crash down against the engine. Windows were broken and a passenger suffered a broken belt and umbrella.

A tragedy that had nothing to do with the Manitou & Pike's Peak Railway occurred on November 21, 1963, after the close of the operating season, when two men were killed in the runaway of a small gasoline-powered unit designed and built by a City of Colorado Springs employee at the Ruxton Park intake. It had been in use for some years, and six men were using it on that day while working on the city's power lines that parallel the track. Coming down, they were slowing for an inspection stop, when the machine broke loose and started downgrade rapidly. Four of the men jumped and were not injured, but the car left the track and struck a utility pole about a mile farther down and about half a mile above the Manitou shops, killing the other two men. While the local newspapers were careful to emphasize the fact that the car was neither owned nor operated by the Cog Road, this was unfortunately not made clear in the national press.

After 80 seasons of operation and millions of passenger miles, the toll has amounted to one tourist and one employee killed, and none seriously injured, a fine operating record, indeed.

During August 1951, several large boulders crashed down on the track from Lion Rock at the Half Way House, with the result shown above. (BELOW) The Ways and Means Committee of the Cog Road stop to consider what to do with these huge boulders and just how to do it. In the background the work train waits patiently, with the safety valve blowing steam skyward. — BOTH WILLIAM W. ABBOTT

PEOPLE

Clinton W. Sells, a smallish and very nervous and energetic man, was general manager from about 1895 and president from 1902 until he left the road in 1917. He had succeeded Hiram S. Cable as president when that gentleman became general superintendent of the Rock Island. Sells began his career as a railroader in telegraph service with the Santa Fe, later was traveling auditor for the Kansas City, Fort Smith & Memphis, and held the same position with the Rio Grande Western. He became traveling passenger agent for the Colorado Midland, from which line he joined the M. & P. P. as assistant manager in 1891. He left the Cog Road to become a fruit grower, operating Sells Orchards at Beaver Park, Colorado, and died in October 1941 at the age of 76.

Most of the other men who were associated with the road in its early days are only names today. Some of them were regular railroaders from other lines; for example, conductor Douglas Hughes of Missouri, who spent the rest of the year working on the Missouri Pacific. Doubtless some of the others were from the Colorado Midland and the Denver & Rio Grande.

The engineer in charge of the locomotive used when the two-coach tests were made in 1891 was Ed Quinlan. He also took the governor and his party to the summit in a special train that summer.

When a party of newsmen made the trip in 1891, the *Pueblo Chieftain* mentioned that the crew consisted of conductor J. F. Gamber, brakeman W. H. Tucker (the one who was killed in an accident that fall), engineer P. H. Mestler and fireman A. H. Mathews. An old train order book now in the library of the State Historical Society of Colorado gives the names of some of the men who kept things going in the 1917-22 period, as follows: Conductors (who acted as brakemen on slow days, or might have been shopmen pressed into service on busy days) Stearns, Hughes, Hennessey, White, Schoeberlin, Kitloe, Dotterer, Kirk, Ferris, Lynn, Cobb, Adams, Nichols, Clark, Tilton, Pentruff, Lester, Padgett and Jordan; Engineers Gosling, Bouchey, Tilton, Jones, Weigand, Fisher, Jamison, Odgers, Turner, Edwards, Smith, Hiner and Bush.

Back in the earlier years of the century the senior engineer was Herman C. Gosling, known to all as Herm. In 1927 it was recorded in the local press that he had made an average of 260 trips per year for 32 years, or 8,320 trips, and that at that time

Unveiling the memorial to General Pike on the summit in 1906, just one hundred years after his sighting of the peak. — PROCTOR W. NICHOLS COLLECTION

he was the road's oldest employee in years of service. In 1939 another local paper gave the figure as 9,280 trips. Conductor Frank Ferris, who died in the 1940's, began with the Colorado Midland as fireman in 1888, was engineer from 1892 till 1895. In 1910 he became conductor on the M. & P. P., stayed until 1914, returning in 1919 and remaining until ill health forced his retirement. His "spiel" to the tourists on the up trip will long be remembered by old timers, beginning with "Them two rocks on top of the mountain ahead of the car is Gog and Magog."

T. J. "Ted" Weigand, who retired not so many years ago, was an engineer who joined the M. & P. P. about 1915, and finally stopped running locomotives when a back injury forced him into the shop. The old steamers were very rough riders. Frank Smith, who joined the road in 1918, retired as senior engineer October 23, 1970, and doesn't look the 40-odd years he has spent going up and down.

Recently death took the dean of M. & P. P. old timers, Brough J. Taggart, who practically cut his teeth on a rack bar, having been born in the original frame section house at the Saddle in 1895. Though he can claim no credit for the event, other than having been present, he has the distinction of being the only person known to have been born on Pike's Peak. The altitude record for the United States probably goes along with that, as the Sad-

Zalmon G. Simmons had this medal designed and struck for the occasion of the 1905 Encampment of the G.A.R., presented each attending member with one of them and a trip to the summit on his Cog Road. — GRANT G. SIMMONS, SR.

dle is some 12,500 feet above sea level. His father, John B. Taggart, who died in 1935, was for years section foreman and employed by the road during construction days. The family lived in Cascade during the cold months, and operated a livery business there. Brough began railroading as timekeeper for the Colorado Midland when he was 16 years old, but went with the Cog Road in 1918. Until a bad heart made it advisable to stay at a lower altitude, he was conductor for years. He served for some years as station agent at Manitou, which included dispatching. In 1949 his son, John E. Taggart, became an engineer on the road, the third generation of cog railroaders.

CHANGING TIMES

In, say, the first 30 years of the Cog Road, vacationers were a different and hardier breed than now. Automobiles were few and there were even fewer good roads for cross-country driving. For this reason, people came by train, settled down in a hotel or rooming house, and proceeded to see the area thoroughly. None of this dropping in at a motel for a night or two and then racing on to do Yellowstone Park and the Tetons in a day.

Just suppose you were an early twentieth century tourist with a comfortable income of perhaps $3,000 per year. You arrived in Colorado Springs from the east (which probably meant east of the Missouri River) via the Union Pacific, the Burlington, Santa Fe, or Missouri Pacific by way of Denver or Pueblo, or directly by the Rock Island. If affluent, you took a room or two at the Antlers Hotel, each room being slightly smaller than a tennis court. (If you wanted to play tennis indoors, you might have tried the hallway.) This was your headquarters for a week or two. The hotel was the pride of the city, with a French chef and the finest of everything. The busses from all hotels met every train and urged the arrivals to get aboard for the best in town.

The next day, having unpacked the inevitable trunk, you set out to see the sights. Horse-drawn surreys with sagging springs, "rubberneck wagons," saddle horses and burros were readily available. The sights included the Garden of the Gods, the Cave of the Winds, the Grand Cavern, Seven Falls, Helen Hunt Jackson's grave (she had long since

The Denver & Rio Grande depot at Colorado Springs as it looked years ago, where many tourists got their first view of Pike's Peak. Hotel liveries await the train, as does the Manitou Branch local on the siding. —DONALD DUKE COLLECTION

Looking west on Pike's Peak Avenue, Colorado Springs, in the days of the original Antlers Hotel which burned in 1898. Colorado Springs & Interurban trolley No. 12 rolls down Pike's Peak Avenue, while No. 31 heads northbound on Tejon Street. — DONALD DUKE COLLECTION

The hiking costumes of yesteryear were protective, if not practical. The bipedal beast of burden in the center by the rack rail is a mere man, heading up from Manitou in the 1890's. — MORRIS W. ABBOTT COLLECTION

been removed to Evergreen Cemetery), Stratton Park, and finally Pike's Peak, which luckily was too large to be fenced in.

The fare on the Cog Road varied from a low of $3.50 for the round trip to a high of six dollars. If you wanted to, you could make it on the hurricane deck of a burro, or afoot. Hundreds did it both ways every season, and, though stiff and sore for a few days, they were soon as good as new again.

In those days of tourists who used their legs for walking instead of for operating a throttle and brake, there was hardly an hour in the day or night in summer when there weren't people trying to climb Pike's Peak on the M. & P. P. right-of-way, and a lot of them made it. A lot more didn't. Some of them walked all night to see the sunrise, which could be magnificent, others did it by day. Many turned back before they really got started, and many kept on when they should have turned back. Most were ill fitted for such a strenuous climb, most were too lightly clad for the high altitudes, and some even carried babes in arms.

Disregarding, as all did, the sign warning trespassers to keep off the right-of-way of the M. & P. P., and climbing what seemed endlessly, the hiker reached the Half Way House depot, having in mind that he was half way. It was a bitter disappointment to read the sign on the depot, which said that he had come only 2.63 miles and climbed about 2,400 feet. Ahead were 6.27 miles and about 5,200 feet of climbing.

Determination is a fine thing, when mixed with judgment, but one couple didn't know that. Late in August 1911, Mr. and Mrs. William A. Skinner of Dallas, Texas, perhaps 50 years of age, set out to climb Pike's Peak. They stopped to talk with Tom Wilson, publisher of the *Pike's Peak Daily News* at Mountain View, and he tried to dissuade them, as the temperature was low and they were poorly clad for mountain climbing. In spite of his warning of a possible snow storm higher up, they plodded on. Their frozen bodies were found later about a half a mile below the summit house. One account credits Herm Gosling, while another says a boy hiker found them. Curiously, a letter found in the dead man's pocket was from a friend in Dallas, and closed with the words, "I hope you have a good time in Colorado, and that you won't freeze to death on Pike's Peak." A special train carried the coroner to the scene, and then the remains to Manitou.

Howard H. Robison (or perhaps Robinson), employed at the summit house by J. G. Hiestand and a resident of Colorado Springs, claimed the walking record from the Manitou depot to the summit in 2 hours, 31 minutes on August 19, 1904. One George W. Patterson, reported to be a New York opera singer, claimed that the previous year he had made the round trip in 4 hours 31.5 minutes (up in 3:05, rested 0:05, down in 1:21). Through the sporting pages of the *Colorado Springs Gazette,* Robison had offered to wager $2,000 on himself to defeat all comers, but had no takers. In 1906 Patterson suggested that they compete in a foot race as part of the Colorado Centennial Celebration planned for September, which would appear to have been 100 years after Pike's sighting of the peak. A Creede silver miner named Neil McQuaide was also scheduled to race Robison for a $1,500 purse. Apparently nothing came of either proposal. The writer remembers seeing Howard Robison striding up the roadbed, and had he been old enough would gladly have bet on him. After all, 2:31 is faster than 3.5 miles per hour for 8.9 miles that average 16 percent gradient. However, in March 1928, Dolphus Stroud, Phi Beta Kappa, onetime Colorado College athlete and Harvard student, made the distance afoot in 2 hours 5 minutes. He said that the hike was nothing when compared with his 4 hours and a half hike up the peak through deep snow, over icy glaze and against frigid winds on the last day of December 1931.

By burro, the trip differed mainly in that the burro did the work, but even so it was quite an ordeal. A burro party left Manitou daily from Jones & Drennan's burro barn, rain or shine, about midafternoon, and stopped for lunch and a rest at the Half Way House late in the afternoon. Women were provided with ill-fitting and ugly divided skirts (for in those days pants were not worn by women, let alone ladies), broad brimmed straw hats, a yellow slicker and what passed for a blanket. The slicker bore large painted letters "J & D" on the back, lest the tourist try to go away with it, one supposes. None of these things even pretended to fit, the skirts and blankets were probably clean at the start of the season, and the slickers were more or less water-repellant. The men got overalls, if they wanted them, slickers, hats and blankets.

A guide or guides went along with each party, and some of them were really large. There was usually one guide for each 20 or 25 riders. While the average party 60-odd years ago might have been 25 to 40 people, on some days it ran as high as 100 or more. Unless it rained, the ever-present life-of-the-party would keep their spirits up until they reached "burro camp", which was not far from Mountain View and consisted of some log and canvas shelters. About midnight all hands were roused by the guide, and the procession started for the top, hoping to see the sunrise. Come rain, sleet, snow or hail, on they went, and when they reached the summit, tired and probably half frozen, each rider had to pay 25 cents to get into the warm summit house. If the clouds permitted they saw the sunrise.

The trip down was harder in some ways, since burros, when descending, are able to hold back only by taking mincing steps which jolt and jar the rider unmercifully. Knees give out and dependence must be placed upon the hands, one forward and one aft, to try to keep one's weight off the sorest parts, and 12 miles means a lot of jolts.

Tourists flocked the streets of Manitou (originally and now, again, known as Manitou Springs), patronizing the curio stands and drinking the iron, sulphur and soda waters. Today the tourist roars up Ute Pass on a four-lane highway, where once the Indians had a trail to the hunting grounds in South Park. The automobile changed all this and now comparatively few tourists linger among the curio shops. The people of the region loved the

The first automobile to make it to the summit of Pike's Peak was this 1901 Locomobile Steamer. (LEFT) W. B. Felker with his machine on the old carriage road to the summit. (BELOW) W. B. Felker and C. A. Yont with the sturdy steam car beside the Summit House. — BOTH MORRIS W. ABBOTT COLLECTION

tourist with a deep and abiding love as long as he stayed in the city, but when he wandered off the reservation and upon the watershed of Ruxton Creek he became a menace to the public health, so that now he follows the straight and well-paved paths provided for him, and sees a lot less.

Speaking of automobiles, it is interesting to note that, up to 1913, only two cars had reached the top of Pike's Peak, both via the old carriage road from Cascade. On August 12, 1901, a 1901 Locomobile steamer driven from Denver by W. E. Felker made it. By then the road had fallen into disuse after the opening of the Cog Road, so the trip was quite an ordeal. One may read further about the event in the April 1905 issue of *Motor Field*, or the *Colorado Springs Gazette-Telegraph* of August 2, 1951.

Another assault was made in a 20 horsepower Buick "Bear Cat," which reached the summit July 17, 1913, under the skillful guidance of H. Brown in 5 hours 35 minutes from Colorado Springs.

An interesting entry appears in an old train order book, which contains copies of train orders put out by the dispatcher of the Cog Road in Manitou. This particular order reads as follows:

No. 2 **Ki 9/13/20**
Turner, Eng 6 Ki
Engine 6 (six) will run light Manitou to Minnehaha and Look Out for Extra Engine 2 and automobile ahead

H J H

OK 2:15 PM
Turner HJH

The car referred to was a Paige "6-66" touring car, piloted by none other than Ralph K. Mulford, a noted race driver who had placed second in the 1911 and third in the 1916 Indianapolis 500 Mile Race. He was for a time head of the Paige racing team, and this was obviously a publicity stunt for the company. The "H J H" on the train order was Harrison J. Holt, then president and general manager of the road.

A Buick "Bear Cat" in an impossible position at the Summit House in 1913, driven by H. Brown. — DENVER PUBLIC LIBRARY, WESTERN COLLECTION

Indianapolis 500 Mile Race driver Ralph K. Mulford made it to the summit of Pike's Peak on September 13, 1920, by driving up the Cog Road track in a Paige "6-66" automobile. At the right, the Paige machine at Half Way House switch. Not far behind the automobile came steam locomotive No. 2, evidently as a rear guard. In the other illustration, the triumphant Paige car at the Summit House, amid the cheers of the onlookers. —BOTH PROCTOR W. NICHOLS COLLECTION

As the auto highway improved, more and more tourists reached the summit via the four wheels of the family automobile rather than aboard the coaches of the Cog Road. In this illustration, a family from California poses on the summit in their new Packard Model 3-25 of 1917 vintage. The running board is laden with tents and miscellaneous duffle, with more tied to the trunk rack at the rear. —MALLORY HOPE FERRELL COLLECTION

This map of the city of Manitou Springs shows the terminal facilities of the Manitou & Pike's Peak Railway in relationship to the town. It was retraced from a fading huge blueprint in the archives of the Cog Road. The original maker failed to date his work, but various landmarks identify it between 1895-1900. Specific points of interest are indicated by a number in a circle.

1. Denver & Rio Grande Railway Manitou Depot — Track extended from Colorado Springs to Manitou in 1880 to handle the tourist traffic. This location was once considered as an extension point of the Cog Road from Engelmann Canyon.
2. Point where D&RG "Y" passed under the track of the Colorado Midland.
3. Manitou Depot of the Colorado Midland Railway.
4. Tunnel 1 — Colorado Midland Railway.
5. Tunnel 2 — Colorado Midland Railway.
6. Colorado Midland iron bridge spanning Engelmann Canyon.
7. Manitou Iron Springs Depot of the Colorado Midland — Point where M&PP steam locomotives and equipment were unloaded.
8. Terminals of the Manitou Electric Railway & Casino Co. trolley line. The terminal by the Cog Depot shows the line next to the cog track, then later moved across Ruxton Creek. The downtown terminal was at the corner of Ruxton Avenue/Manitou Avenue. The Colorado Springs & Interurban Railway built a balloon turn-around here in 1900.
9. Manitou & Pike's Peak Railway — Depot
10. Cog Road shops and coach shed.
11. The Mt. Manitou Incline Railway was later built at this site.
12. The Colorado Springs Rapid Transit built a horse car line to Manitou in 1888. The line was electrified in 1890, and double tracked the following year. The Colorado Springs & Interurban Railway took over in 1900 and built the balloon loop at Ruxton/Manitou Avenues.

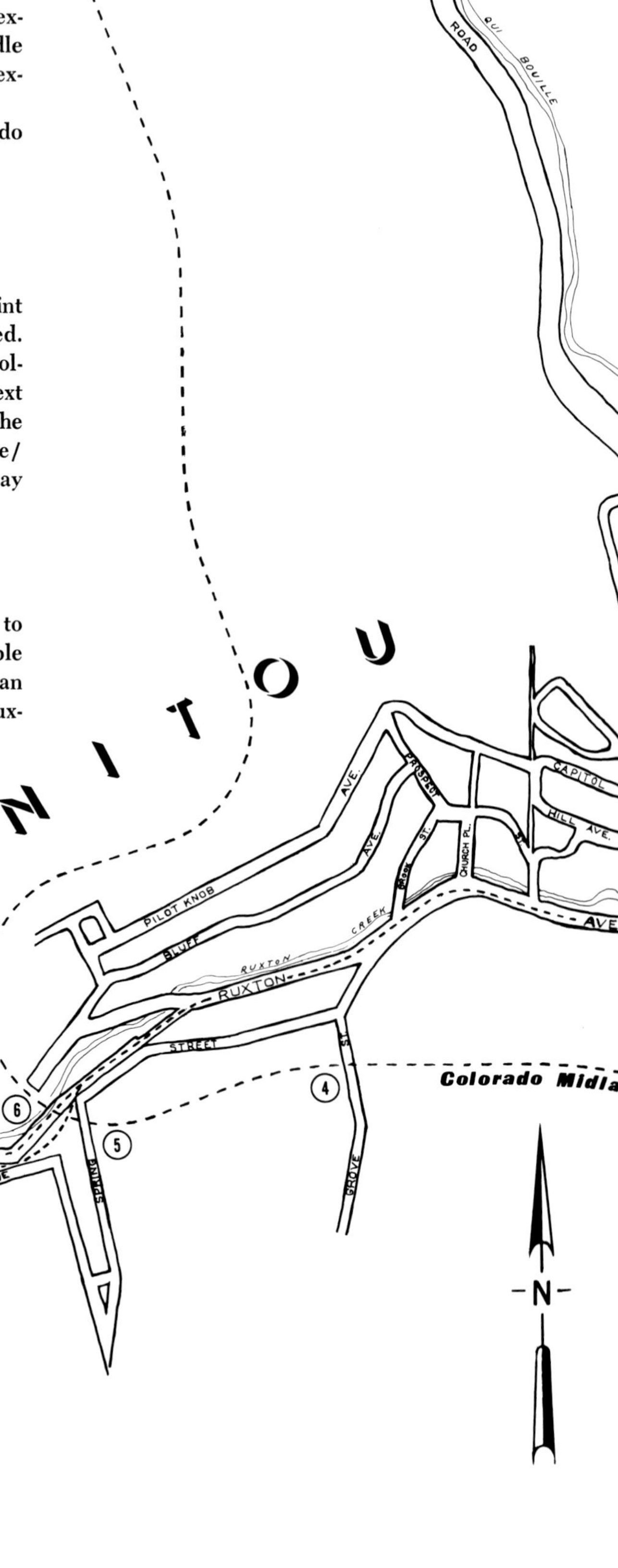

Manitou Springs, a resort city lying in the forested foothills that swell upward toward Pike's Peak, was founded in 1872 by Dr. William A. Bell and General William J. Palmer, railroad builder who formed the Denver & Rio Grande Railway. The proposed name of Villa la Font was changed to Manitou (Indian word meaning Great Spirit or Great Healer) when a resort hotel was opened, then to Manitou Springs in 1912 when the town enjoyed its greatest popularity as a watering place for eastern upper middle class tourists. Hotels, guest houses, restaurants, curio shops, and the usual variety of resort amusements line the main thoroughfares. The whole town of Manitou Springs hibernates from October to June when the majority of the hotels and shops are closed.

The great springs here were long known to the Indians, who marked off the area surrounding them as a sort of sanctuary. It remained for George F. Ruxton, an adventurous Englishman, to be the first white man to explore the region in 1847. For what purpose other than the pleasures of discovery is not known — and it is evident from his writings that in his own mind his most important find was Manitou, which he pictured with exactness and enthusiasm. Ruxton enjoyed the waters and wished to linger in this enchanting spot, but the Utes, though not particularly savage, resented his intrusion into their Holy place, and Ruxton was obliged to move on.

Of the numerous developed springs four claim to be the original Manitou Springs Ruxton wrote about and for which the community is named: Navaho Springs in front of the Navaho Hotel; Soda Springs at the rear of the Manitou Mineral Water Co.; Manitou Springs at Manitou Bath House; and Ute Iron Springs in Engelmann Canyon.

Until the construction of the Manitou & Pike's Peak Railway, the town centered primarily along the foothills on both sides of Manitou Avenue. As activity increased in the Engelmann Canyon region due to the Cog Road, lots were staked out and homes built near the Cog Depot.

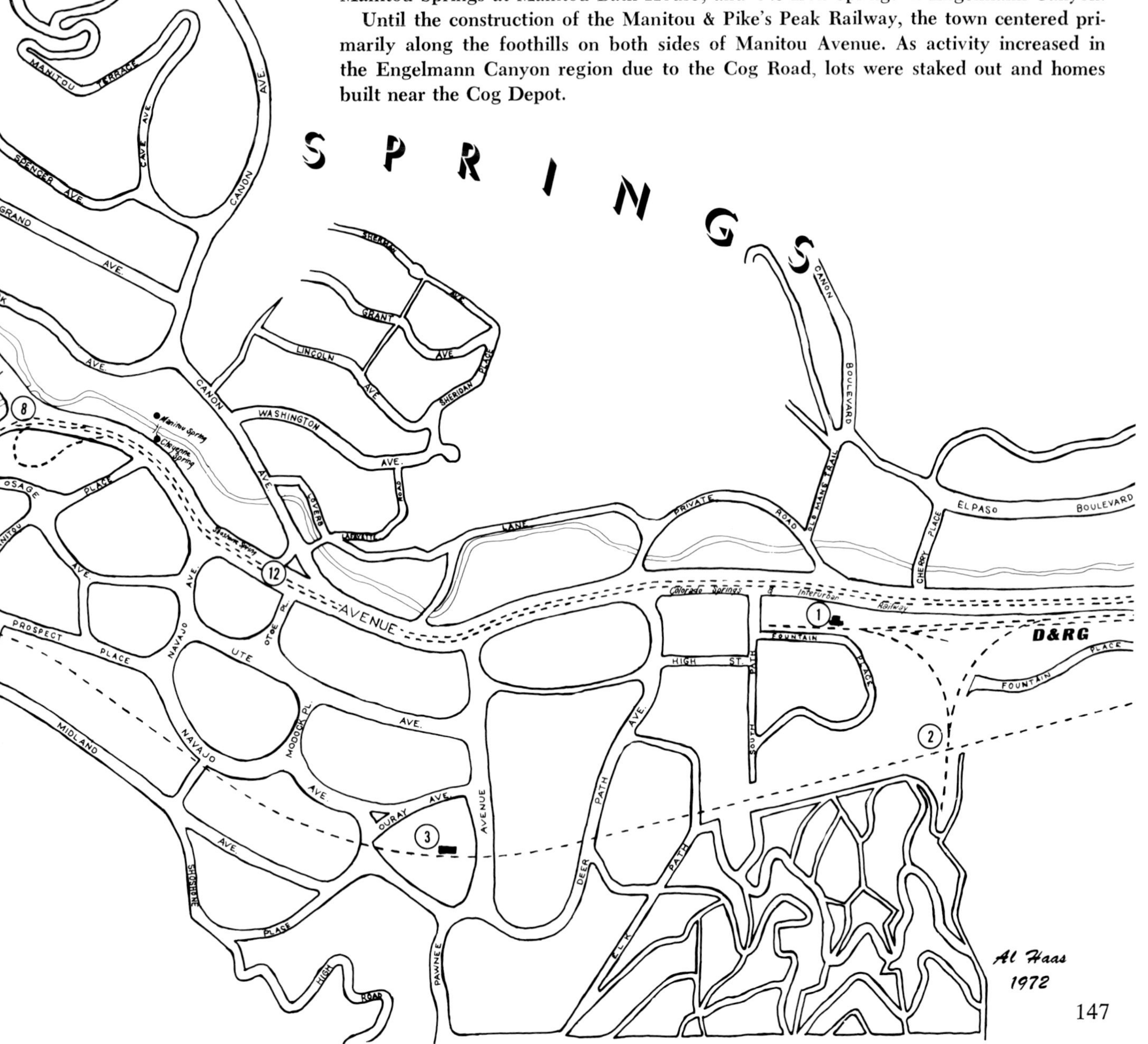

THE "DINKY"

The lower terminus of the Cog Road was built quite a distance from the center of activity in Manitou, and at first horse drawn busses and carriages brought passengers to the depot. In June 1893 Senator M. A. Leddy, late mayor of Manitou, got a "free franchise" to build a standard gauge electric line from the Denver & Rio Grande station in Manitou to the Iron Springs Hotel (adjacent to the Cog Road depot) and also "up to the Ute Pass." No street railway company was formed at that time, and no plans were announced. By 1895, however, the Manitou Electric Railway & Casino Company was in business and had a mile and a half of track. Leddy became president, John Hulbert vice-president, and H. S. Cable secretary-treasurer, and it was obviously a very close relative of the M. & P. P. In February 1895 a lease was executed giving operation of the line to the Colorado Springs Rapid Transit Railway Company for a term of ten years from the first of the following June. This agreement probably was not renewed; at least the Manitou Electric Railway & Casino Company was operating its own property in 1918, when the In-

The heart of Manitou some 50 years ago. The Cliff House in the background was a famous hostelry owned and operated for many years by the Nichols family. Across the street is the Soda Spring pavilion. The Colorado Springs & Interurban Railway trolley is about to turn left into a loop and head back to Colorado Springs. — DONALD DUKE COLLECTION (BELOW) Car No. 1 of the Manitou Electric Railway & Casino Company, known as the *Dinky*, awaits passengers at its lower terminus. — STEPHEN D. MAGUIRE COLLECTION

terstate Commerce Commission report showed that the M. & P. P. owned all of its stock, par value $125,100, book value $52,000, and bonds with a face value of $15,000.

This was a single track trolley line from the Colorado Springs electric line's balloon turn-around opposite Soda Springs in Manitou up to the cog depot, with a passing track at the halfway point. The writer recalls that the road owned two open cars and one closed car, all four-wheeled affairs with hand brakes. The closed car was run in inclement weather after the tourist season was over, for the benefit of the home-folks who lived up Ruxton Creek, and who fondly referred to the line as "the Dinky."

The fare was five cents, collected by the one-man crew at the passing point, but reduced fare tickets were available to regular patrons. In later years the Dinky went the way of all street cars, and a bus ground its way up the long hill, under the Colorado Midland's iron viaduct that curved across Ruxton Creek (dismantled in the early 1960's), past the ghost of a once busy Iron Springs Pavilion and up to the cog depot. Now passengers for the cog drive up in their own cars.

Car No. 2 of the Manitou Electric Railway & Casino Company stands beside the stone waiting station opposite the Cog Road depot, built over Ruxton Creek. Two open cars and one closed car constituted its entire roster of rolling stock. The trolleys shuttled back and forth as fast as possible in the busy season with passengers for the Cog Road. — DONALD DUKE COLLECTION

The Cog Road depot and restaurant, and a train ready to depart. Tie marks show where the trolley tracks were before being moved across Ruxton Creek.—DR. L. L. WILLIAMS COLLECTION

The Manitou Electric Railway & Casino Company's *Dinky* between trips at the foot of Ruxton Avenue. President C. W. Sells stands between the two trolleymen. — DONALD DUKE COLLECTION

The passing switch of the trolley line on Ruxton Avenue, half way between the depot and Soda Springs.—DONALD DUKE COLLECTION

MORE TRIVIA

It is surprising how many little incidents can come to light that seem unimportant but are interesting. One must not take them all as gospel; through the passage of the years the separation of chaff from wheat isn't always easy.

For example, the *Colorado Springs Gazette* reported on June 14, 1890 that "the rails are of steel painted red and are only about 8 feet long." Perhaps we are safe in assuming that the rack rails were delivered red-leaded, and that their 80 inches somehow got changed to 8 feet in the telling.

The *Locomotive Engineer* for February 1891 featured an article about the new locomotives, and the first paragraph read, "It is more than a decade of years since a western poet wrote a wild and fantastic article on how disgusted a Rocky Mountain burro was at finding a Rio Grande locomotive at the summit of Pike's Peak — western people would not have thought the fact more ridiculous if he had made the meeting place in the moon. Yet the locomotive is there."

The *Denver Times* for August 3, 1898, under a "scare head" reading "COG ROAD DANGEROUS," spoke of the lightest travel on the M. & P. P. of any season since it opened, and went on to say that the roadbed and rolling stock were in bad condition, being neglected by the management. It was alleged that the normal jolting had worsened, and that there had been three accidents the previous summer, "when an engine broke away from a carload of passengers while descending . . ." This must have been a reference to the wreck of first No. 4 in 1896, but the paper goes on to say that news of the two other accidents had been suppressed by the management. This seems most unlikely, as old timers would have heard of them and not failed to comment in later years.

The *Colorado Springs Gazette* carried the news on January 14, 1893, that Major Hulbert had announced that a good hotel of stone would be built at the summit to accommodate 50 to 60 persons, near the signal station. Pike's Peak stone was to be used, walls were to be three feet thick, and the hotel to be completed by the summer of 1893. Also "a Half Way House" would be erected at the Mountain View siding, where Hulbert had bid on 130 acres of land that was about to be sold by the State of Colorado.

The first motion pictures in history of a storm from above the clouds were made from the summit on June 10, 1902. In October 1901 Commodore Vanderbilt (William K., no doubt) made the round trip in a private train in two hours and 45 minutes, which sounds a bit exaggerated for publicity purposes. The author recalls having seen a Vitagraph movie camera mounted on the front platform of one of the passenger trains before 1910.

Lightning in the mountains is nothing if not terrifying. Cameron's Cone, one of the mountains past which the Cog Road runs, always seems to attract more than its share of lightning. In July of 1908, for instance, a minister of the Gospel from Colorado Springs was struck by lightning on the Cone, it being no respecter of parsons. It melted the gold rims of his spectacles and part of his watch chain, tore his clothing and high boots, besides burning him. Although he weighed 210 pounds, his 23 year old son carried him down to the Cog Road, and he subsequently recovered.

Somewhat less serious but directly connected with the Cog Road was the near-cremation of conductor Art Brown in August 1903, when a bolt struck him as he was about to highball his train down from the summit. The freak flash stripped off his outer clothes, set his fleece underwear afire, and burned a blue line across his chest, knocking him unconscious to the ground. He promptly revived, borrowed a Navajo blanket, which he wrapped around his person like a Roman toga, and took his train down, the while collecting tickets and regaining his dignity. It is understandable that he laid off a few days after that.

In October 1900 the National Funeral Directors Association made an excursion to the summit that could have been more enjoyable. The party left Manitou at 9 a.m., and after a mile or so the engine broke down on the first of two trains. An hour and a half later it was repaired and started up again, went 50 feet and broke down a second time. After the next start, according to the newspaper account, "it blew out a flue" and steam put out the fire. Many of the passengers started to walk on ahead of the train and the two trains picked them up later in all stages of exhaustion. Most were ill before they reached the top at 2 p.m. Of course the exhausted passengers wanted to remain in the cars and rest, but this was contrary to company rules. They all had to file out, stand to have their picture taken, and stay out in the cold until departure time, which procedure provoked arguments that nearly led to a fight.

Henry Park, trick cyclist, rode down the Cog Road right-of-way from the summit to Manitou on a unicycle, which had no handle bars, no seat, and no pedals. The axle was extended far enough on both sides that he could stand on it. He wore a pair of heavy gloves, and braked the thing by grasping the tire with his gloved hands. Park finally arrived at the lower station at 7 p.m., having worn out a pair of shoes and several pairs of gloves. He also had fallen off the wheel many times, and was badly lacerated, though victorious. Even in those days there must have been an easier way to make a living.

In 1906 a large electric searchlight was installed on the summit by H. H. Buckwalter of Denver, to be powered by "a 25 HP electric machine from Fairbanks-Morse & Co., a combination gasoline engine and dynamo." The estimated cost was said to have been $100,000, which indicates that somebody's decimal point slipped. The late Carl F. Mathews of Colorado Springs, wrote, in his *Early Days Around the Divide*, "One more memory of those old days recalls the powerful searchlight on Pike's Peak. They said it was the world's largest. When it was directed your way, you could read a newspaper on the darkest night, even if you were 40 miles from the Peak."

In August 1946, Max D. Miller of Wichita, Kansas, had the distinction of being declared the one-millionth passenger to ride the Cog Road to the summit of Pike's Peak. In token thereof, the M. & P. P. presented him with a piece of granite from the summit. As he could have obtained one by the simple process of bending over and picking it up, one must assume that there was something unusual about the memento, such as an incrustation of iron pyrites or an embroidered cogwheel, or something. Denver's *Rocky Mountain News* didn't specify.

On Pike's Peak the barometer stands at about 17 inches of mercury, water boils at 184 degrees, Fahrenheit, and freezes at 34 degrees. Cooking is more than art in high places, as it is practically impossible to boil beans, potatoes, etc., and a three-minute egg leaves a lot to be desired.

This beautiful model of John Blenkinsop's locomotive of 1812 is located in London's Science Museum. It was the first of several locomotives built for the Middleton Colliery Railway, the first railroad to use steam power commercially. Propulsion was through a single cog wheel, which engaged a rack that was an integral part of the left running rail, the flanged wheels serving only to support the engine. The two vertical cylinders were located within the boiler. The whole locomotive weighed about five tons and was used between the colliery and Leeds, Yorkshire, England, some three and one-half miles. — THE SCIENCE MUSEUM, LONDON

11

GRADE CLIMBERS

A VOLUME featuring the Manitou & Pike's Peak Railway is hardly the place to describe in any detail all the ways that have been devised or suggested to conquer grades, but the subject seems of sufficient interest to warrant a brief look at some of the more important methods. These are the systems originated by Blenkinsop, Stevens, Marsh, Riggenbach, Strub and Locher, as well as the non-rack systems of Sellers, Fell, and Wetli.

When railways were first conceived and built for the use of steam locomotives, originally for hauling coal in England, engineers could not bring themselves to believe that smooth wheels would not slip excessively on smooth rails. In 1812 John Blenkinsop operated a steam locomotive which was geared to a combination adhesion and rack rail on the left side, while the right rail was smooth. The engine weighed five tons and ran between Leeds and the Middleton Colliery, a distance of three and one-half miles.

In the same year, William Hedley of the Wylam Colliery built a manual-powered engine by which he proved that racks were unnecessary on normal gradients, but the problem of steeper grades remained. He built the "Puffing Billy" in 1813 and it was able to run under its own power in England in 1925.

Never used commercially and perhaps for that reason often forgotten is the steam locomotive built and operated at Hoboken, New Jersey, in 1825 by Colonel John Stevens, for whom Stevens Institute of Technology is named. It had one cylinder operating a gear which in turn drove another gear that engaged a rack rail in the center of the track. This was America's first rail locomotive and first rack engine.

In 1830 Charles B. Vignola and John Ericsson, English inventors and engineers, devised a way to assist locomotive propulsion on grades by means of a central rail. Although patented in England, no practical application seems to have been made. A rack-and-pinion 0-6-0 type locomotive was put into service in 1832 at the Dowlais Iron Works in Wales.

Another attempt to solve the problem was the subject of patents issued in the United States to George Escod Sellers for his "grade climbing locomotive." Sellers and his immediate ancestors were noted Philadelphians, a family of builders of machinery of all kinds, including fire engines, papermaking and textile machinery. In 1835 and 1836 they completed two locomotives for the Philadelphia & Columbia and Alleghany Portage Railroads. After the depression of 1837, George Sellers moved to Cincinnati, Ohio, and thereafter was actively

Replica of Colonel John Stevens' locomotive of 1825, built and shown at Stevens Institute of Technology in 1927. The original locomotive operated in Hoboken, New Jersey, to prove the feasibility of steam powered railways. — SMITHSONIAN INSTITUTION (BELOW) The Baldwin Locomotive Works built this 5-cylinder rack-and-adhesion machine in 1848 for use on the steep grade of the Madison & Indianapolis Railroad. — MORRIS W. ABBOTT COLLECTION

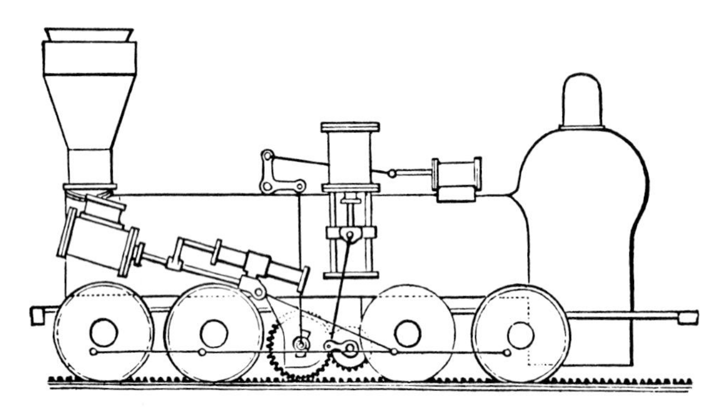

engaged in the manufacture of heavy machinery. In the period 1846-47 he proposed a scheme to increase a locomotive's adhesion by means of a central rail, on either side of which were horizontal wheels.

On the level Sellers' locomotive operated as did standard engines, but when a grade was reached, two smooth gripper wheels operated by a separate pair of inside-coupled cylinders gripped the central rail between them, and provided additional adhesion. The plan was practical, and the Panama Railroad ordered three locomotives of this plan. They were built in 1851 and 1852, but never used, since an easier route across the isthmus made them unnecessary. Sellers, having other interests, made no effort to promote his plan further.

After experience showed that toothed wheels were unnecessary, the interest in racks and pinions in America slumbered until the need arose for a locomotive to operate on a gradient of 5.89 percent on the Madison & Indianapolis Railroad, later part of the Pennsylvania Railroad. At first, in 1847, this road used a 12-ton 0-4-0T built by the Baldwin Locomotive Works, but it could handle only one car at a time. The next year a specially designed 5-cylinder 0-8-0T combination adhesion-rack locomotive was tried out. Two of the cylinders drove the conventional drivers, two others, which were placed vertically over the boiler, drove a train of cranks and gears that eventually meshed with a central rack rail. The fifth cylinder was used to raise and lower the cog wheel to engage it with or disengage it from the rack rail. The original 0-4-0T was then rebuilt as a rack locomotive, and the two operated for 20 years, when more powerful adhesion engines replaced them.

The Fell System was also designed to increase adhesion, and it too involved a third rail in the center of the track. This rail can best be described as a double-headed rail laid on its side and elevated above the level of the standard running rails. Two vertical shafts carried horizontal wheels that bore on the central rail, one on each side of it, increasing the rail surface and hence the adhesion. This also served to improve braking when descending grades. The Fell System was installed on a locomotive placed in operation in 1868 on the Mont Cenis Pass line between France and Italy, where the average grade was about six percent, the maximum about eight percent. Its use was discontinued in 1871, when a tunnel was completed, eliminating the heavy grade. This system is used today on the Snaefell Mountain Railway on the Isle of Man, for braking only.

The Wetli System was another attack on mountain grades. Anatole Mallet, who should have known whereof he spoke, described Wetli as "a distinguished engineer," but his plan to overcome grades looks nothing less than unbelievable today. The Wetli System involved the use of V-shaped sections of rail placed between the running rails and elevated above them, which would engage similarly shaped spiral ridges on a large cylinder beneath the locomotive. The Wetli System was actually tried on the Waedenswil-Einseideln Railway in Switzerland in 1876, but was abandoned after tests proved unsatisfactory.

The first successful mountain climbing system came when Sylvester Marsh, a retired meat packer from Chicago, decided to build a railway to the

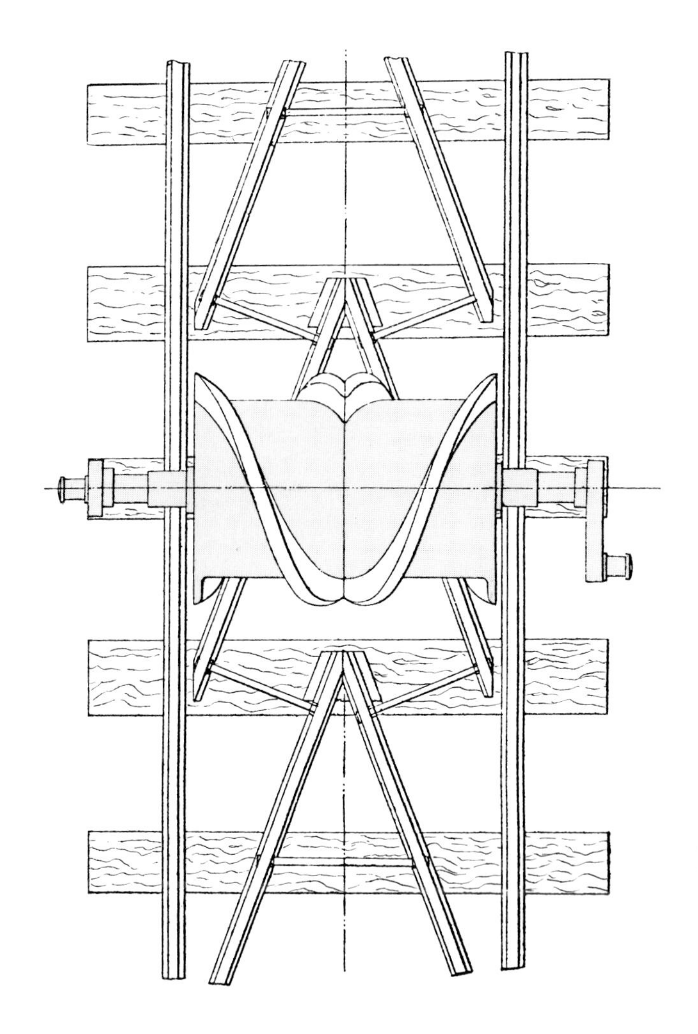

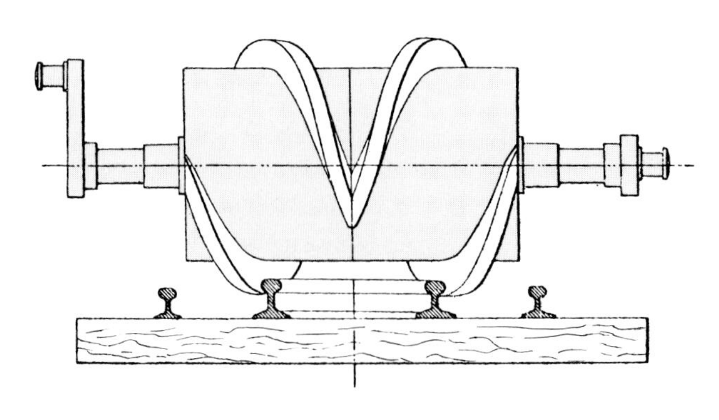

An engineer named Wetli devised this ingenious system of propulsion in the 1870's. The bird's-eye view shows the large driving cylinder of the locomotive, whose complex spirals meshed with the V-shaped arrangement between the running rails. The drawing directly above shows this cylinder, its axle, and one crank, together with the relationship of cylinder spirals and V-rails. — MORRIS W. ABBOTT COLLECTION

Early stereo photograph of the Mt. Washington cog track showing its ladder-like Marsh rack. The entire line, built between 1866-69, is laid on timber trestlework. The line is the granddad of all mountain rack railways.

top of New Hampshire's Mt. Washington, much as Simmons later did to Pike's Peak. The main difference was that Marsh had to blaze the trail himself, nobody having gone before to show him the way. As compared with Pike's Peak, Mt. Washington is a mere anthill if one simply looks at the figures. Mt. Washington is only 6,288 feet in elevation compared with the 14,110 feet of Pike's Peak. But that doesn't tell the story, for Mt. Washington is extremely rugged and is so far north that it towers high above timberline, and the weather up there can be the foulest imaginable part of the year.

Marsh had to design both engines and track, and his early locomotives had vertical boilers so hung that they remained upright on steep grades. A patent was issued to him September 10, 1861 on both engines and track. The engines were geared, for more power and less speed, and between the standard running rails was a rack rail, which consisted of two wrought iron angle bars set three inches apart and connected by pins or bolts one and one-half inch in diameter spaced four inches apart, the whole forming a sort of ladder. The teeth of the cog or pinion wheels meshed with the ladder pins and the engine was thus enabled to climb up hill. In America this is known as the Marsh type rack, but elsewhere is called the Riggenbach type, as Riggenbach made certain improvements in it.

The Mt. Washington road is three and one-half miles long, with a short stretch of 37 percent maximum gradient. It opened in 1869 and has been operating successfully ever since.

Marsh may or may not have known that patents were issued in 1832 to William Bent of Philadelphia for a way of propelling locomotives and cars "by means of cog wheels," and that one was granted in 1836 to Nathan Read of Belfast, Maine, a scale model of whose invention is now at the Essex Institute in Salem, Massachusetts. He might have been aware of them, as his first application for a patent was denied, the Patent Office being of the opinion that cog railways were nothing new.

Marsh organized the Mt. Washington Steam Railway Company in 1865, and the road opened in 1869 to the summit, rising from 2,569 feet of elevation at the lower station to 6,288 feet at the top. To defeat the tendency of the cog wheel to ride up and out of the rack, Marsh had the teeth of the wheels cut extra deep, so that two of them would engage the teeth of the rack at all times. In addition to this, one account says that "grippers" were installed to prevent derailment in case the cog wheel did so behave, but if this device is still in use it did not prevent a serious derailment in 1967.

Working independently of Marsh, but concurrently, a Swiss engineer named Nicklaus Riggenbach developed a system very similar to Marsh's. When he heard of the successful installation on Mt. Washington, he came to the United States to see it. Returning to Switzerland, he proceeded to build the Vitznau-Rigi Railway, which opened in 1871. Like the Mt. Washington road's, his locomotives at first had vertical boilers, but later they were horizontal. The line was electrified in 1937. These early Swiss rack locomotives were built by the Swiss Locomotive & Machine Works at Winterthur, which, 90 or 95 years later, built four diesel-electric rail cars for the Manitou & Pike's Peak Railway, Nos. 14 through 17.

One main difference between Marsh's and Riggenbach's rack is that the latter consists of two channel irons laid on edge and connected by pins, while the Marsh rack used two angle irons. The overhang of the Riggenbach channel irons permits the addition of grippers or hooks which depend from the locomotive or car and travel along beneath the tops of the channel irons, preventing derailment. At least this was true of the original Vitznau-Rigi Railway.

Nicklaus Riggenbach built this locomotive in 1871 for Europe's first rack railway, the Vitznau-Rigibahn. — SWISS NATIONAL TOURIST OFFICE (BELOW) A steam locomotive on the same road, still used on occasion, though the line was electrified in 1937. — SWISS MUSEUM OF TRANSPORT

Riggenbach's success led him to organize his own rack locomotive manufactory, Maschinenfabrik der Internationalen Gesellschaft für Bergbahnen. The company built only 12 locomotives, but it should be noted that he appointed as manager of the works another Swiss engineer, Dr. Roman Abt, who later invented the rack system used all over the world, including the installation on Pike's Peak. A goodly number of rack roads used the Riggenbach system, a dozen or so in Switzerland, a few in Germany and Austria, at least three in Brazil, and a number of others.

The Abt system was well received, and by 1894 there were 19 lines built following this plan, either alone or in conjunction with adhesion operation, for a total of 194 miles. These included, among others, the Snowdon Mountain Railway in Wales,

The Gornergratbahn, a meter gauge Abt system rack line, was opened in 1898, the first rack railway in Switzerland to be operated by electricity. It is nearly six miles long and reaches an elevation of 10,134 feet above its Zermatt station, with a maximum gradient of 20 percent. Spectacular views of the Matterhorn and Gornergrat glacier make it a popular attraction. — SWISS NATIONAL TOURIST OFFICE (BELOW) The Japanese 3 foot 6 inch gauge line between Yokokawa and Karuizawa, though now entirely adhesion, until 1963 used the unusual 3-rail Abt rack. Completed in 1892, it was electrified in 1912. — JAPANESE NATIONAL RAILWAYS

Before electrification, the Glion-Rochers de Naye line (shown on the left) used steam power. This locomotive is an 0.8 meter gauge (31.5 inches), with its cylinders below the steam dome, the pistons working ahead of them. This 6.5 mile road was built in 1890, uses the Abt rack system and climbs 5,164 feet above Montreux to an elevation of 6,460 feet, with a maximum gradient of 22 percent. — SWISS MUSEUM OF TRANSPORT

The Arth-Rigibahn, shown on the right, was opened in 1875 to compete with the pioneer Vitznau-Rigibahn. It also is standard gauge with Riggenbach rack. The maximum grade is 20 percent. — SWISS MUSEUM OF TRANSPORT

The ill-fated Green Mountain Railway had two engines built in 1883, and also two cars with transverse benches, similar to an open trolley. After the road failed, the engines went to the Mt. Washington Ry., where they are still in service. One locomotive was damaged in a derailment in 1967, but was rebuilt.

the Harz Mountain line in Germany, the Rama-Serajevo in Bosnia (now in Jugoslavia), a section of the Transandean Railway between Argentina and Chile (using 3-bar rack), and one in the West Indies, and, of course the Manitou & Pike's Peak Railway. There was also an electric Abt system railway up Mont Salies in France, and the Beirut-Damascus Railway was to use the Abt plan. Others were built in South America, Japan and elsewhere.

The Green Mountain Railway was built and opened in 1882 to the top of Green Mountain, which is now called Cadillac Mountain, on Mt. Desert Island near Bar Harbor, Maine. It used the Marsh system, but was financially unsuccessful, ceased operating about 1891, after which its two locomotives went to the Mt. Washington line, which had lost some of its motive power in a fire.

The Snowdon Mountain Railway had an unfortunate accident in its early days, and proceeded to install guard rails on either side of the rack, with grippers on the locomotives and cars which rode under the guard rails to prevent derailments.

The very earliest Abt racks had single bars, but very soon two bars became standard, and, as we have mentioned, some lines used three. The secret of the success of this system seems to have been the design and accuracy of manufacture of the rack bars.

The Snowdon Mountain Railway in Wales is the only rack railway in Great Britain. It is just over 4.5 miles in length and reaches an altitude of 3,492 feet above the sea and 3,140 feet above the lower station. The line uses Abt rack, has a gauge of 2 feet 7½ inches (800 millimeters) and operates with coal-burning steam locomotives built by the Swiss Locomotive & Machine Works. The maximum gradient is 18.2 percent. (ABOVE) The Snowdon rack train at the summit. — MORRIS W. ABBOTT COLLECTION (RIGHT) A scene near the summit. — ROBERT B. ADAMS COLLECTION

The Brienz-Rothornbahn is now the only rack railway in Switzerland exclusively steam powered. The Abt system is employed and the line has a maximum gradient of 25 percent in the 4.75 miles of length, reaching 7,388 feet of elevation just shy of the summit of Rothorn. (ABOVE) Locomotive No. 3 pauses at Brienz in 1965, ready for a run. At the upper right, the same train leaving for the summit. — BOTH GERALD M. BEST (RIGHT) A switch at the summit of the railway in 1971. — ROBERT B. ADAMS

This 0-6-0 was a combination rack-adhesion, meter gauge locomotive, built in 1905 by the Swiss Locomotive & Machine Works for the Bruniglinie. It featured two pairs of cylinders, one of which powered the adhesion drive wheels, while the other drove the pinion. The road has a length of about 46 miles, of which less than six are rack. It is the only narrow gauge segment of the Swiss Federal Railways, uses Riggenbach rack, and is now electrified. The maximum gradient is 12 percent. — SWISS MUSEUM OF TRANSPORT

The Strub system of rack rail, which is used on the Jungfraubahn and a few others in Switzerland and France, consists of a heavy central T-rail, higher than the running rails, the top of which has broad teeth into which mesh the teeth of the cog wheels.

A unique and very interesting system is the Locher, which is used only by the Pilatusbahn in Switzerland. It was long believed that a 25 percent grade is the steepest on which the other systems can be used with safety, because of the tendency of the cog wheel to climb out of the rack (yet the Mt. Washington line has a 37 percent maximum grade). Devised by Colonel Edouard Locher, this system was designed for use on the 48 percent grade on Mt. Pilatus. It consists of a heavy central rail, on both *sides* of which are cut teeth into which mesh those of two horizontal pinion wheels. It is impossible for them to escape from the rack rail, and they also prevent derailment. It is said that they obviate the need for flanges on the wheels, but will be noted that the original steam-powered rail car had wheel flanges outside the rails. The line has been electrified, of course, but the original conveyance was like nothing else before or since. A single unit, the rear or lower end carried a steam power plant whose small boiler was placed crossways of the track. The rest of the car consisted of four compartments arranged in steps.

In 1892 the first purely rack railway in Italy was opened, the Sant' Ellero-Saltino Railway, with a gradient of about 23 percent. The rack was the Telfener type, consisting on the lighter grades of two steel angle bars rivetted together in four to six foot lengths, in which teeth were cut. On steeper grades, the thickness of the teeth was increased by placing flat steel bars between the angle bars, making an inexpensive form of rack.

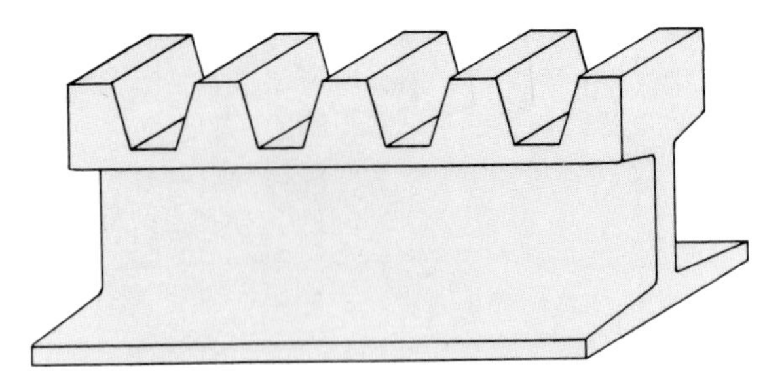

The Strub system of rack is used on six Swiss rack railways, three of which are combination rack-adhesion. All are meter gauge. It is simply a heavy T-rail, higher than the running rails.

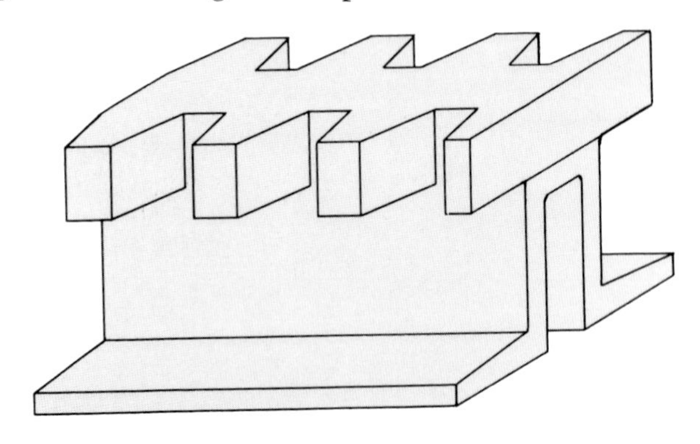

The Locher rack rail is unique, with its teeth cut into the sides rather than the top of the rail. It was designed expressly for use on the Pilatusbahn, where the steepest gradient is 48 percent and it was feared that the pinions or cog wheels would tend to climb out of the rack, with resultant catastrophe. (ABOVE LEFT) This unusual affair ran on the Pilatusbahn in its early days. The boiler was set crosswise of the car, which had its passenger compartment in four steps. The wheels of this vehicle had outside flanges. — SWISS MUSEUM OF TRANSPORT (LEFT) Unusual arrangement used in lieu of conventional switches, which the Locher rack renders impractical. Curved sections of track mounted on trucks are moved bodily to lead the car in the desired direction.

APPENDIX

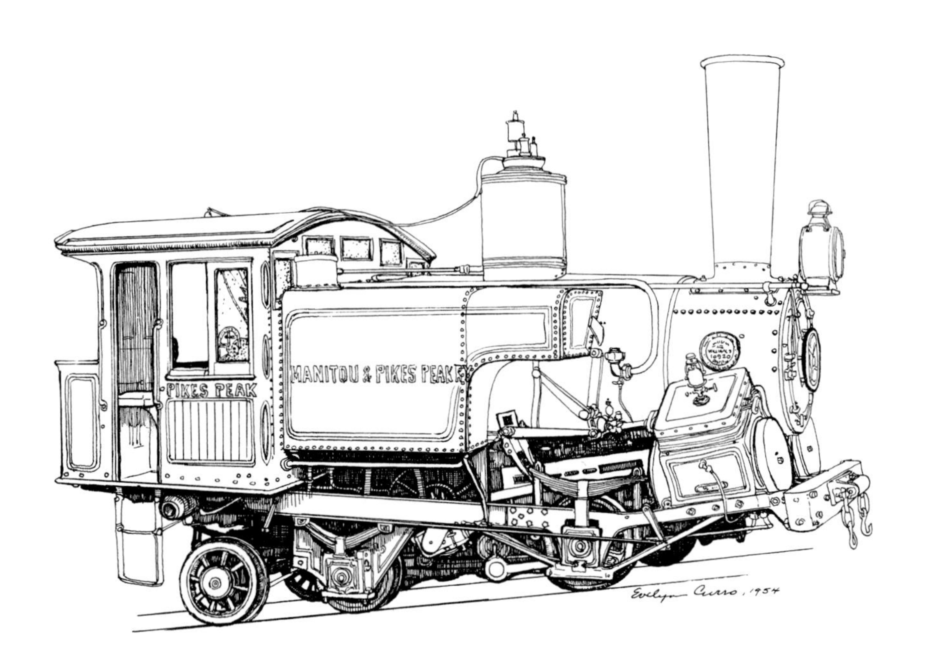

STEAM LOCOMOTIVES

No.	Name	Type	Builder	Builder No.	Date Built	Drivers	Cylinders	Engine Weight	Boiler Pressure	Note
	John Hulbert	Rack	Baldwin	10835	4/1890	22.4"	17x20"	53,600	160	A
	Manitou	Rack	Baldwin	10919	5/1890	22.4"	17x20"	53,600	160	B
	Pike's Peak	Rack	Baldwin	10920	5/1890	22.4"	17x20"	53,600	160	C
1		Rack	Baldwin	13318	3/1893	22.4"	10x15x22"	52,680	180	D
2		Rack	Baldwin	13319	3/1893	22.4"	10x15x22"	52,680	180	E
3		Rack	Baldwin	13324	3/1893	22.4"	10x15x22"	52,680	180	F
4		Rack	Baldwin	12681	5/1892	22.4"	9x15x22"	48,850	180	G
2nd 4		Rack	Baldwin	15173	1/1897	22.4"	10x15x22"	62,455	180	H
5		Rack	Baldwin	18939	4/1901	22.4"	10x15x22"	58,500	180	I
6		Rack	Baldwin	28401	6/1906	22.4"	10x15x24"	60,000	210	J

A. Rebuilt 3/1893 as No. 1. Became a 4-cylinder Vauclain compound.
B. Rebuilt 3/1893 as No. 2. Became a 4-cylinder Vauclain compound. Renamed *T. F. Richardson* before 1893 rebuilding.
C. Rebuilt 3/1893 as No. 3. Became a 4-cylinder Vauclain compound.
D. Former *John Hulbert*. Rebuilt as Vauclain compound. Retired. On exhibit Cheyenne Mtn. Zoo, Colorado Springs.
E. Former *Manitou* and *T. F. Richardson*. Rebuilt as Vauclain compound. Retired 1939. On exhibit Manitou Springs.
F. Former *Pike's Peak*. Rebuilt as Vauclain compound. Scrapped for parts.
G. Wrecked in a runaway 8/31/1896 – scrapped.
H. Vauclain compound locomotive to replace No. 4. Retired operable. Donated to Colorado Railroad Museum – 1968.
I. Vauclain compound. Retired. On exhibit at Cog Depot, Manitou Springs.
J. Vauclain compound. Built as oil burner, converted to coal burning in 1907. Retired – scrapped in 1955.

NOTE: All locomotives were rebuilt in 1912 with new frames and rod arrangement in the Manitou & Pike's Peak Railway shops using parts acquired from the Baldwin Locomotive Works. Before this rebuilding, stronger, fluted rods had been installed in place of the original plain rods on locomotives Nos. 1, 2 and 3.

The diameter of the driving pinions is measured on the pitch line. No. 6 was built with three driving pinions and no trailing wheel. The boiler pressure of No. 6 was reduced to 193 lbs. and the other engines had their boiler pressure increased to 193 lbs. when rebuilt. All engines had boilers of 44 inches diameter, with 19.7 square feet of grate area, and total heating surface of 576 square feet. Water capacity of saddle tanks – 600 gallons.

STEAM LOCOMOTIVE No. 2

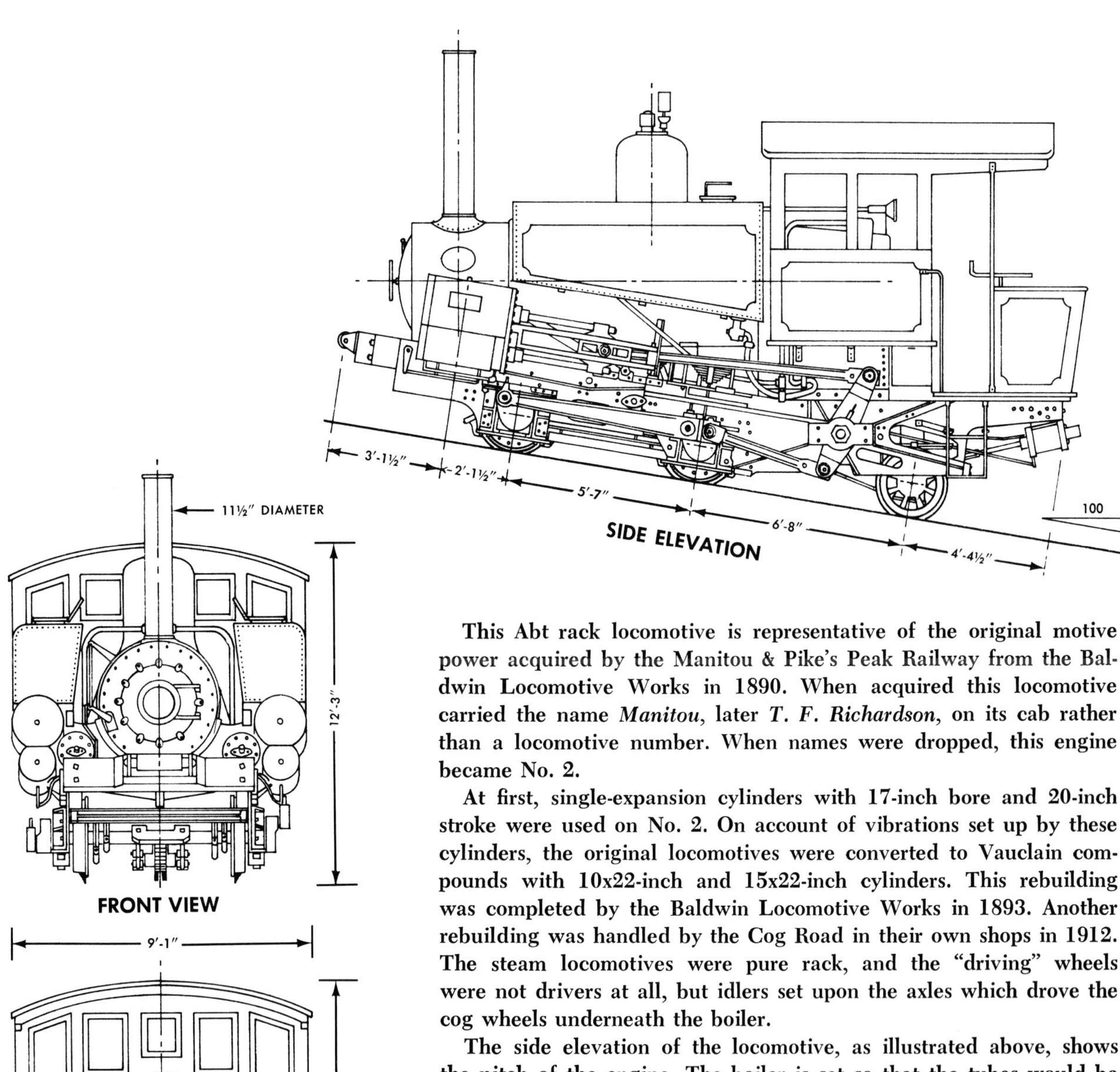

This Abt rack locomotive is representative of the original motive power acquired by the Manitou & Pike's Peak Railway from the Baldwin Locomotive Works in 1890. When acquired this locomotive carried the name *Manitou*, later *T. F. Richardson*, on its cab rather than a locomotive number. When names were dropped, this engine became No. 2.

At first, single-expansion cylinders with 17-inch bore and 20-inch stroke were used on No. 2. On account of vibrations set up by these cylinders, the original locomotives were converted to Vauclain compounds with 10x22-inch and 15x22-inch cylinders. This rebuilding was completed by the Baldwin Locomotive Works in 1893. Another rebuilding was handled by the Cog Road in their own shops in 1912. The steam locomotives were pure rack, and the "driving" wheels were not drivers at all, but idlers set upon the axles which drove the cog wheels underneath the boiler.

The side elevation of the locomotive, as illustrated above, shows the pitch of the engine. The boiler is set so that the tubes would be horizontal when the engine was upon a 16 percent grade.

With the water tanks on each side, the engine carried 600 gallons of water and sufficient coal for one round trip, in a bunker behind the cab. The coal was located at the rear of the cab. Maximum speed loaded was about 8 miles per hour on an 8 percent grade. As the grade increased the speed decreased to about 5 miles per hour.

The locomotives were painted the standard engine black with a graphite smoke box front during most of their life. A bit of silver trim was added during the "Streamline" era. The inset panel under the cab window was trimmed in red and black with the locomotive number, the name in white on the side tanks. The road number also appeared on the rear, on the coal bunker. During the years of steam locomotive operation, there was no cog wheel painted on any part of the locomotive. This feature was added when the locomotives became monuments.

SCALE — 3/16 inch to the foot

DIESEL/GASOLINE LOCOMOTIVES

No.	Type	Builder	Builder No.	Date Built	Engine Weight	Engines	No. of Engines	H.P.*	NOTE
7	A - A	Manitou & Pike's Peak	–	1938	–	General Motors 707	1	200	A
8	A - A	General Electric	12454	1939	40,000	General Motors 71	3	420	
9	A - A	General Electric	28372	1946	48,000	Cummins NHS	2	440	
10	A - A	General Electric	30279	1950	48,000	Cummins NHS	2	440	
11	A - A	General Electric	30280	1950	48,000	Cummins NHS	2	440	
12	A - A	Manitou & Pike's Peak	–	1955	50,000	General Motors 110	2	440	B
14	A - A	Swiss Locomotive & Machine Works	4441	1963	76,900	Cummins NHHRTO	2	500	C
15	A - A	Swiss Locomotive & Machine Works	4442	1963	76,900	Cummins NHHRTO	2	500	C
16	A - A	Swiss Locomotive & Machine Works	4778	1968	70,300	Cummins NHHRTO	2	500	
17	A - A	Swiss Locomotive & Machine Works	4779	1968	70,300	Cummins NHHRTO	2	500	

*Actual horsepower rating at site (Pike's Peak) since units never operate below 6,500 feet.

A. Gasoline powered. Original engine was General Motors 707, replaced by Cadillac V-8 type.
B. Placed in service in 1956.
C. Originally built with Swiss diesel engines. Replaced in 1964 with Cummins 6-cylinder horizontal type NHHRTO-6-B1.

No.	Type	Builder	Builder No.	Date Built	Engine Weight	Engines	No. of Engines	H.P.*	NOTE
20	A - A	Manitou & Pike's Peak	–	1934	–	Pierce Arrow	1	160	D
21	A - A	Manitou & Pike's Peak	–	1953	–	General Motors	2	400	E

D. Gasoline powered work car. Built with Pierce Arrow engine, replaced with General Motors 707 from No. 7.
E. Rotary snowplow.

WOOD COACH "ASPEN"

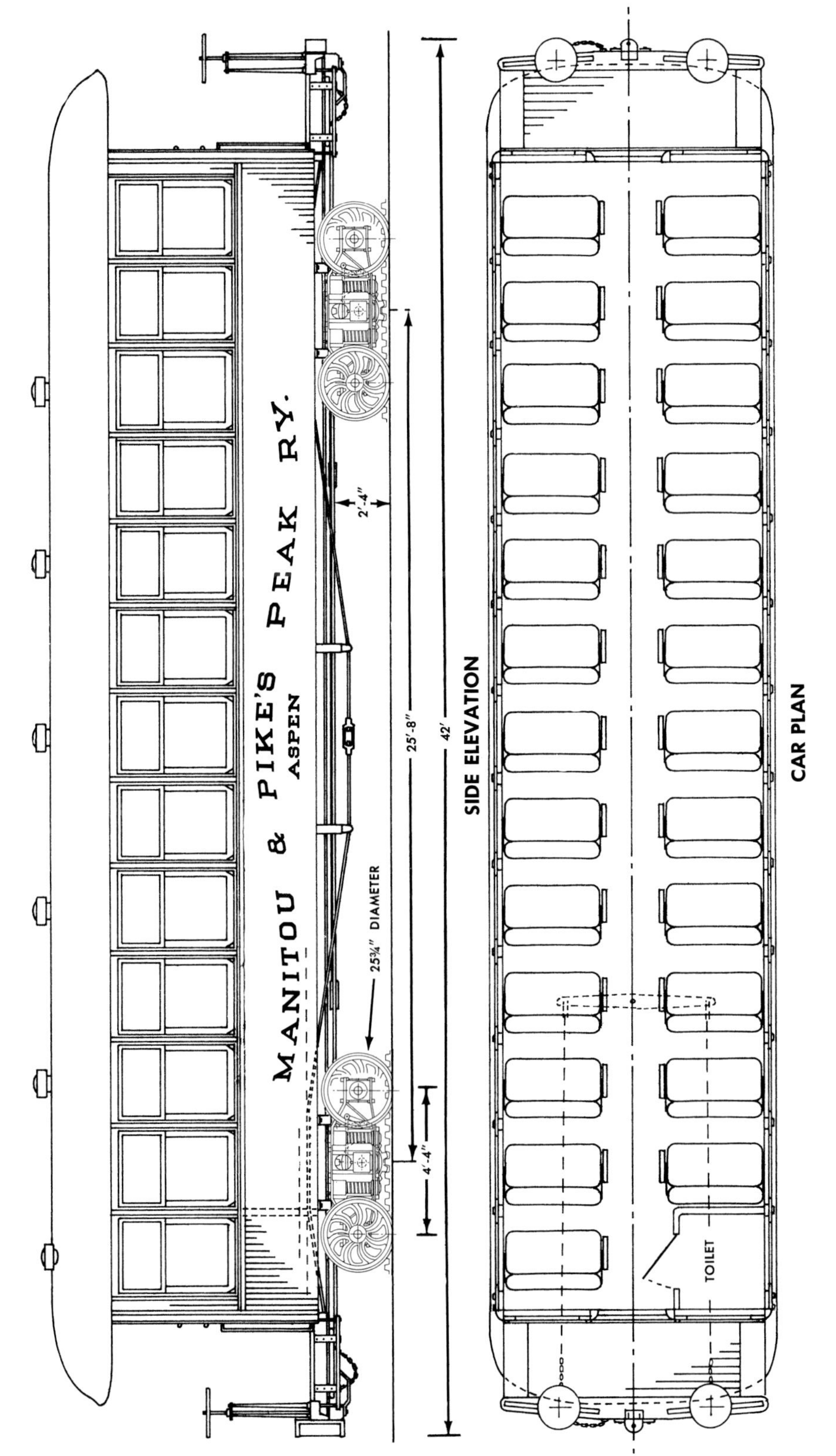

SIDE ELEVATION

CAR PLAN

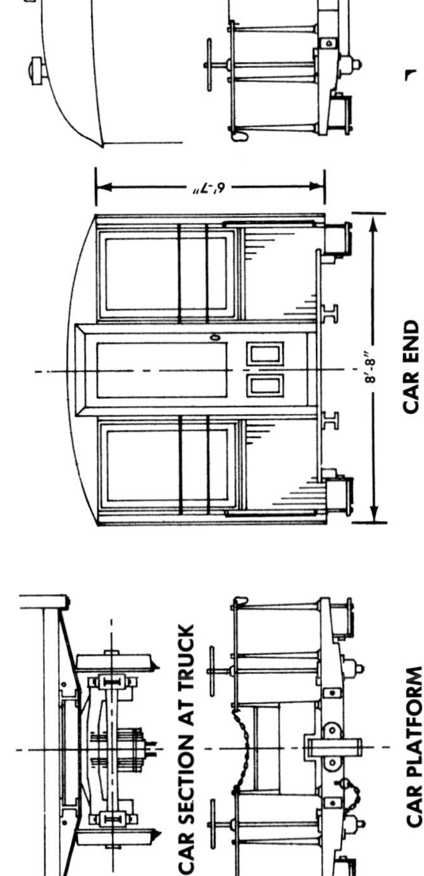

CAR END

CAR SECTION AT TRUCK

CAR PLATFORM

SCALE — 3/16 inch to the foot

The Manitou & Pike's Peak Railway began operation with six wood constructed coaches built by the Wason Manufacturing Co. The original cars carried names rather than car numbers and were equipped with a single axle under each end. Due to poor tracking the single axles were replaced by four-wheel trucks after one year of operation.

Each coach carried 50 passengers and had a small toilet compartment at the lower end. The seats, like the steam locomotive firebox and boiler, were level on a 16 percent grade. Each coach was equipped with two independent brake systems for safe operation.

(continued on next page)

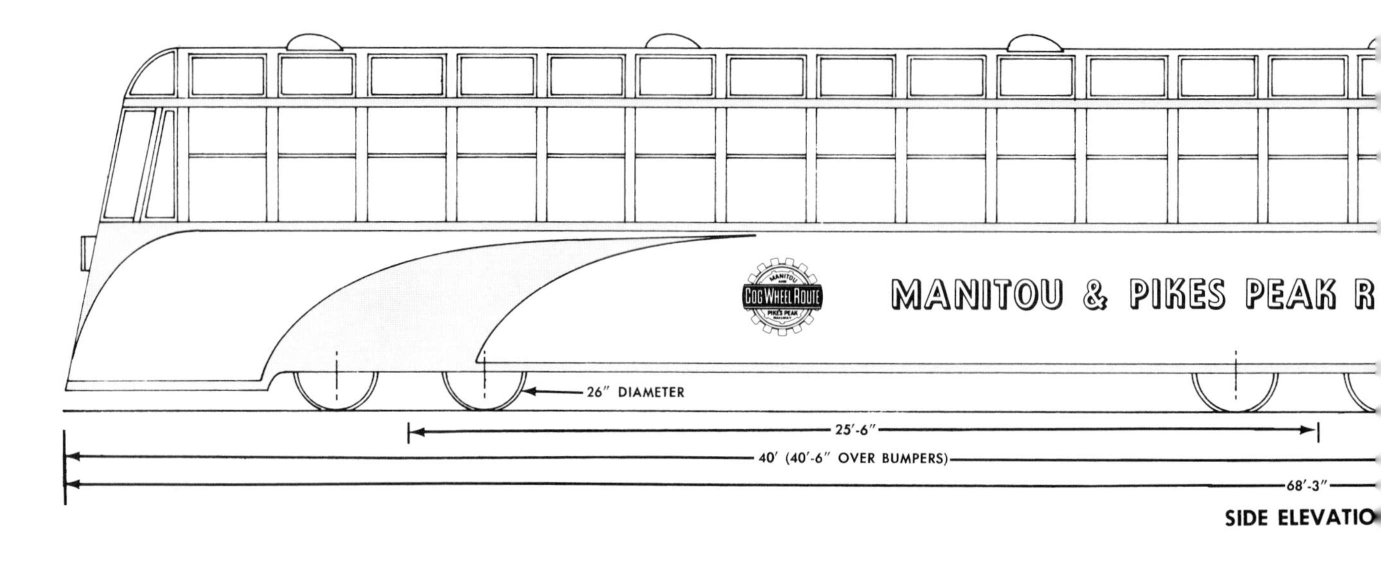

SIDE ELEVATIO

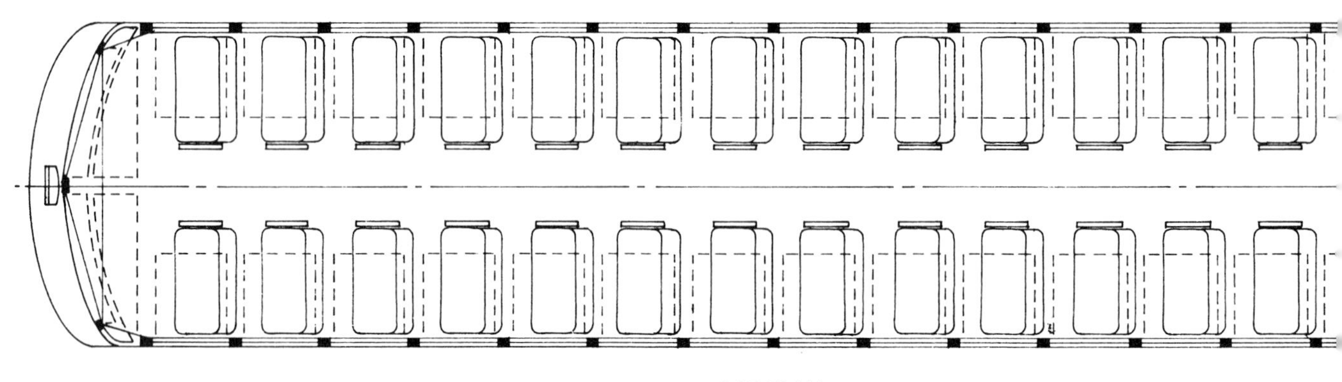
CAR PLAN

WOOD COACH (continued)

The exterior of the coaches were handsomely finished in dark Pullman green with ornate gold striping just below the windows and at the bottom of the car. Gold leaf and color work were also applied around doors and at the corner posts. Lettering was in gold leaf with red and black shading. Window frames were natural wood that was varnished to a high shine. The roof was painted a sort of box car red color, with underbody and frames dull black.

With the coming of the "Streamliner" era in the mid-1930's, the coaches were painted silver or aluminum with a black underbody. To finish off the car, the coach lettering was a shaded red and black.

DIESEL TRAIN NO. 10

The Manitou & Pike's Peak Railway was one of the early users of gasoline and diesel powered cog trains. This diesel train set is representative of the first phase of the road's "Streamline" era.

The locomotive unit was built by General Electric at Erie, Pennsylvania, in 1950 and equipped with 2 Cummins 440 h.p. NHS diesel engines which supplied the power for four General Electric 1204 type traction motors, two on each axle. The locomotive unit contains all of the operating equipment except for the mufflers and braking resistors which are mounted on the roof. Each train set is equipped with three brake systems: electric, air and hand brake.

The coach section has a capacity of 52 passengers, and was built in Denver by Winter-Weiss Co. Each seat has its own window and this train unit has glass extending into the roof section for better viewing en route. The car is equipped with electric lights, but there is no toilet.

The locomotive and coach have steel underframes with aluminum body construction. The train was originally aluminum color with a red decorative trim. The portions painted red appear as a screen on this model plan. The locomotive unit and coach carried the railroad emblem on the side in addition to the lettering which was black with red trim.

With the arrival of the new Swiss trains, these "Streamliners" were painted a fire engine red with a white stripe below the windows. The roof is aluminum color and the underbody black.

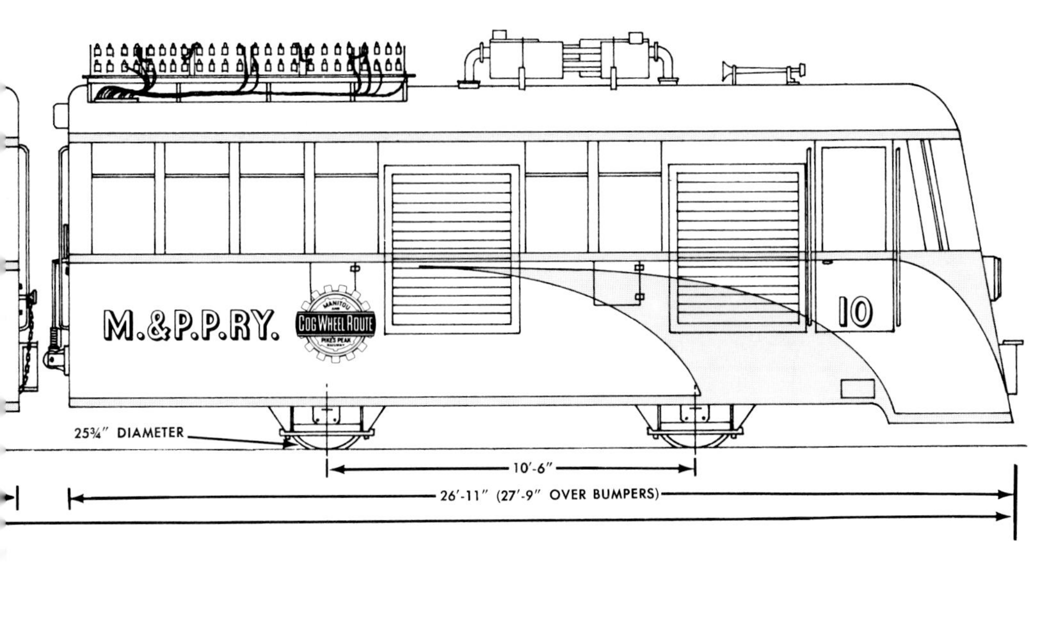

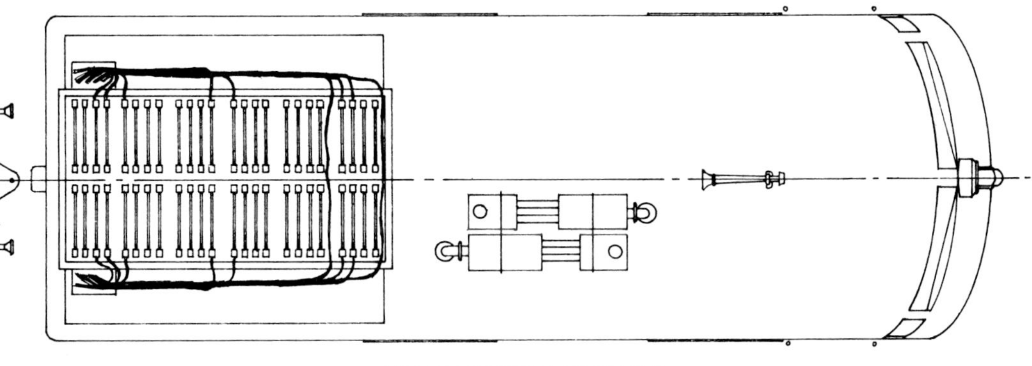

LOCOMOTIVE ROOF DETAIL

DIESEL TRAIN No. 10

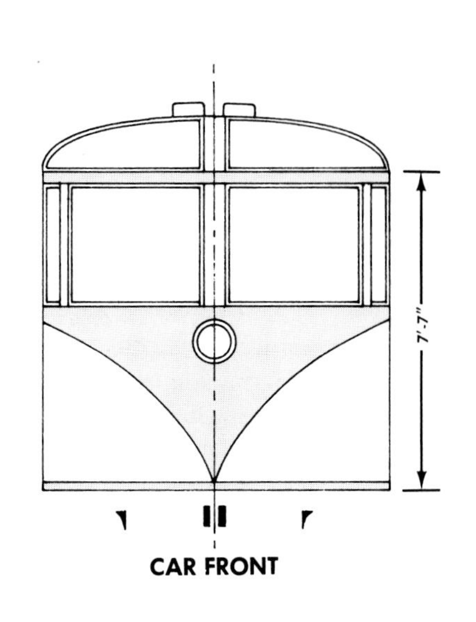

CAR FRONT

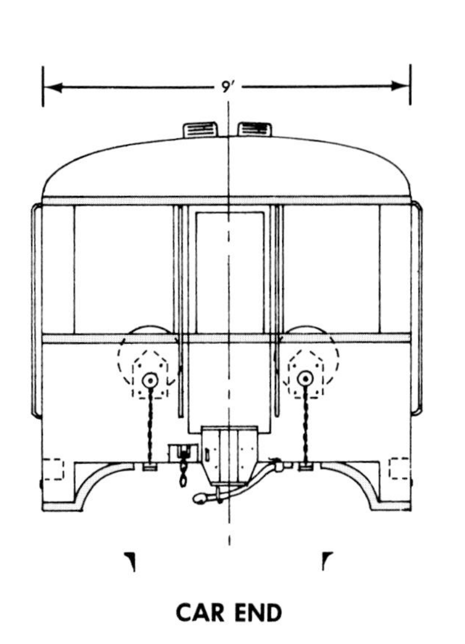

CAR END

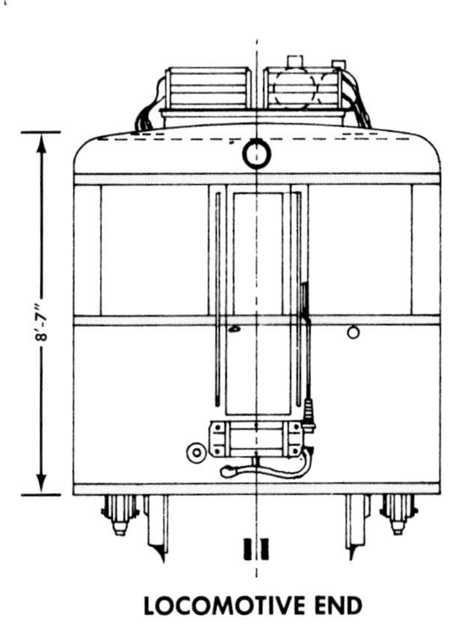

LOCOMOTIVE END

SCALE — 3/16 inch to the foot

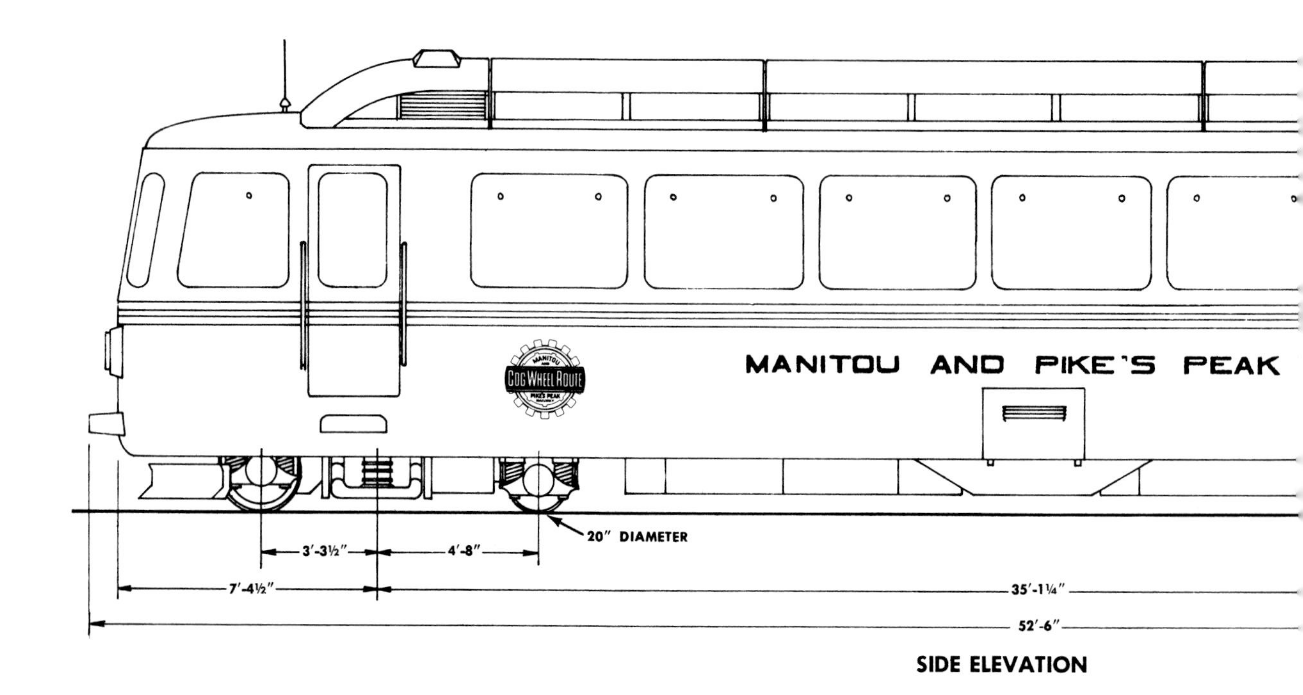

SIDE ELEVATION

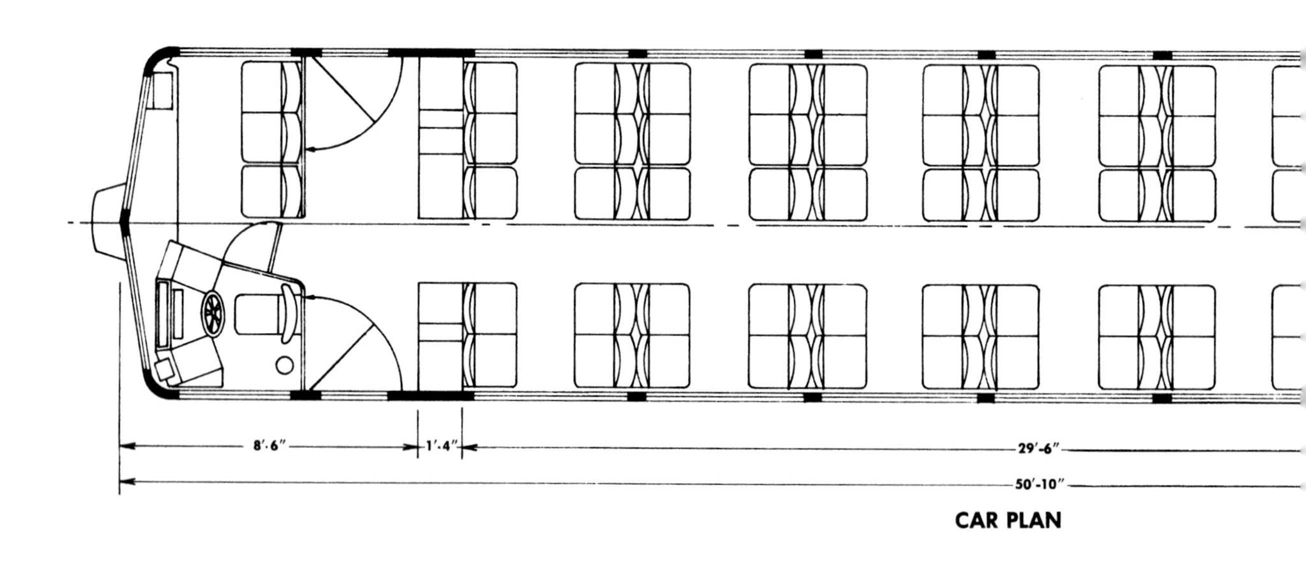

CAR PLAN

SWISS DIESEL TRAIN No. 14

SCALE — 3/16 inch to the foot

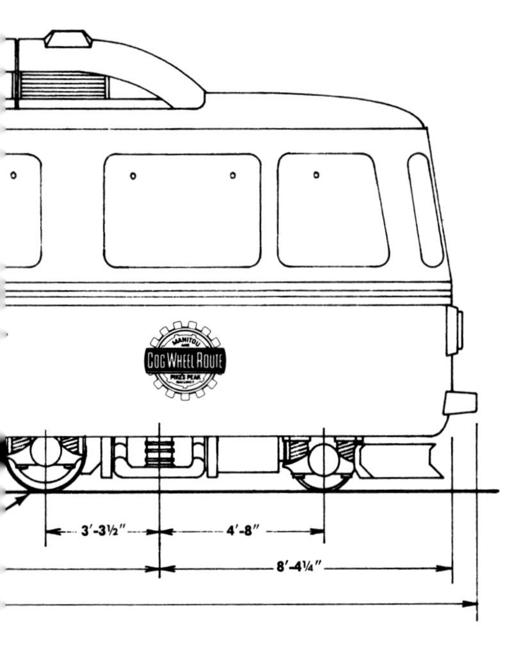

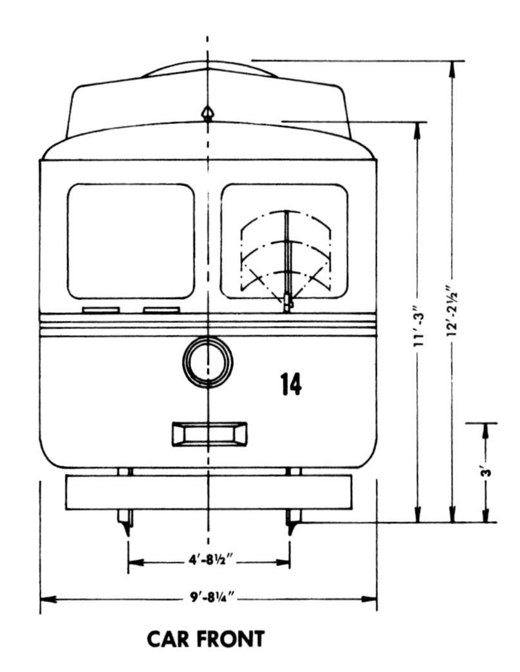

CAR FRONT

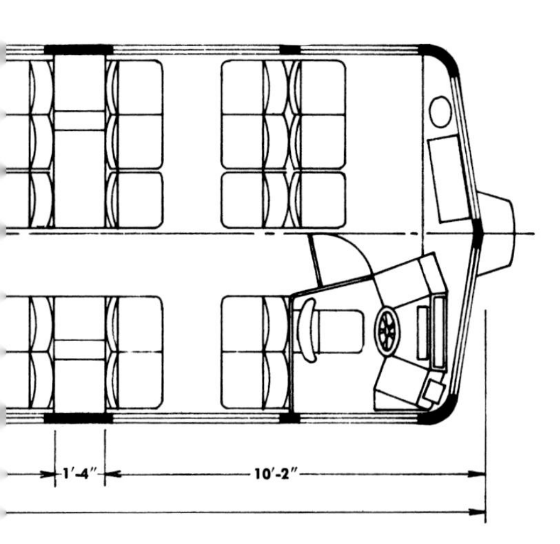

After several years experience with the diesel train sets like No. 10, the Manitou & Pike's Peak Railway found it more practical to have the coach and locomotive all in one unit.

The Swiss Locomotive & Machine Works designed this new train, of which No. 14 is one of four like units. Originally built with Swiss diesel engines, they were soon replaced by 2 Cummins NHHRTO 500 h.p. diesels after one year of operation. All mechanical equipment is located underneath the floor of the car body except for coolers on the roof.

Each train carries 80 passengers, three passengers per seat on one side and two on the other. The car has electric lights, but no toilet facilities.

The Swiss diesel trains are painted fire engine red, with the roof an aluminum color, and underbody equipment a dull black. Each train has two white bands which run completely around the car just below the windows. The road name is in raised chrome letters applied to the car center. At each end the Manitou & Pike's Peak Railway name, a raised Cog Road herald has been applied.

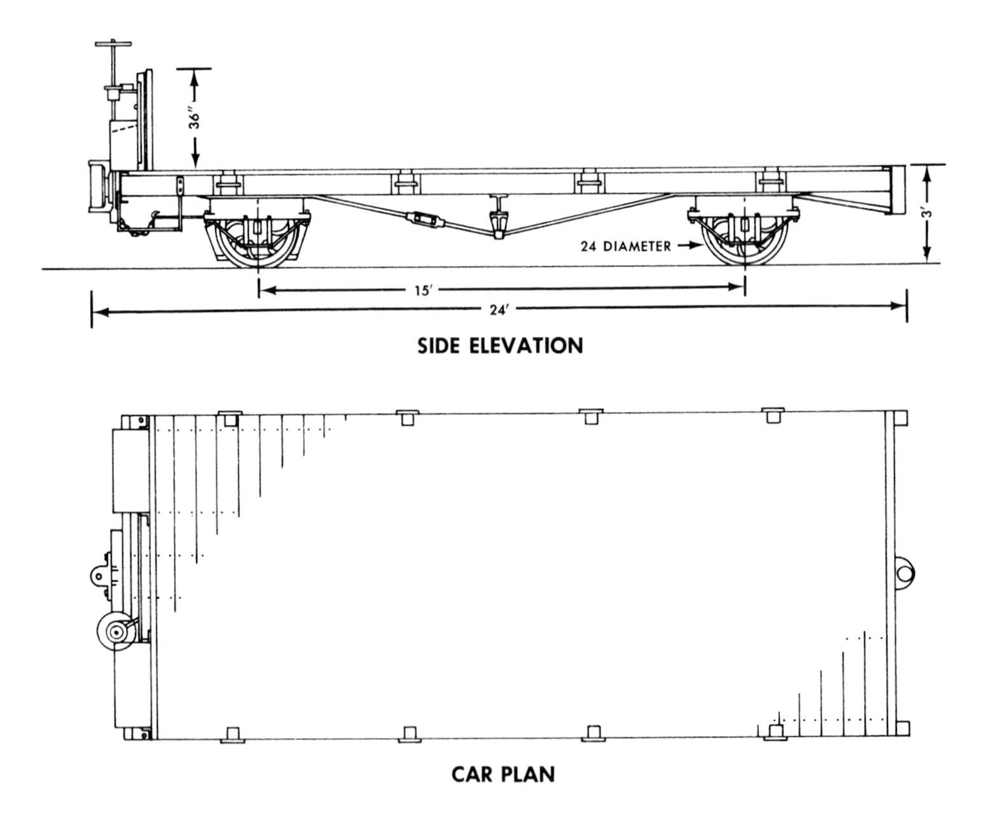

SIDE ELEVATION

CAR PLAN

FLAT CAR

The original order for rolling stock included two flat cars built by the Wason Manufacturing Co. These cars were used to carry company equipment and supplies to various resorts and residents along the line, as well as to the Summit House. During the 1930's the cars were rebuilt with a steel underframe, but were used mostly in maintenance-of-way service.

It is believed the flat cars were always boxcar red in color. When built they carried the road name and a possible number as is evidenced by the illustration on page 56-57. During the author's lifetime the flat cars carried neither lettering nor road numbers.

In 1967-1968 the only flat car still on the roster was equipped with a steel bed and a hydraulic lift to speed up snow removal.

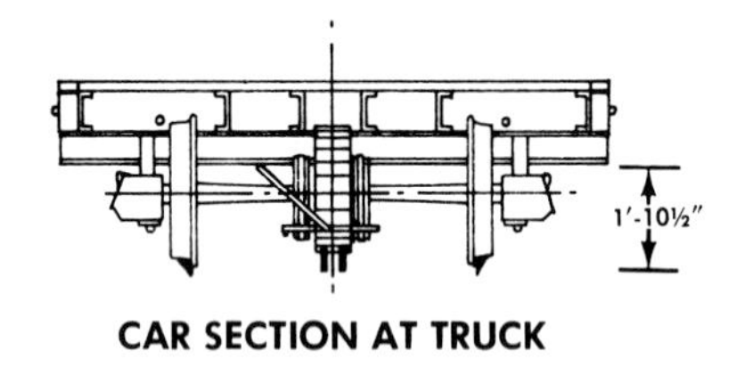

CAR SECTION AT TRUCK

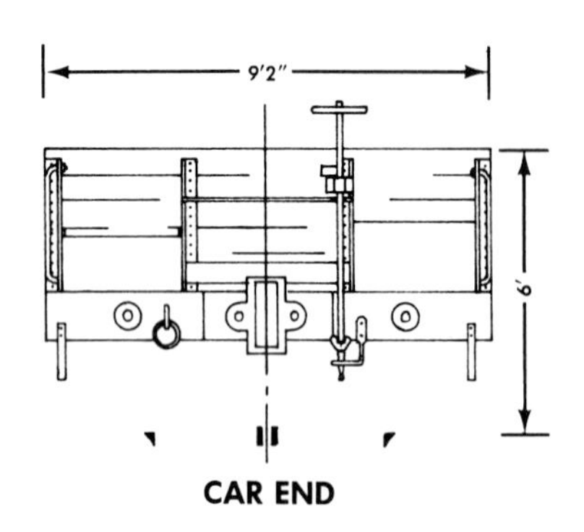

CAR END

SCALE — 3/16 inch to the foot

THE RACK SYSTEM

The Abt rack system, to whose specifications and requirements the Manitou & Pike's Peak Railway and its rolling stock are designed, is the invention of the celebrated Swiss engineer, Dr. Roman Abt of Lucerne, who, in collaboration with Francis Rinecker, of Wurzburg, Germany, has been responsible for some three-quarters of the world's total rack railway mileage.

The main feature of the Abt system is a mild steel rack with open upstanding teeth, into which mesh two or more driving pinions carried on the locomotive. At first sight, a steel cog or tooth hardly seems to call for much designing, but the tooth of the Abt system is a work of finesse, plotted and profiled with great care to meet the strains. It is rounded to precise radii on top, bevelled at the sides, and undercut at the root, the latter to ensure that the cog of the driving pinion will not bind.

Locomotion on the Manitou & Pike's Peak Railway is "pure rack," which means that all the drive is conveyed through the rack pinions or cogs, without any help from the road wheels of the locomotive. Thus the engine climbs up Pike's Peak cog by cog, and the carrying wheels are loose on their axles. This is the basic reason that the rack is so important.

Thomas F. Richardson, construction engineer for the Manitou & Pike's Peak Railway, presented some interesting details about the rack system in his report on the construction of the Cog Road. The original rails are ordinary 40 pound T-rails laid on wooden ties with the rail spacing to the standard gauge measure of four feet eight and one-half inches. The Abt rack is laid in the center between the running rails, and consists of two toothed steel bars as already described. These are fastened side by side in specially designed chairs. The chairs in which the bars are seated are of steel, die-forged from a half inch thick plate, but have a core of T-iron which is 3½ x 3 inches. Each chair is 13 inches long, 7.5 inches wide and 4.5 inches high, of which height 3.5 inches are above the top of the tie and one inch below it. Each chair weighs 23.5 pounds, though slightly smaller ones were used on the lesser grades and weighed 23 pounds. They originally cost $5.645 per hundred pounds.

These chairs are spaced 40 inches apart, and each has holes for two seven-eighths inch bolts for the two lighter weight bars or one inch for the heavier ones, with one-sixteenth inch clearance in each hole. As the rack bars are 80 inches long, each one reaches from the middle of one chair to the middle of the second one beyond, and of course they are arranged so

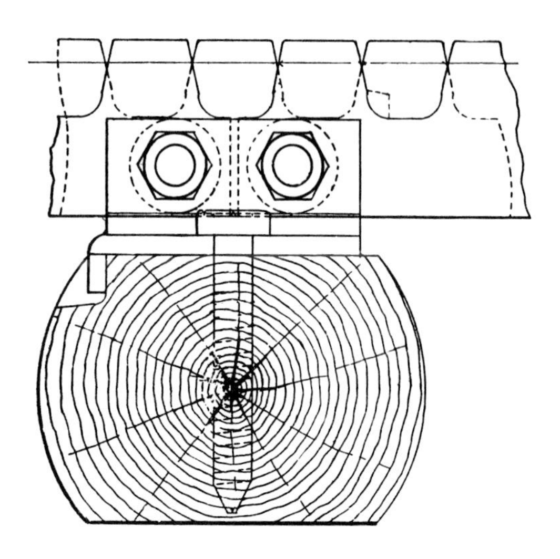

ELEVATION

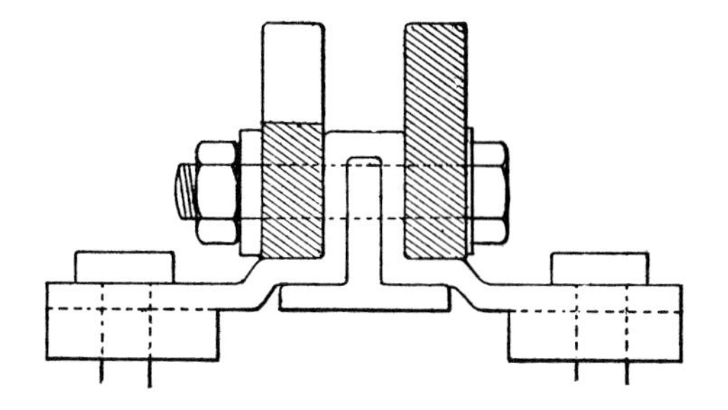

SECTION

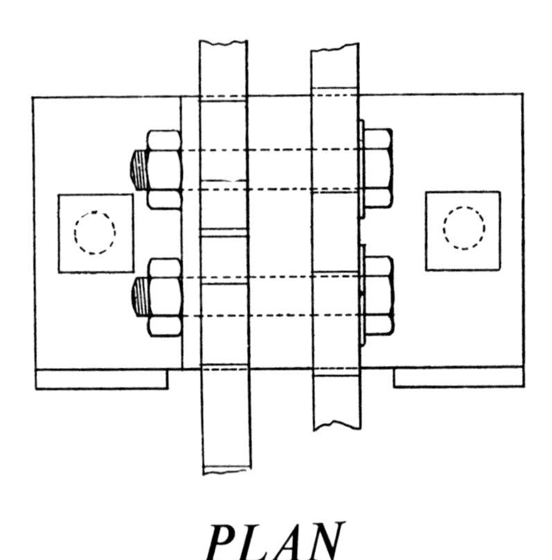

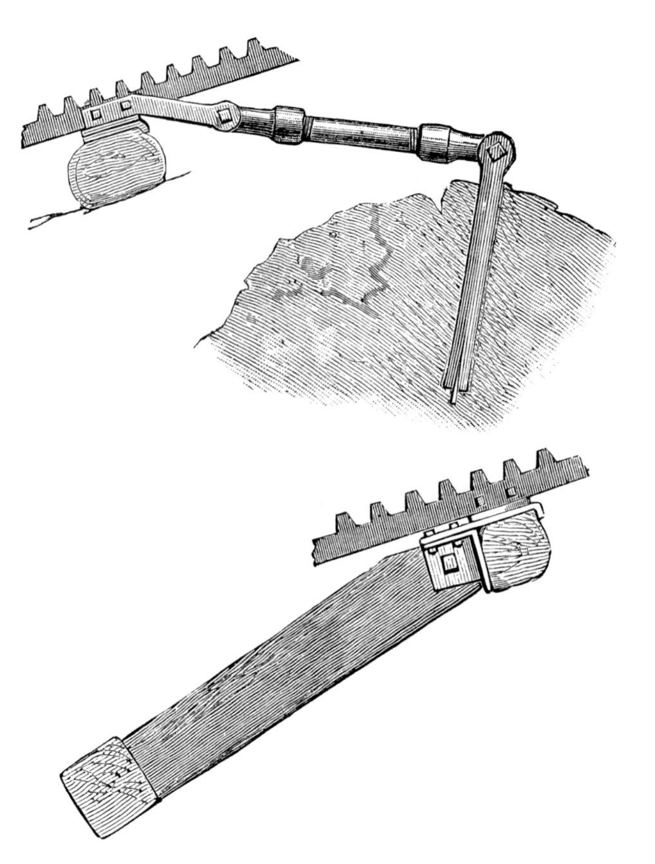

These two old line drawings, appearing in the January 24, 1891 issue of *Scientific American*, show the two methods used in the original construction to anchor the track to prevent it from sliding downhill. The top drawing is of an anchor where solid rock was available, while the lower drawing shows an anchor in a fill with a timber butting against a "dead man" buried beneath the track. — DONALD DUKE COLLECTION

as to break joints and the teeth of one bar are opposite the spaces in its companion bar. Each bar is held to the chair by one bolt at each end and two at its middle part.

While the two holes at the center of each bar had one-sixteenth allowance for expansion, those at the ends had one-tenth inch, and Richardson thought that one-thirty-second inch at the middle would be better and allow less play. The chairs are fastened to the ties by wood (lag) screws, one inch by seven and one-quarter inches, and also by a one inch lip on the uphill edge of the chair, which extends down over the edge of the tie. In addition to these parts, there is a 7 x 2½ x ½ inch plate which is used to cover over the broken joint at the ends of the bars. The bars and cover plate are bolted together and to the chair with two bolts. Spring washers were used, which were one-eighth inch thick, but Richardson found that they simply took a permanent set, and recommended lock nuts.

There was a saving of about $140 per mile by using lighter bolts, chairs and cover plates with the seven-eighths and one inch bars, but as it turned out there was a confusion of sizes, and the savings were more than overcome by the complication of always having too many of the wrong sizes on the job, and not enough of the needed size.

It was thought necessary to use an anchoring system to prevent the rack rail from creeping downhill, and these anchors were spaced 200 to 600 feet apart, depending on the grade. A total of 145 were used, but it was Richardson's opinion that this principle was wrong, as they caused certain unforeseen troubles. The rack bars next above the anchorages crowded together, while those next below them stretched out. This meant that the cog or pinion wheels of the locomotive did not mesh properly with the teeth of the racks, and the result was excessive wear on the rack rails at each anchorage. This was apparent even during track laying, and the following spring it was necessary to regauge the rack rail and move the chair ties to where they belonged. In addition, a two by eight inch plank was spiked with boat spikes to the chair ties on each side of the rack rails, and these were carefully placed so that each plank butted firmly against the one below it. Richardson says that after these planks were placed, the excessive wear on the rack teeth ceased almost entirely. This may be true, but when the planks eventually rotted away, they were not replaced. They appear in the oldest photographs, but by the early 1900's had mostly disappeared, especially at the lower altitudes.

No special provision was made to prevent the smooth rails from creeping. However, it was intended to use supported square joints for these rails, the joints to come always on a chair tie. For this reason, rails 29.8 and 30.2 feet in length were provided for use on curves as the inner and outer rails of 16 degree curves. For curves of greater radii, they were used as required in combination with ordinary 30 foot rails. Thus, on an 8 degree curve, half of the rails were 30 feet long, a quarter of them 29.8 feet and a quarter 30.2 feet.

Richardson listed the quantities and weights of the various materials used per mile of track. The following excludes anchorages.

		Lbs.
1,584	rack bars, each 87.8 lbs.	139,080
1,584	chairs, each 23.25 lbs.	36,830
3,168	rack rail bolts, 197 lbs. per 100	6,240
3,168	wood screws, 164 lbs. per 100	5,200
1,584	cover plates, 189 lbs. per 100	2,990
3,168	spring washers, 14.6 lbs. per 100	460
352	T-rails, each 400 lbs.	140,800
352	pairs angle bars 38″ long, each 32¾ lbs.	11,530
2,112	bolts for above, 48 lbs. per 100	1,010
12,672	spikes, 55 lbs. per 100	6,970
	Total per mile	351,110

(Plus 3,168 ties.)

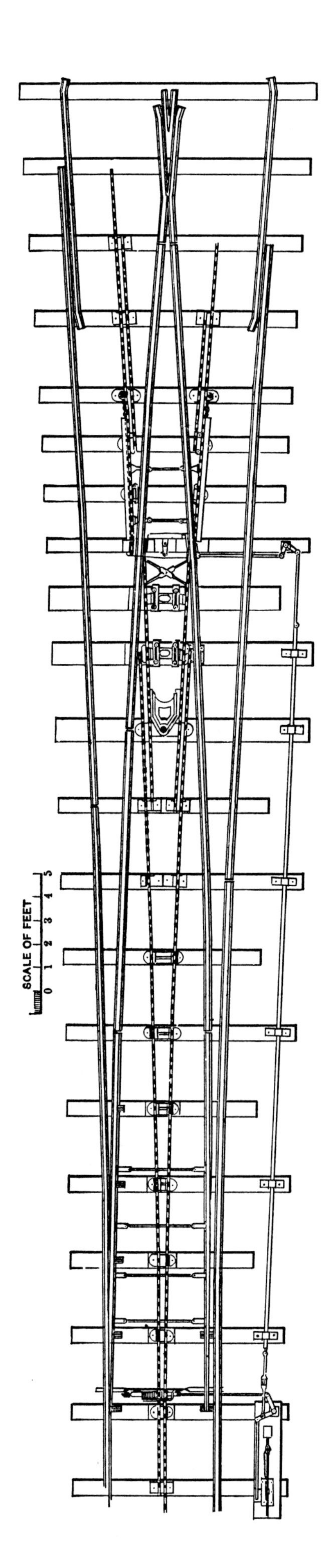

If the reader is familiar with the workings of an ordinary railway switch, it will not be too difficult to understand the operation of the Abt switch shown above. When the switch is thrown, it aligns the running rails as with an ordinary switch. The action of throwing the switch also simultaneously moves the rack bars to positions where the one to be followed is centered in the track, while the other is brought away from the running rail to allow the wheels flanges and treads to clear. This drawing is reproduced from Richardson's paper, and the switch is set here for the main or the track on the horizontal. — MORRIS W. ABBOTT COLLECTION

Hildebrand, Abt's representative, furnished wooden patterns, which reached over three chairs and were provided with steel clips fitting the bolt holes in the chairs. Richardson soon found the use of these patterns unsatisfactory, for, when the pattern was removed in order to install the rack bar, there was only loose ballast to hold the tie in place, and this resulted in too much variance from the exactness required. Instead, he devised drift pins to hold the assembly in place while the bolts were inserted and secured. This gave almost perfect results.

There were seven switches, located only where the grade was no more than 12.5 percent, and they worked very satisfactorily. Richardson says, "So far as the bearing rail is concerned, they are similar to ordinary split switches. When the points of the switch are thrown, four pieces of rack rail are also thrown at the crossing of the rack and bearing rails. This is accomplished by rods and a suitable arrangement of levers. For a switch on a 16 degree curve, the rods are 38 feet long. Two of the pieces of rack rail are thrown close up to one of the bearing rails, making a continuous rack rail, while the other two pieces are thrown away from the bearing rail, allowing room for the wheel flanges and tread of the bearing wheels of the engine and cars to pass."

A close-up section of a switch where the rack bars are shifted. Note that the rack bars on both sides of the X-brace are moved one way or the other, depending on the direction desired. The lever which moves this section is clearly visible running along the ties. — RICHARD B. JACKSON (BELOW) A good view of a switch located at the summit of Pike's Peak. — AL ROSE

BIBLIOGRAPHY

BOOKS

Abbott, Morris W., "The Rise and Fall of the Half Way House," in Denver Posse of the Westerners *Brand Book*, Denver, 1969.

Allen, Cecil J., *Switzerland's Amazing Railways*. Thomas Nelson & Sons Ltd., London, 1965.

Baldwin Locomotive Works Catalog. Philadelphia, J. B. Lippincott & Co., 1872.

Cafky, Morris, *Rails Around Gold Hill*. Denver, Rocky Mountain Railroad Club, 1955.

Catalog of the Centenary. Baltimore, Baltimore & Ohio Railroad Co., 1927.

Cragin, F. W., *The Francis W. Cragin Notes* — Book XIV, Colorado Springs, Pioneers Museum.

Davis, E. O., *The First Five Years of the Railroad Era in Colorado*. Denver, Sage Books, 1948.

Fetler, John, *The Pikes Peak People*. Caldwell, Caxton Printers, Ltd., 1966.

Hale, R. W., *The Story of Bar Harbor*. New York, Ives-Washburn, Inc., 1949.

Hollenback, F. R., and Russell, Wm. Jr., *Pikes Peak By Rail*, Denver, Sage Books, 1962.

Hooper, S. K., *The Story of Manitou*. Chicago, Denver & Rio Grande Railroad, 1892.

Kerr, James H., *Brief Statement Relating to the Pike's Peak Railway*. Colorado Springs, Privately Printed, 1884.

Mallet, Anatole, *Etude sur les Chemins de Fer de Montagnes avec Rail á Cremaillere*. Paris, 1876.

Moody's Manual of Railroads and Corporate Securities. New York, Moody's, 1928.

Mt. Washington Cog Railway. Mt. Washington, Mt. Washington Cog Railway, 1964.

Neue Deutsche Biographie. Berlin, Duncker-Humblot, 1953.

Oliver, S. H., *The First Quarter Century of Steam Locomotives in North America*. Washington, D.C., Smithsonian Institution, 1956.

Poor, Henry V., *Manual of the Railroads of the United States*. 1890-1930, New York.

Ranson-Wallis, P., *Snowdon Mountain Railway*. London, Ian Allan Ltd., 1964.

Records of Recent Construction No. 26. Philadelphia, Baldwin Locomotive Works, 1901.

Roethlisberger, Peter W., *Bergbahnen der Schweiz*, Zurich, Obersee-Verlag, Druckerei, 1959.

Sprague, Marshall, *Money Mountain*. Boston, Little Brown & Co., 1953.

Sprague, Marshall, *Newport in the Rockies*. Denver, Sage Books, 1962.

Stone, Wilbur F., *History of Colorado*. Chicago, S. J. Clarke Co., 1918.

Sulzer, Elmer G., "Locomotives of the Madison Hill," in Railway & Locomotive Historical Society *Bulletin No. 123*, Boston, October 1970.

Vauclain, Samuel M., *Steaming Up*. New York, Brewer & Warren, Inc., 1930.

White, John H., *Cincinnati Locomotive Builders*. Washington, D.C., Smithsonian Institution, 1965.

NEWSPAPERS

Chronicle-News, Trinidad, Colorado, December 27, 1937.

Colorado Springs Evening Mail, Colorado Springs, Colorado, 1901.

Colorado Springs Evening Telegraph, Colorado Springs, Colorado, 1882-1922.

Colorado Springs Free Press, Colorado Springs, Colorado, April 27, 1964.

Colorado Springs Gazette, Colorado Springs, Colorado, 1882-1923.

Colorado Springs Gazette-Telegraph, Colorado Springs, Colorado, 1925-1964.

Denver Post, Denver, Colorado, 1900-1963.

Denver Republican, Denver, Colorado, 1889-1904.

Denver Times, Denver, Colorado, 1890-1891.

Manitou Springs Journal, Manitou Springs, Colorado, 1891-1939.

New York Times, New York, New York, May 7, 1961.

Pike's Peak Daily News, Manitou, Colorado, August 27, 1905, August 1, 1910.

Pike's Peak Herald, Colorado Springs, Colorado, 1891-1893.

Rocky Mountain Herald, Denver, Colorado, August 15, 1896.

Rocky Mountain News, Denver, Colorado, 1889-1963.

Sun, Schuyler, Nebraska, September 25, 1913.

PERIODICALS

American Engineer & Railroad Journal, Philadelphia, Vol. LXVIII (1894).

Beckwith's Almanac, New Haven, 1917.

Cassier's Magazine, London, 1902-1919.

Colorado Railroad Annual, Golden, Vol. 1, No. 7, 1969.

Engineering Journal, Philadelphia, Vol. LXVI (1892).

Industrial News, Gates Rubber Co., Denver, August 1939.

Iron Horse News, Golden, 1958-1970.

Japanese Railway Engineering, Tokyo, March 1964.

Journal of the Association of Engineering Societies, Philadelphia, August 1894.

Locomotive Engineer, New York, February 1891.

Magazine of Western History, New York, Vol. XI (1889).

Narrow Gauge News, Alamosa, January 1949.

Official Guide of the Railroads of the United States, New York, 1891, 1893, 1907, 1968, 1970.

Railroad and Engineering Journal, New York, Vol. LXIV (1890) and LXVI (1892).

Railroad Magazine, New York, 1938-1970.

Railroad Stories, New York, 1930-1937.

Railway & Engineering Review, Chicago, 1898-1899.

Railway & Locomotive Engineering, New York, Vol. 9-40 (1896-1927).

Railway Age, New York, 1890-1970.

Railway Gazette, New York, 1887-1907.

Railway Review, Chicago, February 7, 1891.

Scientific American, New York, January 24, 1891.

Trains, Milwaukee, Vol. 1-29 (1940-1969).

MISCELLANEOUS

Various booklets, literature, public timetables, and employees timetables of the Manitou & Pike's Peak Railway.

United States Geological Survey maps covering the route of the Manitou & Pike's Peak Railway.

Original location map filed with the United States Land Office, Denver, Colorado.

INDEX

These corrections and additions were suggested by the author, Morris W. Abbott, prior to his death in 1978...

Jacket, front flap, first line- delete "erstwhile"

Jacket, back flap, third line from bottom- change "researches" to "research"

page 11, col. 2- authorities differ as to whether Pike was on Cheyenne Mountain or another

page 12, the current James Peak is not higher

page 14, change "Evans" to "Ellis"

page 27, col. 1- there are only three switches, the Half Way House switch was removed and reused at a lower elevation

page 31, lower photo- the whiskered man is not Moffat, he looks like Simmons in the photo on page 36

page 44, next to last line, change "relieved" to "solved"

page 48, the second No. 4 cost $8250.00, FOB Philadelphia, plus $471.08 for freight, moving and setting up

page 52, bottom photo caption, change "1892" to "1893"

page 55, col. 2, par. 2- the doors, not the windows, rolled

page 56, lettering on flat car appears to have initials only, in agreement with the photo on page 54

page 58, upper photo- chains were later hooked to brakes

page 59, caption- the negative, not print, was a "time exposure"

page 62, the Iron Springs Pavilion does not appear in this photo

page 69, according to Martin Frick, the incline is only one mile long and rises 2000 feet

page 71, on far side of creek is a burro trail

page 79, change "perpendicular" to "vertical"

pages 80 and 81, lack of trees is evidence of fire about the time of the Civil War

page 81, caption- change "1920" to "1912"

page 83, name of author and grandfather are in col. 2 of passenger lists

page 94, date that north end of Summit House became two-story is unknown

page 104, a RMRRC member stated that they had steam power on their trip

page 111, McKay is second from right, not left

page 127, caption- change "Engelmann Canyon" to "Ruxton Creek"

page 137, presumably it was No. 3 throughout

page 139, it took three days and two nights to build a "shoo-fly" around the mess, and it was used for the rest of the season

page 156, col. 1, par. 3- grippers are no longer used on Mt. Washington

page 163, par. 1- change "representative of" to "strongly resembles"
par. 2, line 8- change "drove" to "drive"

Newest railcar reaches the top

Cog railway celebrates

By **Rick Ansorge**/Gazette Telegraph

Minutes before Railcar No. 25 rolls out of Manitou Depot on its inaugural trip to the summit of Pikes Peak, Martin Frick smiles, makes a fist and knocks wood.

Frick is president of the Manitou and Pikes Peak Railway Co., and he doesn't want any problems.

Later, it's obvious why he felt compelled to appease the wood sprites. In 1963, during another inaugural trip, the railcar broke down midway through the trip. The passengers twiddled their thumbs for an hour before railroad crews repaired the damage. "There were all these dignitaries on board," Frick says, shaking his head. "We just laugh about it now."

There are plenty of dignitaries on board this Wednesday, including executives from the Swiss Locomotive Works in Winterthur, Switzerland. Railcar No. 25 — 125 feet long and with 216 seats — was custom-built in Switzerland, shipped to Houston and trucked to Colorado Springs.

The odyssey went smoothly, Frick says, until the three-truck caravan carrying the disassembled twin-unit railcar reached Academy Boulevard, where it sparred with a couple of low-hanging traffic lights, and won.

Railcar No. 25 has been in service since May 25, and it still looks like it just came out of the crate. The bright red exterior gleams, and the polished wood seats are devoid of bubblegum, soda-pop stains and other ravages of tourism.

Frick affectionately refers to it as a "$4 million toy."

Powered by four U.S.-made diesel engines, Railcar No. 25 noisily chugs up the steep slope to the summit. Some grades are 25 percent. Averaging 7.5 mph, it makes the nine-mile, 7,500-foot ascent in less than an hour-and-a-half.

On its way, it passes by canyons, reservoirs and rocky slopes that support herds of bighorns. This day, however, the bighorns are in hiding. The only critters that venture near Railcar No. 25 are marmots, thick-bodied rodents with long, bushy tails.

The air is thin near the summit, with only 60 percent of the oxygen found in Manitou Springs, but it doesn't stop Railcar No. 25 or Jim Heidelburg.

Heidelburg, an engineer for the Manitou and Pikes Peak Railway Co., is in training for the Aug. 20 Pikes Peak Marathon. The passengers gape as they watch Heidelburg run down the tracks in blue jogging shorts on his way back to Manitou Springs.

When Railcar No. 25 reaches the 14,110-foot summit, the fog is so thick that it looks like the mountain has been sprayed by a huge dry-ice machine. The clouds fire pellets of snow into the slush that surrounds the gift shop.

During the 40-minute layover, engineer Barry McDaniel stands next to Railcar No. 25 and lights a cigarette. After 13 years of driving railcars for the Manitou and Pikes Peak Railway Co., he's accustomed to the altitude.

Before the inaugural trip, McDaniel took Railcar No. 25 up and down the mountain about a dozen times. "I helped break it in," he says.

The company didn't buy Railcar No. 25 to increase the number of runs, he explains, but to give the other three railcars a break. "They're like people," he says. "You gotta give 'em a day of rest."

In past seasons, he says, crews sometimes had to work all night to repair a damaged railcar. If they didn't succeed, they were forced to put two smaller railcars in service, and that meant less revenue. With a combined capacity of 160, two small railcars hold 46 fewer passengers than one big one.

McDaniel figures that, with proper maintenance, the railcars could last 30 years or more. If so, it could be 2020 or so before the company files another order with Swiss Locomotive Works and holds another inauguration ceremony.

Two of the company's railcars went into service in 1976. The third began making the rounds in 1984.

If McDaniel had a choice, he would stay at the controls of Railcar No. 25. "It handles real well going downhill," he says. "You don't have to play with the (brake system). You just leave it set and enjoy a nice, smooth ride."

GAZETTE TELEGRAPH

SATURDAY, JUNE 10, 1989

French Creek
North Fork
TELLER CO.
EL PASO CO.
South Fork
Bottomless Pit
Barr Trail
Cabin
14,110'
PIKE'S PEAK
SUMMIT HOUSE
Water Tanks
8 Mi.
MANITOU
The Crater
11400'
5 Mi.
PIKE'S PEA
MOUNTAIN VIEW
10,012'
SADDLE
Reservoir No. 7
7 Mi.
Timber
GRECIAN BEND
Ruxton
6 Mi.
12400
Sachett Mtn.
12580'
Water Tanks
Section Ho.
12,129'
THE BIG HILL
WINDY POINT
Reservoir No. 8
Reservoir No. 2
Lake Moraine
MANITOU AND PIKE'S PEAK RAILWAY
COG WHEEL ROUTE
Boehmer Creek
EL PASO
TELLER
Dead Lake